From Generation to Generation

While on the road, a traveller once saw an old man planting a carob tree. He asked the old man when he thought the tree would bear fruit.

"After seventy years," was the reply.

"Do you expect to live seventy years and eat the fruit of your labour?" the traveller asked.

"I did not find the world desolate when I entered it," said the old man, "and as my fathers planted before I was born, so do I plant for those who will come after me."

– Talmud

From Generation to Generation

A History of Toronto's Mount Sinai Hospital

Lesley Marrus Barsky

Canadian Cataloguing in Publication Data

Barsky, Lesley Marrus, date.
From generation to generation : a history of Toronto's Mount Sinai Hospital

Includes bibliographical references and index.
ISBN 0-7710-1061-3

1. Mount Sinai Hospital (Toronto, Ont.) – History.
I. Title.

RA983.T6M68 1998   362.1'1'0899240713541   C97-931615-4

The publishers acknowledge the support of the Canada Council for the Arts and the Ontario Arts Council for their publishing program.

Typesetting by M&S, Toronto
Printed and bound in Canada

McClelland & Stewart Inc.
The Canadian Publishers
481 University Avenue
Toronto, Ontario
M5G 2E9

1 2 3 4 5   02 01 00 99 98

In loving memory of my mother and father,
Lillian and Elliott Marrus

Mount Sinai Hospital gratefully acknowledges the generous assistance of Mr. W. Bernard Herman and family for making possible the creation of this book chronicling our history. This gift is in recognition of the Herman family's seventy-five-year association with Mount Sinai Hospital.

Contents

Preface

My first involvement with Mount Sinai Hospital occurred in the spring of 1992, when *Chatelaine* magazine invited me to write a special report on Canadian hospitals. The purpose of the feature was to assess acute-care hospitals large and small, from coast to coast, and to profile twelve institutions that objective observers from a wide variety of health-related associations and professions agreed were outstanding. Like all of the magazine's "service pieces," this one was meant to benefit readers; in this instance, the goal was to alert potential patients to the characteristics that defined high standards for hospitals. A lengthy appendix to the article provided a list of 330 institutions across Canada that had been granted an unconditional three-year accreditation. This was the highest award given by the Canadian Council on Health Facilities Accreditation. Having the designation meant that the hospital met or exceeded this independent body's standards of performance without reservation in all essential services, as well as in policies of safety and risk management, and that the hospital did not require further evaluation for three years.

My research for this report began with a visit to the Ottawa office of the Canadian Council on Health Facilities Accreditation (CCHFA) to investigate the function of the watchdog organization and its role in maintaining standards for Canadian hospitals. What I also learned was that, after the most recent round of inspections, one hospital was about to be awarded an unconditional *four*-year accreditation, a distinction never before bestowed on a Canadian health-care facility. The CCHFA executive director, Ambrose Hearn, was lavish in his praise for this hospital, which he revealed was in Toronto, but, consistent with the council's confidentiality code, he did not name. Only after subsequent telephone interviews and my sworn oath not to advise anyone other than my editors, who required the early scoop because of the magazine's lead time, was I entrusted with the information that the country's highest accreditation ever would be awarded to Mount Sinai Hospital in the fall of 1992.

It was with a good deal of interest, therefore, that I accepted the commission to write the history of Mount Sinai as it approached its seventy-fifth anniversary. Welcoming the opportunity to delve into the past and present workings of the hospital in much more depth, I was absorbed by several questions, the most compelling of which was how this particular Toronto hospital had achieved so much in such a short time. But there were other themes to ponder. How did a disparate, and largely struggling, Jewish community create this institution at a time when there were clear obstacles to ethnic success? Who were the key individuals who formed the cast of the drama? What circumstances in the city of Toronto, in government and in academe, influenced milestones at Mount Sinai over the years?

The answers to these questions, and to the many others that they inspired, make up Mount Sinai's story. There are no formal hospital archives cataloguing the early years, with the exception of board minutes dating from the 1940s and a few files of newspaper clippings from a decade later. Public archives contain virtually nothing about Mount Sinai's first thirty years. Although regrettable, this dearth of primary archival material did not come as a total surprise. As Stephen Speisman pointed out in *The Jews of Toronto: A History to 1937*, the early working-class Jewish community had little historical awareness, being both too preoccupied with daily survival to attend to preservation of records and fully content to dispatch a painful and turbulent period to the ether.

As a result, much of the information in this history pertaining to the first Mount Sinai Hospital on Yorkville Avenue is based on personal interviews with surviving pioneers of those days, and, in some instances, with their family members, descendants, or later colleagues. Whenever possible, I attempted to verify one individual's recollections with another's or to corroborate incidents with the scanty documentation that does exist. Ultimately, however, the interpretation of events is my own, for which I accept full responsibility. The historical record of Mount Sinai Hospital would have been even further depleted had it not been for the lively accounts in the unpublished personal memoirs of Dorothy Dworkin and Drs. Aaron Volpé and Joseph Gollom, and in the monograph *Toronto's Jewish Doctors*, written by Dr. David Eisen, who, throughout his lifetime, was a dedicated guardian of Toronto Jewry's history. I am exceedingly grateful for the efforts of these individuals and for the invaluable documents they left behind. I would also like to commend the Herman family, not only for their generous support of this project, but for their determination that this story be told.

While researching and writing this book, I was greatly assisted by several people who took a keen interest in the subject and availed themselves of every opportunity to provide me with useful information. For this I wish to extend my sincere thanks to Harry Arthurs, Michael Bliss, Michael Marrus, Ruth Mather, Ned Shorter, Stephen Speisman, Dora Track, and Joy Wolfson. I was also guided through unfamiliar territory by the thoroughly professional and unfailingly helpful staff at the National Archives of Canada, the Archives of Ontario, the City of Toronto Archives, the University of Toronto Archives, the Ontario Jewish Archives, the Thomas Fisher Rare Book Library, and the Toronto Historical Board.

I am happy to acknowledge the help of those who read all or parts of the manuscript as it took shape, and offered fruitful suggestions and criticisms: Jeffrey Ashley, Lorne Barsky, Theodore Freedman, Jodi Macpherson, Joseph Mapa, Michael Marrus, Gerald Tulchinsky, and Gerald Turner. Paul Bleiwas provided patient computer-related advice throughout this project, and Paula Ashley assembled a good deal of essential background material about Ontario hospitals. I owe them both a great debt of gratitude.

I want to extend special thanks to all members of the administration of Mount Sinai Hospital, who warmly invited me into their fold and then left me to go about my work independently. It is a tribute to them, and to the hospital they represent, that they had sufficient confidence in the record to let it speak for itself. My day-to-day existence at Mount Sinai would have been far less pleasant and productive were it not for the prompt and cheerful assistance of Elizabeth Barry, Elaine Danells, Linda Devore, Donna Gage, Irene Geras, Ira Grossman, Nadine Hubert, Rose Jones, Valerie Jones, Gordon Lindsay, Trish O'Reilly, Bernard Schulman, Johanna Sheerin, Sharon Vanderwerff, and Michael Vokins. Both the photographic services and the enthusiastic support of John Hendrix, Ken Meats, Randy Precious, and Irene Schmidt of the hospital's Image Centre are gratefully acknowledged. My sincere appreciation as well to Avie Bennett, Doug Gibson, and McClelland & Stewart for their support, and to Pat Kennedy and Heather Sangster at McClelland & Stewart for their encouragement and sage counsel throughout.

Finally, my deepest debt of gratitude must be reserved for my husband, Lorne, and children, Paula and Jeffrey, Sara and Paul, and Joanna, who never tired of hearing about "the hospital" and who shared my unflagging zeal for rescuing this little-known story from oblivion. Their loving support is my fortune.

1

Why a *Jewish* Hospital?

If it were fiction, the story of Mount Sinai Hospital would be a classic coming-of-age novel, for there is more in this tale than the growth and development of a mere institution. The story of Mount Sinai is also the remarkable record of the young Jewish community of Toronto and its full flowering into adulthood. It is a chronicle of sacrifice, of struggle for acceptance, of dogged pursuit of excellence. It is a story of individual men and women whose journey through life was steered by a selfless concern for the well-being of their neighbours. It is a story of inspiring vision and hard-won cooperation. It is a story that was, and continues to be, non-denominational in plot and structure, but thoroughly Jewish in spirit. Mount Sinai Hospital's seventy-five-year ascent from the most humble of beginnings in a small house on Yorkville Avenue to its present status as a leader in Canadian health care and a world-renowned medical and research institution is a story that is as rare as it is astonishing.

Unlike the case with other hospitals, it was not the provision of health care alone that necessitated the creation of Mount Sinai. Rather, what became apparent in the two decades preceding the opening of Mount Sinai's doors in 1923 was that Toronto urgently required a *Jewish* hospital. One compelling reason for this was that the specialized needs of a burgeoning immigrant population were not being adequately met within existing facilities.

At the dawn of the twentieth century, Toronto was reasonably well endowed with general hospitals, most of which functioned as houses of refuge for the sick poor, as opposed to centres for medical treatment.[1] The largest and most influential of these, the Toronto General, had opened in 1829, rapidly growing to several hundred beds before undergoing major expansions in 1855 and 1913. The Children's Hospital, later the Hospital for Sick Children, came on the scene in 1875, St. Michael's in 1892, the Toronto Western in 1898. For the well-heeled there were also privately owned hospitals such as the Wellesley, which opened in 1912. Furthermore, several smaller, specialized institutions were already serving the city before Mount Sinai came into existence.

Hospitals in those early years were fearful places, to be avoided whenever possible. Despite the publication of Joseph Lister's revolutionary methods of chemical asepsis in the mid-1860s – followed in the last decade of the century by the sporadic introduction of autoclaves, sterilized dressings, and rubber gloves – infection and mortality rates within hospitals remained high. Certainly, the usual expectation if one fell sick was to depend on loved ones for care rather than accept the ministrations of strangers, albeit professional ones. It was common practice, especially among the middle class, for those who took ill to summon a doctor to their homes. Delivery of babies, setting of broken bones, even some surgery was customarily performed at the sickbed by a frock-coated medical man who attended at all hours of the day or night, rolling up his sleeves and administering whatever limited nostrums he had available. Often the patient's own kitchen table functioned as an operating table, with family members serving as assistants and nurses. Following the initial treatment, the doctor would return several times each day to monitor the patient's progress and instruct the family caregivers. Consequently, though the list of known diseases and effective treatments was short, those who found themselves in hospital were generally very ill, very poor, or both.

It was the utter transformation of Toronto's Jewish community, which began shortly after the turn of the century, that consigned many of its members to these unfortunate categories. Until then, the handful of Jewish immigrant families that had first settled in the city in the 1850s were British-born, of Spanish, German, and Polish ancestry.[2] Most were middle-class merchants or artisans who were strictly Orthodox in their religious practices. English Jews, in fact, had founded the city's first synagogue in 1856, the Toronto Hebrew Congregation (Sons of Israel), later renamed Holy Blossom Temple.[3] Seeking economic betterment in North America, these early immigrants came equipped with language and occupational skills, as well as modest capital, enabling them to assimilate with relative ease and begin to grow prosperous.

The economic climate of Toronto prior to the First World War was a golden one.[4] Vying with Montreal as the banking centre of Canada, Toronto surpassed all other cities in wholesaling, manufacturing, mining, and retailing.[5] A housing boom whose magnitude wouldn't be equalled again until the 1950s created new suburbs, which would later form part of the inner city. An explosion of new streetcar lines closely followed the activity in construction, and transportation became more efficient as a result of the municipal creation of the Toronto Transit Commission in 1918 and the increasing appearance of automobiles on bustling city streets.[6]

Politically, Toronto was indelibly conservative and gripped by the ideology of the Orange Order, an organization that was a stronghold of Protestantism, originally imported to British North America by Irish settlers in the eighteenth century but quickly amplified into a universal symbol of the glory of the British Empire. In practice within Toronto, the numerous Orange lodges and the city administration that they tightly controlled noisily championed everything British, viewing with suspicion and xenophobia all that was "foreign." Annually on the twelfth of July, this partisan fervour was celebrated in an elaborate Orange Day Parade through the main streets of Toronto.

For the city's British-born Jews, such Union Jack waving and Empire-centric propaganda was familiar and, for the most part, non-threatening. But by 1900, the sun prepared to set on this Canadian extension of the noble British Empire, when Toronto began to undergo a sudden and dramatic increase in its Jewish population, part of a massive exodus from Eastern Europe that has been labelled the greatest population movement of post-biblical Jewish history.[7]

Conditions in Poland and in the part of the western Russian Empire known as the Pale of Settlement, which were inhabited by the greatest concentration of Eastern European Jews, had swiftly deteriorated following the assassination by revolutionaries of Tsar Alexander II. In the aftermath of the murder, the new tsar, Alexander III, enacted the provisional emergency May Laws of 1882, which actually remained in effect until 1917 and resulted in harsh, restrictive measures against Jews. Among other restraints, they were denied the right to professional education, worship, public assembly, and property ownership. Not only were Jews forbidden to settle in any rural area of the Russian Empire, but towns where they had lived for generations were systematically reclassified as rural villages, effectively driving the inhabitants toward urban centres that were already experiencing widespread impoverishment as a result of industrialization. Subsequent government-sanctioned pogroms, the notorious mass evacuation of Jews from Moscow in 1891, and the accession of the militaristic Tsar Nicholas II sealed Jewish fate in the Tsarist Empire. In the Austrian province of Galicia, a less-developed part of the region where there was, nevertheless, significant Jewish settlement, mounting economic hardship was causing Jews to uproot in great numbers. Meanwhile, in Romania, the combination of extreme poverty and anti-Jewish action was fuelling a similar exodus.[8]

In vast numbers, Jews from all of these regions fled to the *goldene medina*, the golden land of North America. In Toronto, the Jewish population, which had numbered 534 in 1881, trebled within the succeeding two decades, soaring to more than 3,000 by 1901. Ten years later, the influx of Jews gathered even more momentum, vaulting another 401 per cent compared to a general population increase of 72 per cent. In the decade to follow, there was another 90 per cent rise in Jewish citizenry. By 1921, incredibly, 34,619 Jews were residents of Toronto.[9] But in stark contrast to the city's first Jewish settlers, the English-speaking stalwarts of Holy Blossom who had so rapidly integrated into the city's cultural, economic, social, and even religious existence, these Jewish families were destitute, fleeing persecution in their homelands. Mostly Yiddish-speaking, and

A group of Jewish immigrants to Toronto, circa 1910. Women were especially fearful of hospitals. (Archives of Ontario)

The corner of Elizabeth and Albert streets in the heart of the Ward, circa 1917. The Yiddish sign advertises a service that sends money and parcels to Poland and Russia. (City of Toronto Archives)

Out-patient clinic at the Hospital for Sick Children, circa 1919, was "for the poor only." (Hospital for Sick Children Archives)

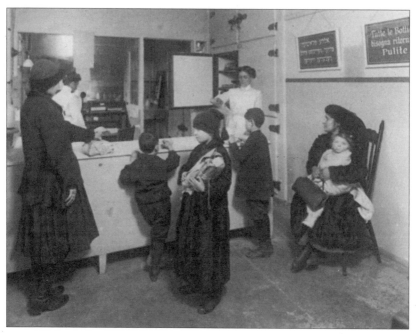

A dairy within the Hospital for Sick Children where pasteurized milk was available, circa 1915. Signs in Yiddish and Italian read, "All bottles must be returned clean." (Hospital for Sick Children Archives)

exotic both in appearance and demeanour, they disembarked with few skills, no money, and usually several mouths to feed.

The first immigrant arrivals crowded into cheerless cottages and boarding houses in the part of the city west of Yonge Street known as St. John's Ward, bounded by Queen and Gerrard streets and University Avenue. Long considered a city slum, this neighbourhood housed the old House of Industry at Chestnut and Elm streets, the privately run workhouse designated for the "deserving" and "undeserving" poor – a judgement routinely applied by Victorian charities.[10] With a population density of eighty-two persons per acre, "the Ward," as it was known, was the subject of an investigation into slum conditions in the 1911 report of Medical Officer of Health Dr. Charles Hastings.[11] An even more brutal indictment of social neglect in the area appeared in the 1918 report of the Bureau of Municipal Research, which cited widespread evidence of malnutrition, squalid housing, poverty, and disease among its residents.[12] Until 1925, when the City of Toronto voted to borrow $14 million to upgrade existing municipal waterworks, typhoid fever was a common occurrence in the Ward.[13] By that time, however, new Jewish arrivals began migrating west of University Avenue, soon populating many of the streets between McCaul and Bathurst.[14]

At first, many Jewish immigrants became pedlars, rag-pickers, or scavengers of some other form of salvage. They chose these menial occupations with a view to eventually establishing themselves in independent shops. Perhaps more important, such jobs also preserved the autonomy required by these poor-but-religious Jews for strict observance of the Sabbath. Later, Jewish refugees in great numbers sought employment in the sweatshops of the numerous needle trades or the factory lofts of the two retailing giants, Eaton's and Simpson's, where arduous piecework was plentiful, but seasonal layoffs frequently the norm. With harsh working conditions, low pay, and financial burdens that usually included scrimping to provide passage for relatives still languishing in Europe, the economic status of most refugee families was precarious indeed.

In the majority of cases, the early wave of immigrants possessed only the most elementary grasp of English, which made them even

F229-308-0-1837

Piece-work, tailoring, and cutting in clothing factories were among the most common occupations of immigrant Jews to Toronto. (Archives of Ontario)

more vulnerable, as illustrated by the experience of the Solarz family of Gerrard Street, refugees from Poland who first arrived in Toronto in 1904. When Kalman Solarz was five years old, he was eligible to begin kindergarten at Victoria Street Public School. But, because his parents spoke only Yiddish, they entrusted their eldest child to the care of six-year-old Abe Track, a neighbour boy who by virtue of having already completed kindergarten was deemed responsible enough to march little Kalman off to school and navigate the impenetrable labyrinth of Canadian school registration. "What's the boy's name?" asked the teacher. Abe, whose spelling skills at the time were embryonic, proceeded to pronounce Kalman's name, which the teacher then spelled out phonetically: COLEMAN SOLURSH. Given the stamp of officialdom by the public school, the name stuck and was adopted by the entire family, a not-uncommon outcome of language misunderstandings during these insecure times.[15] (Coleman Solursh and Abe "Al" Track went on to play major roles at Mount Sinai Hospital; the former being the first chief of General Practice and the latter, a senior surgeon.)

Among other repercussions, the plight of the East Europeans in Toronto became a catalyst for the growth and development of philanthropic services within the Jewish community. Although established Jewish aid societies, notably a women's group associated with Holy Blossom called the Ladies' Montefiore Society, already existed in Toronto

Reverend Maurice Kaplan, cantor of the McCaul Street synagogue, attempted to provide medical services that were culturally and religiously appropriate for Jewish immigrants to Toronto. (Courtesy Bea and Max Wolfe Library, Beth Tzedec Synagogue)

prior to the grand influx of refugees, their number expanded rapidly thereafter. One vital communal service was inspired by the efforts of Reverend Maurice Kaplan, a *mohel* (ritual circumciser) and cantor of the McCaul Street Synagogue.* In 1909, under his direction, a Jewish dispensary opened in the centre of the Ward at Elizabeth and Agnes (now Dundas) streets offering the first free institutional medical services geared to new immigrants. (An earlier Jewish dispensary under the auspices of a doctor from Cleveland, Ohio, S. J. Kaufman, who was then living in Toronto, had charged half of the one-dollar fee levied by other city dispensaries. It closed when the free dispensary opened in 1909.)

The Elizabeth Street dispensary operated daily in the afternoons as a sort of out-patient clinic, providing treatment and dispensing medicine for Yiddish-speaking patients, who, for the most part, regarded hospitals with great trepidation as places to go to die. Often sixty to seventy patients a day attended the clinic. The first nurse in charge of the dispensary was a young Toronto woman, Dora "Dorothy" Goldstick, who was to become a driving force behind Mount Sinai Hospital. Born in Windau, Latvia, in 1890, Goldstick had gone to Cleveland, Ohio, at the urging of Dr. Kaufman to train in midwifery. After receiving her

---

* The use of the honorific "Reverend" by some rabbis and cantors was a custom originating in England, and merely signified membership in the clergy.

Left: Toronto's first Jewish doctor was Dr. Samuel Lavine, an 1899 graduate of Trinity University before its amalgamation with U of T. (Eisen, Toronto's Jewish Doctors) *Right: Bessie Pullen, the first Jewish female doctor in Canada, graduated from the Ontario Medical College for Women in 1910. (Hart,* The Jew in Canada)

diploma from the Medical State Board of Ohio in 1909, she returned to Toronto to operate the free Jewish dispensary. Besides Goldstick, others involved in establishing the clinic were community activists Ida Siegel and her brother Abraham Lewis, Dr. Samuel Lavine, the first Jewish doctor to practise in Toronto, and Drs. A. I. Willinsky, Solomon Singer, L. J. Solway, and Bessie Pullen, Toronto's first Jewish female doctor.[*] Several non-Jewish doctors also contributed their services, notably three local practitioners: Drs. J. Churchill Patton, George Sylvester, and S. Mortimer Lyon. It is interesting to note that these individuals became involved because they took offence at the aggressive Christian conversion missions operating in the Ward at the time.[16] Drugs were dispensed by A. B. Hashmall, the first Jew to graduate from the University of Toronto College of Pharmacy.[17]

In addition to treating patients at the clinic, the free dispensary

---

[*] Dr. Pullen graduated in 1910 and practised medicine only briefly until her marriage to L. M. Singer.

Dorothy Goldstick (later Dworkin), a young midwife trained in Cleveland, operated the free Jewish dispensary at Elizabeth and Agnes (Dundas) streets between 1909 and 1911. (Courtesy Professor Harry Arthurs)

made house calls. Many were obstetrical cases, necessitating a furious bicycle ride to arrive on time. It was on one such race to beat the stork that Dorothy Goldstick, in the company of Dr. Lavine, experienced her first ride in a motor car. Here is her account of a maternity call to an immigrant home in the Ward:

> In those days, women were terrified of hospitals. I remember a deserted mother who lived in abject poverty in a home which seemed to lack everything. The doctor in charge anticipated trouble and insisted that the patient go to the hospital; but the poor woman was frightened and refused to leave her home, where she remained in labour for two days. Finally, with the help of Mrs. Pasternack and Mrs. Bockneck (two devoted members of the Maternity Aid Society), I persuaded her to go to hospital. The ambulance arrived, the patient was on the stretcher – but at the last minute, she panicked. Her baby came quickly after that, and, with the assistance of the above-named dedicated ladies, I delivered a healthy, normal child.[18]

The terror of this expectant mother at the prospect of hospitalization was by no means unique. In fact, it was shared by most Jewish newcomers to Toronto, especially women. As mentioned, the general aversion to institutional as opposed to family-centred care was commonplace at the time. But aside from this, Jews had special reasons to be fearful. Without the availability of kosher food in the existing general hospitals, they were unable to observe the most basic of their essential daily religious practices. Furthermore, language barriers prevented them from adequately communicating with the medical professionals in the hospitals, none of whom spoke Yiddish. Since hospital patients had extremely limited visiting privileges in those days, their near-total isolation was assured. Add to this the prevailing belief that a hospital was almost certainly the last stop before the cemetery, and it's little wonder Jewish immigrants such as this woman reacted as they did.

After her marriage in 1911, Dorothy Goldstick (now Dworkin) left the dispensary, which soon closed. Not long after, however, several Jewish charitable organizations formed the Associated Jewish Charities, a forerunner of the Federation of Jewish Philanthropies. With their combined resources, they purchased a large building on Simcoe Street to house an orphanage on the upper level and a new, even better equipped dispensary in the basement. No records of this third Jewish clinic survive, and, despite its reputed popularity, it also folded after a short time, leaving institutional medical care for the community in disarray.

So much was this the case that, during the terrible worldwide influenza epidemic of 1918, when people were dying like flies, the only available support within the Ward was an emergency clinic organized on McCaul Street, near the synagogue. Aaron Volpé was a senior medical student at the time, and he was recruited to pitch in during the crisis. Several years later, Dr. Volpé recalled his makeshift medical role: "I was given a car with a chauffeur, a satchel full of Aspirin, and a list with two or three hundred people to see every day. I attended them all by the simple process of entering a home, showering the entire family with Aspirin, and running off to the next. It was not physically possible to examine them. Pregnant women were rushed to the hospital, as they were almost sure to die."[19]

Other social services for poor immigrants, aside from the series of dispensaries, were provided by mutual-benefit and free-loan societies. These organizations, some religious and others secular, were formed by the newcomers themselves to assist their own *landsleit*, or kinsmen,

Before beginning medical studies at U of T, Dr. Aaron Volpé, a pioneer of Yorkville Mount Sinai, acted as "secretary-superintendent" of the short-lived third Jewish dispensary on Simcoe Street. (Courtesy Jenny Volpé Klotz)

from a particular region in the Old Country. One well-established organization that acted as a link between the *shtetl* and the Ward was the *Folks Farein* (People's Association), which originated shortly before the First World War as a Yiddish literary society. Through necessity it later came to undertake certain medical services, such as supplying artificial limbs and dentures and paying hospitalization costs for indigent members. From time to time, this group also attempted to organize kosher meals for Jewish patients in general hospitals, a project that met with limited success.[20]

Many of these fraternal groups employed their own doctors to attend to members, each of whom contributed a small amount, perhaps a dollar a year, toward the doctors' modest annual salaries. Originally, these "lodge doctors" were exclusively non-Jews, but, in 1907, Dr. Samuel Lavine was elected lodge doctor of the Pride of Israel Benefit Society, initiating a great boost in that organization's membership. In his autobiography, *A Doctor's Memoirs*, A. I. Willinsky recalled that, in consideration of his small stipend, the lodge doctor was obliged to heed every call from a member or any one of his predictably large family. If a lodge doctor failed to attend, he had to incur the cost of any other physician the member consulted. And while a premium charge of fifty cents was applied for any calls between midnight and 6 A.M., the lodge doctor's basic salary was meant to cover all other medical services he

Abraham Isaac Willinsky, Toronto's third Jewish doctor and the first chief of Surgery at Yorkville Mount Sinai, began his practice as a "lodge doctor" at College and Henry streets in 1910. (Eisen, Toronto's Jewish Doctors*)*

provided, no matter how numerous.[21] This primitive form of medical insurance (for lodge members) and capitation (for doctors) was clearly more beneficial to the former than the latter, as lodge doctors were mercilessly exploited, earning less than $500 a year for the privilege of being at the beck and call of the lodge members twenty-four hours a day, seven days a week. But the arrangement provided two significant advantages, which illustrate why physicians eagerly campaigned, and indeed, fiercely competed, for election to the humble positions: they acquired immense practices and, at the same time, they came into contact with the leading medical specialists of the day.

For the few Jewish doctors who were practising in Toronto in the first quarter of the twentieth century, these advantages were immeasurable, as they helped to mitigate some of the serious professional roadblocks the doctors encountered because of antisemitism. Sadly, it was this climate of bigotry that constituted the second major impetus to the founding of Mount Sinai Hospital.

Although it was not publicly manifest at first, antisemitism washed onto the shores of Toronto along with the waves of European immigrants. The pioneer Jewish settlers, embodied in the original Holy Blossom membership, had readily assimilated, and, for the most part, they enjoyed congenial relations with the Gentile community. But the slum-dwelling foreigners were another matter entirely.

Before the First World War and even in later years, bearded, traditionally garbed Jews were frequently the victims of physical attacks
whenever they left their neighbourhoods. Vicious antisemitic articles
were not uncommon in Toronto newspapers, and, because these were
widely quoted and commented upon in the Yiddish dailies, even those
immigrants who didn't venture beyond the Ward were fully aware of,
and intimidated by, the threatening mood. Such was the case of Dr. A. I.
Willinsky, who throughout his whole university career admitted to
being mindful of his mother's baleful warning, "Remember, you are a
Jew. You should not make yourself conspicuous."[22] Jews, moreover,
could not seek employment in banks or some department stores, and,
when it came to considering professional education, they discounted
teacher training and engineering courses, because Gentile firms and
school boards would not hire them.[23] When he graduated from high
school, David Eisen, who would later become the first radiologist at
Mount Sinai, intended to study history, for which he had been awarded
a four-year, full university scholarship. But, because he was persuaded
by an older brother that, as a Jew, he would never find work as a history
teacher, he opted to attend medical school instead.[24]

Analysing a number of such conditions in his meticulously com-
piled 1939 statistical study of Jewish life in Canada, demographer Louis
Rosenberg fulminated:

> It is in the economic life of Canada that anti-Jewish discrimination
> is most marked and most serious in its results. In seeking employ-
> ment by public bodies, a Jew must be so outstandingly brilliant that
> his qualifications swamp the obstacles raised by his birth. It is taken
> for granted that for a Jew to secure an appointment in competition
> with non Jews, he must be ten times as good as the average applicant
> in order to have a tenth of the average applicant's chance.[25]

Other non-economic spheres of life were rendered difficult, too. On
the occasions when Jews were admitted to public hospitals, they often
were treated with indifference by nurses who couldn't understand
them. Vigorous efforts to inculcate Christianity, as well as insensitivity

to other religions, though not officially sanctioned, were widespread in schools. Missionary activity was at its height in the years prior to the First World War, during which a variety of Christian organizations zealously sought converts by preaching on street corners, providing all manner of charitable services to the poor, and generally singling out hungry Jewish schoolchildren and their needy families for proselytizing by Yiddish-speaking missionaries. The most notorious, and successful, of these groups was the Presbyterian Jewish Mission, directed by an apostate Jew from Glasgow, Scotland, Sabeti Rohold, who arrived in Toronto in 1908. The son of a rabbi, Rohold became an ordained Presbyterian minister and soon established a conversion centre at Elm and Terauley streets, the goal of which was to convert the new East European immigrants. When Rohold moved his operation to larger accommodations at Elizabeth and Elm streets, the mission, renamed The Christian Synagogue, included in its many social services a popular free dispensary.[26] No doubt the need to combat the relentless threat that this mission posed to the survival of the vulnerable Jewish community was a compelling factor that spawned the free Jewish dispensary.

Those immigrant Jews who possessed a limited ability to speak English were easy targets for anti-Jewish expression. Their mother tongue, Yiddish,[27] so closely identified by Orange-bred Torontonians with German, and after the First World War with Bolshevism, coupled with the prevalence of Jews in the garment unions contributed to the widely held notion that all Jews were Communists. In fact, although social activism was commonplace among working-class Jews, and there was indeed a small Jewish presence in the Communist Party of Canada (whose largest foreign membership was Finnish, followed by Ukrainian),[28] most of the rank-and-file garment workers supported the two major American unions, both of which were solidly anti-Communist.[29]

Still, the association prevailed. A postwar editorial in the *Globe*, which labelled Jews "the brains of the Communist movement in Germany, as in Russia and elsewhere," was typical of the hostility levelled against foreigners in general, and Jews in particular.[30] In the midst of the Red Scare that engulfed Toronto following the 1917 Bolshevik

Revolution and the 1919 Winnipeg General Strike, Alderman John Cowan declared during a 1920 legislative committee debate over whether to prohibit non-English (read Yiddish) advertising signs, "If foreigners who come here to make a living could not conform to English ways and customs, they could return to their native countries."[31] *Saturday Night* magazine was less subtle: Canada, it proclaimed, was a "white man's country" that had become "the dumping ground of Europe."[32] This malevolent climate worsened throughout the 1920s, particularly as the economy began to fray at the edges and come unravelled toward the end of the decade.[33]

Ironically, one place where Jews were not excluded, at least between 1910 and 1940, was the University of Toronto medical school. It is often suggested that quotas existed to restrict Jewish students from medical training in Toronto. While such a hostile environment did exist in certain other Canadian universities between the wars (and actually did flourish at U of T *after* the Second World War), this was apparently not the case throughout these critical years at the University of Toronto and another academic refuge, Dalhousie University.[34] As a public provincial institution, the policy at U of T was to admit any citizen of Ontario who presented the requisite qualifications of senior matriculation.[35] In fact, records show that the number of Jewish students at Toronto's medical school began to grow at an extraordinary rate once large-scale immigration got under way. In 1910, only 2 per cent of students were Jews. By 1920, that number rose to 7 per cent; by 1925, Jewish students made up 17 per cent; in 1929, 21 per cent; and by 1932, over a quarter of all medical students were Jewish, an astonishing figure at a time when Jews made up only 7 per cent of the city's population.[36] As well, the academic performance of Jewish students during this period was exemplary, and thus gave little support for systemic prejudice within the medical faculty.

Once Jewish students graduated as doctors, however, they faced the full force of discrimination. For instance, there were twelve internships available in Toronto for the graduates of 1908, four at St. Michael's Hospital and eight at the Toronto General. None was available to Jews, despite their high academic achievement. That policy

In 1930, Abraham "Al" Track became only the second Jewish medical graduate permitted to intern at the Toronto General Hospital. (Courtesy Dr. and Mrs. A. Track)

persisted until 1929, when the Toronto General began to admit one Jewish intern per year, a meagre concession that was soon adopted by other Toronto hospitals.[37]

The first Jewish intern accepted at a Toronto hospital was Dr. Adolph Appell; the second was Dr. Abraham "Al" Track. Neither was offered postgraduate training in Toronto, despite their history-making internships, which were only made possible, it was widely believed at the time, by the successful public-relations efforts of Rabbi Ferdinand Isserman, spiritual leader at Holy Blossom during the 1920s.[38] The winner of the Faculty of Medicine's gold medal in 1931, Dr. Harold Taube, was forced to go to Cleveland to intern when no Toronto hospital would have him.[39] More fortunate was *Miss* Evelyn Breslin (*not* Dr., according to hospital records), one of the few female graduates of 1930, who was recommended as an "extern" in the Out-Patients' department of St. Michael's. Her duties, however, were restricted to that department, with no responsibility for in-patients.[40]

If all doors were closed to Jewish interns, they were similarly barred to those seeking specialty training.[41] Any Jewish doctor who desired further medical education, therefore, had to go to Europe or the United States, an option few could afford.

Establishing a practice meant additional obstacles. In the fashion-
able areas of Toronto, where Anglo-Saxon doctors had offices, Jews were
firmly shut out, with the result that most had to set up shop within the
immigrant neighbourhoods. Since they had no attending privileges in
public hospitals, Jewish doctors had no other recourse but to hand over
the care of those patients needing hospitalization to Gentile colleagues.

The bigotry that poisoned the profession at this time was frequently
overt. Years after one Jewish physician was first stung by the rebuke in
the 1920s, he bitterly recalled the words of a staff member at the
Hospital for Sick Children: "You may as well know that I'd hate to see
any Jew get on in this hospital. Once you opened the door, they'd be
running the place in no time."[42] Even today, the hateful memory of a
classmate's reprehensible treatment at the hands of a gynecological
surgeon in the 1930s leaves a retired Jewish specialist shaken. The
surgeon demanded to know the identity of the medical student preparing to attend one of the senior man's operations. When the student gave
a Jewish-sounding name, the surgeon imperiously announced, "Get out.
I don't scrub with Jews."[43] Despite the protests of a few enlightened
Establishment doctors who deplored such ugly policies, no Jew was to
hold an indoor staff position[*] at a Toronto teaching hospital until after
the Second World War, with the exception of two doctors who held
posts at the Western Hospital in the 1920s.[44] Under such circumstances,
one begins to understand why the chance to land an oppressive, yet
dependable, job as a lodge doctor might start to look appealing.

As mentioned earlier, it was the combined pressures of a radically
changed Jewish population plus this intolerant mood within the wider
medical community that prefigured the opening of Mount Sinai
Hospital. But before we turn to that début, it is interesting to note the
one earlier attempt to provide for Jewish hospital patients in Toronto.

When the free Jewish dispensary that he had founded closed in 1911,
the community-minded cantor, Reverend Maurice Kaplan, began
another campaign to establish a Jewish wing in an already-existing

---

[*] An "indoor" appointment meant that the physician was on hospital staff and
could admit and treat patients there.

institution. As one of the busiest *mohelim* in the city, Kaplan was familiar with most of the downtown hospitals and known to their administrators, and, as a benefactor of many worthy causes within the Jewish community, he was obviously well placed to conduct negotiations between the two groups. Only too aware of the problems facing Jews in general hospitals, Kaplan sought a practical and manageable solution. He determined to raise funds to create a separate ward, under the supervision of a Yiddish-speaking Jewish nurse, in which kosher food would be served to patients. However, authorities at the Toronto General, whom he approached with this proposal, refused to even consider the matter. So, as a report in the *Canadian Jewish Times* declared shortly after the latest snub by the Toronto General juggernaut, "the only thing left for the Toronto Jews to do was to establish a hospital for their own sick."[45]

And that, as we know, is exactly what they did.

2

Mount Sinai Is Born

From the outset, it was women who formed the backbone of social-service organizations for the immigrant Jewish community. Among the newcomers to Toronto were those who, in the midst of their own struggles to adapt to dislocation, nonetheless resolved to help fellow Jews plagued by even greater misfortunes. One such group of women – *Ezras Noshem*, literally, "Ladies' Aid" – was founded on August 9, 1913, by four women whose names have been recorded only as Mrs. Cohn, Mrs. Miller, Mrs. Spiegel, and Mrs. Adler,[1] to focus principally on the special needs of women and families. Mrs. Miller, who was elected president, and her dedicated followers regularly performed the religiously prescribed mitzvah, or divine commandment, of *bichur cholim* – that is, they visited the sick, helping to care for their children and households. Other specific functions of the society were to assist its members financially, and to ensure that each member would be present at the funeral of a fellow member.[2]

The *Ezras Noshem* had embarked on its first major fund-raising project in 1916 as a result of a sad encounter with a certain Pearl Feiman, a ninety-six-year-old religious woman who had been committed to the insensitively named Home for Incurables on Dunn Avenue in Parkdale. When the *Ezras Noshem* found the poor woman, she was crying pitifully,

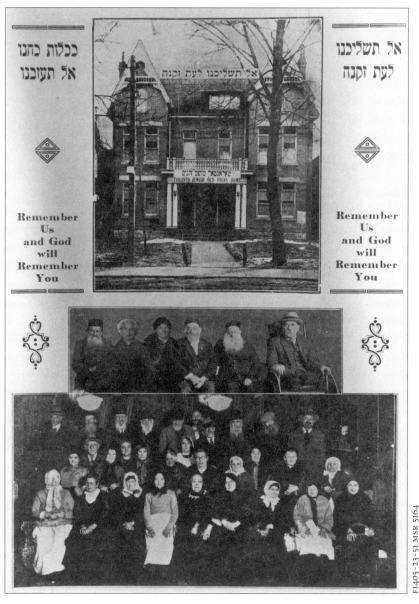

Moshav Zekanim, *the home for the Jewish aged established by the* Ezras
Noshem *society on Cecil Street in 1917 (above), and some of the institution's first
residents. (Signs are superimposed on the photograph.) (Archives of Ontario)*

lamenting the institution's lack of kosher food and Yiddish-speaking
staff, and praying that she might die among Jews.[3] The wretched plight
of Mrs. Feiman and of other destitute elderly induced the group to begin

raising money for a home for the Jewish aged. In 1917, the *Ezras Noshem* purchased a semi-detached rooming house at 31 Cecil Street, acquiring the building next door a year later. That rudimentary institution, *Moshav Zekanim* (The Old Folks' Home), where these tireless volunteers cooked and cleaned for their cherished charges, was the first ethnically distinct home for the aged in Ontario, and became a forerunner of the Baycrest Centre for Geriatric Care.[4]

Encouraged by their success as formidable and persuasive door-to-door fund-raisers for the old-age home, the *Ezras Noshem* next took on the challenge of a Jewish hospital. The original intention was to open a comprehensive general hospital to receive patients of all ages, clearly an ambitious undertaking for an unsophisticated group of non-professional immigrant women. When one Toronto newspaper got wind of the plan, it announced the fact in a scurrilous article containing mock "dialogue" between a nurse and an immigrant patient in which it mimicked the thick Eastern European accent that presented such a barrier for Jewish patients in "Gentile hospitals."[5] But the society's president at the time, Slova Greenberg, knowing that her own son, who was then a medical student, would be denied a local internship,[6] determined to make the hospital a reality. Aided now by the active membership of Dorothy Dworkin, the nurse-midwife from the free Jewish dispensary, the *Ezras Noshem* began another fund-raising campaign in 1921. Jewish doctors, recognizing an opportunity to become part of a hospital where they could treat their own patients, were willing contributors of both money and services. As well, the coffers included funds that had previously been collected for this purpose following the rejection of Reverend Maurice Kaplan's proposal for a kosher ward in the Toronto General.

By May 1922, the *Ezras Noshem* had accumulated $12,000, most of it in nickels and dimes, to put a down payment on a $35,000 building at 100 Yorkville Avenue. Originally constructed in 1871 as the residence of James D. Bridgland, a surveyor in the Crown Lands Department and Inspector of Colonization Roads, it had been occupied since 1913 by the private Lynhurst Hospital.[7] In celebration of the momentous occasion, the Yiddish-language daily newspaper, *Der Yiddisher Zhurnal*, published an effusive tribute, extolling the many features of the fine new

100 Yorkville Avenue as it appeared in 1922 when purchased by the Ezras Noshem *society to house the Toronto Jewish Maternity and Convalescent Hospital.* (Toronto Star – *Metropolitan Toronto Reference Library*)

medical facility. The hospital would open its doors, the paper proudly announced to its many readers in the Ward, just as soon as it was redecorated in *yiddishe gishmacht,* or "Jewish taste."[8]

Within weeks after the property had been purchased, however, it became apparent that launching a *general* hospital was a far more ambitious enterprise than the Jewish community was capable of supporting. Not only was money extremely scarce, but fear of hospitals was still so prevalent, their association with death so difficult to dispel, that to gain acceptance among the immigrants the new institution would have to allay some of these fears, and somehow strike a more positive note. A compromise had to be reached. There was an urgent need for maternity care, an area that until now had come under the wing of the dispensaries as well as the Maternity Aid Society headed by Ida Siegel, an American-born activist who had had a hand in organizing virtually every Jewish social-welfare organization then existing in Toronto. But while Maternity Aid cared for orphans and helped distribute pasteurized milk, food, and baby clothes, and provided household help for poor mothers, there remained a significant need for obstetrical care. The *Ezras Noshem* concession, then, was to declare the new institution a maternity and convalescent hospital rather than a general one. With its deliberately reassuring name, the thirty-bed Toronto Jewish Maternity and Convalescent Hospital opened at 100 Yorkville Avenue in September 1922.

Conditions in the new hospital were, to say the least, primitive. The indomitable Dorothy Dworkin, whose organizational skills were already legendary, took a leading role in managing day-to-day affairs. Without an autoclave in the earliest days, Dworkin personally ferried bandages and instruments to the old Women's College Hospital on Rusholme Road for sterilization. Since there was no elevator, patients had to be carried up and down the stairs. There was no electric refrigerator either, and cooking odours permeated the building because of the location of the kitchen. As hands-on administrators in the fullest sense, the *Ezras Noshem* pitched in wherever help was required, mending bed linen, canning fruit and vegetables for the pantry, washing dishes, and preparing meals.[9]

Aside from the hospital's numerous physical deficiencies, there was the pressing problem of how to attract patients. At times, as few as three people occupied the beds, and on many occasions it appeared that the hospital, like the earlier dispensaries, would not survive. Almost two years passed before the Jewish community began to shed its Old Country fears and trust the new hospital. During that interval, the women laboured mightily to entice patients, using various ploys that sometimes verged on the comical. One gimmick they employed just after opening was to offer a free baby carriage to the first infant born there, an inducement that must have worked, because there was a lucky winner – recorded as "Baby Koranovsky whose parents resided at 89 Borden Street." A more devious, but equally successful, scheme involved public tours of the new hospital. Apprehensive immigrants saw every ward filled to capacity – thanks to staff dressed in nightgowns playing the role of satisfied customers![10]

In addition to these various threats to its survival, there was one other serious impasse the new hospital faced. When it first opened, not everyone in the Jewish community greeted the occasion enthusiastically.

Dr. Maxwell K. Bochner, one of Toronto's most prominent ophthalmologists, was barred from practising at the Hospital for Sick Children because he was Jewish. (Courtesy Ann Bochner Stein)

On the contrary, those financially secure and confident early immigrants who had succeeded in assimilating and gaining some acceptance within the city viewed the creation of a Jewish hospital as a step backward that would only further segregate Jews from the mainstream. English-speaking and unburdened by Old World fears, they were quite comfortable in the city's general hospitals. Furthermore, they were increasingly disinterested in maintaining dietary laws, and readily patronized non-Jewish doctors who enjoyed prestigious hospital appointments. Not only was this acculturated segment of Toronto Jewry completely unaffected by the restrictions against Jewish doctors and the barriers confronting the more-recent arrivals, whom they frequently referred to disparagingly as "greenies," but, to a great extent, it was blithely unaware of all these problems. As a result, there was considerable bitterness in East European circles when these prosperous members of the community failed to support the new hospital.[11]

No better example of this class rift exists than the following imbroglio: Edmund Scheuer, an Alsatian Jew who arrived in Toronto as a young man late in the nineteenth century, became an affluent Toronto jeweller as well as a pillar of the assimilated Jewish community and a pioneer of the German Reform movement. Scheuer founded the first English-language religious schools for Jewish children in Ontario (then called Sabbath schools) and was largely responsible for introducing

English prayer into synagogue services. As a person of considerable influence, therefore, he was known to Maxwell Kurt Bochner, a Toronto-born Jewish doctor who was among the city's first fully trained ophthalmologists, having completed three years of postgraduate work at the world-renowned Wills Eye Institute in Philadelphia. As a result of his having these rare professional credentials, Dr. Bochner was widely regarded as Toronto's top "eye man," the originator of intracapsular cataract surgery, which he performed (on a mostly Gentile clientele) at the private St. Mary's Hospital on Jarvis Street, as well as at Mount Sinai on Yorkville.*

Upon his return from training in Philadelphia in 1926, Bochner had applied for privileges at the Hospital for Sick Children and had been refused. Not long afterward, he operated at St. Mary's on a child known to Scheuer. When Scheuer inquired why Bochner had not performed the operation at the much-better-equipped Hospital for Sick Children, the ophthalmologist explained that Jews were not permitted to practise there. Aghast, Scheuer promptly attempted to deal with the situation. He then recounted the results of his efforts in a letter to Bochner:

Dear Dr. Bochner,

After some delay, I succeeded in getting an interview with Mr. Williams. Just returning from the gentleman's office I report to you that apparently there is not a ghost of a chance of any Jewish doctor being appointed on the Staff of the Hospital.

The reason the gentleman gave to me is that all of every one of the thirty voluntary doctors on the Staff are opposed to having a Jew appointed.

Very much grieved I now feel not to let the matter rest. If you can get me the names of the thirty voluntary doctors, I feel sure that

---

* A small, private Catholic hospital run by the Sisters of Misericorde, St. Mary's expanded in 1956 into the Scarborough General Hospital. Bochner was simultaneously chief of Staff and chief of Ophthalmology at St. Mary's/Scarborough General and Mount Sinai hospitals for thirty-eight years.

some of them are known to me, and I intend appealing to them for
their support in our efforts.

With kindest greetings, I remain

Yours sincerely,

Edmund Scheuer[12]

What is notable about Scheuer's response to Bochner's explanation
of why he had not operated at the Hospital for Sick Children is the sur-
prised, even wounded, tone it conveys, a tone that furnishes ample tes-
tament to the almost complete lack of awareness of some members of
the more assimilated Jewish constituency to the existence of anti-
semitism in medicine. The message, meanwhile, unmistakably confirms
the tenacity of its grip.

Needless to say, the deep division within the Jewish community over
matters of this nature seriously exacerbated problems at 100 Yorkville. As
the immigrant population slowly began to warm to the idea of a Jewish
hospital, it became imperative to modernize and renovate the old building in order to accommodate patients and extend services beyond maternity care. But to do so required far more money than the *Ezras Noshem*
could ever hope to muster by knocking on doors with their *pushkes* (alms
boxes) extended. Already denied a request for a government grant, the
women certainly held no hope of meeting the necessary standards for
provincial assistance until expensive renovations had been carried out.
There was only one solution. If there was to be any future for the budding
Jewish hospital, the immigrant managers had no choice but to harness
their wagons to the wealthier and more-influential Jewish population.

The ultimate decision to do so marked a defining moment, not
merely for the imperilled hospital but for the entire Jewish community.
The social gap that had fuelled various tensions in the first decades of
the century simply had to be breached if the hospital was to remain
open. To do so required the willingness of the *Ezras Noshem* to appeal to
the older, more-assimilated community, which until now had ignored
their efforts. But it also demanded the full cooperation of that wealthier
element, despite its initial reservations.

Ephraim Frederick Singer was president of Mount Sinai Hospital from 1923 until the move to New Mount Sinai on University Avenue in 1953. (Courtesy Harvey Singer)

Enlisted to superintend this harmonious venture was J. J. Allen, a prominent Jew with links to all segments of the community through his membership in both Holy Blossom, the synagogue founded by the more-assimilated English-speaking immigrants, and Goel Tzedec, a large synagogue founded by Lithuanian Jews and therefore closely allied with the East Europeans. Allen, whose wealth came from the new motion-picture industry, had been called on for assistance once before by the redoubtable Ida Siegel, a close friend of his wife, Ray. On that occasion, Allen had helped the disordered Jewish charities consolidate their fund-raising activities into a single Federation of Jewish Philanthropies. Now, he made a donation to the debt-burdened hospital and suggested that others among his acquaintance in the two congregations do the same. A number of well-connected individuals responded to his appeal.[13]

In 1923, these men provided a provisional board for the hospital, headed by Ephraim Frederick Singer, who was elected president, Isadore Levinter, secretary, and Ely Pullan, treasurer. Even then, E. Fred Singer, a lawyer by profession, enjoyed a richly deserved reputation for opening up hitherto inaccessible doors for Jews. He was, among other things, the first Jew to become president of the Ward 4 Conservative Association, the first Jew appointed grand steward in the Grand Lodge

F1405-23-28 MSR 3075

Members of the Jewish medical fraternity Phi Delta Epsilon, 1926–1927,
included many pioneers of Yorkville Mount Sinai. From left: 1st row:
Dr. Joseph Schwab, Dr. Mitchell Kohan, Dr. I. R. Smith, Dr. Louis Kazdan,
Dr. H. P. Fine, Dr. Charles Markson, Dr. Benjamin Cohen. 2nd row: B. Cohen,
N. Rosenberg, Dr. Nathan Shaul, Ben Sakler, Dr. David Perlman, Dr. David
Eisen. 3rd row: David Scher, Archie Fine, P. H. Ticktin, H. Reinhorn.
(Archives of Ontario – David Eisen Collection)

of the Masonic Order, and the first Jewish lawyer in Ontario named
King's Counsel. Within a few years, Singer would also become the first
Jew elected to the provincial legislature.[14] Other members of the revised
hospital board were Samuel Kronick, Rubin Shapiro, Irving Oelbaum,
Haskell Masters, and M. L. Feinberg. A few years later, several Jewish
doctors who were pioneers at the hospital also became part of the new
board. Among this group were Drs. Leon Judah Solway, Benjamin
Cohen, Nathan Shaul, David Esser, Maxwell K. Bochner, Maurice A.
Pollock, and Louis J. Breslin.

In exchange for mobilizing the more-affluent sector of the Jewish
community in the struggle for the hospital's economic survival, the
board members insisted that the *Ezras Noshem* transfer control to them.
Reluctantly, the women agreed, and this resulted in a mostly male

board, with the exception of Dorothy Dworkin and three additional *Ezras Noshem* members. As a gesture of cooperation and in order to maintain a link with the founders, the hospital's new charter stipulated that four seats on the board be designated for women. On October 17, 1923, the hospital was registered with the Province of Ontario and renamed Mount Sinai.

The choice of name was a significant one. It instantly yoked the little institution on Yorkville Avenue with a proud tradition of healing within Jewish communities worldwide. As the name of the biblical site where the Ten Commandments had been handed down to Moses, Mount Sinai signified the wellspring of moral law, the source of all compassion, and thus had already been bestowed on many other hospitals under Jewish auspices, including a well-known institution in New York, which in 1852 became the first hospital in North America to be founded by Jews, the

Although founded by Jews, Mount Sinai has always served more non-Jewish patients than Jewish ones. Seen here at a Christmas party for patients and staff at Yorkville Mount Sinai is Dorothy Dworkin, seated far left, and hospital administrator Dr. Simon Fines, second from left. (Courtesy Joyce Fines Dain)

*Dr. Maurice A. Pollock, co-chief of
Medicine at Yorkville Mount Sinai,
began one of the first clinic practices
operated by Jewish doctors in Toronto
in partnership with his two sons,
Drs. Oscar and Ira Pollock.*
(*Eisen,* Toronto's Jewish Doctors)

Cleveland hospital where Dorothy Dworkin trained as a midwife, and a
sanitarium for Jewish tubercular patients opened in Ste-Agathe, Quebec,
in 1913. The original staff of Toronto's Mount Sinai Hospital consisted of
the nursing superintendent, Miss B. Pickles, described as "a person of
wide experience and reputation whose competence and energy are
evident in every department,"[15] four graduate nurses, two student
nurses, a cook, a laundress, a housemaid, and a janitor.[16]

Initially, the new board's boost in financial clout did not result in
improved circumstances for the hospital. With many early fears dispelled,
the public was now clamouring for beds. While it pledged to serve the
special needs of Jewish patients, Mount Sinai was also committed from
its earliest days to being non-denominational, and many of its patients
were non-Jewish, especially those living on the working-class streets
close to Yorkville Avenue. During the next year, Mount Sinai continued
on its precarious financial course, sustaining an $800 deficit.[17]
Meanwhile, the range of services was beginning to expand, as Jewish
doctors found at Mount Sinai the professional haven they had been
denied elsewhere.

By 1925, all forty practising Jewish physicians formed the Toronto
Jewish Medical Association, which, in effect, was synonymous with the
staff of the hospital. The only specialists – A. I. Willinsky in Surgery, I. R.
Smith in Otolaryngology, and Benjamin Cohen in Obstetrics and

Gynecology – were installed as heads of departments, while the three senior men – L. J. Solway, Maurice A. Pollock, and Louis J. Breslin – were made rotating chiefs of Medicine.[18] Arthur Podnos (later Parker) took charge of Anesthesia. Rules and regulations for medical staff were incorporated into the by-laws. In addition, there were now nine trained nurses on staff, and student nurses were no longer employed. The youngest of a growing number of Jewish institutions, Mount Sinai was proudly introduced to the nation in the landmark survey, *The Jew in Canada*, published in 1926:

> The Mount Sinai Hospital is housed in a three-storey brick building with commodious verandahs and attractive grounds, and is situated in a fine, quiet residential section of the city. The hospital has at present accommodation for 30 patients. There are 5 public wards, 3 semi-private rooms, 1 private room and a sun parlour. The equipment used is particularly well-equipped [sic] and the sterilizer is said to be one of the best in the city.
>
> The visitor to the Hospital is favourably impressed with the cleanliness and tidiness of the place, from the basement up. The procedure employed throughout is in accord with the most

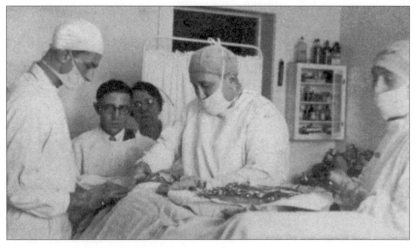

An operating room at Yorkville Mount Sinai, circa 1930. Dr. Simon Fines is seated at the head of the table. Note surgical masks worn below the nose. (Courtesy Joyce Fines Dain)

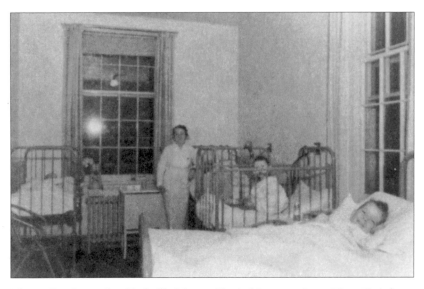

The pediatric ward at Yorkville Mount Sinai. (Courtesy Joyce Fines Dain)

approved scientific hospital methods. The punctilious cleanliness and scientific precision of method is combined with a homelike atmosphere that pervades the institution. There is an absence of cold "institutionalism" so commonly associated with hospitals.

The results obtained in the treatment of patients have been signally satisfactory. Much successful work is being done in the treatment of diabetes through the administration of insulin; and the surgical and general medical work is of a high order. The obstetrical cases are numerous in the hospital, and the nursery is one of the especially busy spots in the institution.

The Mount Sinai Hospital receives both paying and free patients. The leading Jewish physicians of the city are constantly in attendance, and to their unselfish efforts much of the success of the hospital is due.[19]

Among the pioneering practitioners in those early days at Mount Sinai on Yorkville Avenue were the only two Jewish doctors who also had appointments at other Toronto hospitals: A. I. Willinsky and L. J. Solway. Abraham Isaac Willinsky, who divided his time between the new Jewish hospital and the Toronto Western, where he was listed as head of Urology as early as 1918, was well known in Toronto medical circles, and was easily the most prominent of Mount Sinai's original medical staff. Born in Omaha, Nebraska, in 1885, Willinsky was inspired to study medicine after attending a lecture given by the great Sir William Osler at the University of Toronto, where Willinsky was studying biological sciences. Winner of the George Brown Memorial Scholarship at medical school in 1908, Willinsky was nonetheless unable to secure an internship in Toronto and, consequently, had to go abroad to further his education.

Willinsky was extensively trained at such places as the Rotunda Hospital in Dublin, the Polyclinic in New York (where, in frustration at the discrimination he had been subjected to, he registered under the name "Wills," listing his religion as Greek Orthodox), and the Mayo Clinic in Rochester, as well as hospitals in Vienna and Paris. He introduced spinal anesthesia to Toronto and was also the first physician to use a cystoscope for transurethral prostate surgery. Indeed, when the well-known surgeon Dr. Herbert Bruce, founder of the Wellesley Hospital, urgently assembled the finest team of specialists in the city to operate on his brother, who had been injured in an accident, it was Willinsky he called upon to administer the spinal anesthesia. Yet, despite his considerable reputation and a lifetime of exceptional achievements at the Western Hospital, which had been affiliated with the University of Toronto since 1914, Willinsky was never offered a university appointment.

A greatly revered early practitioner who later came to be regarded as the "dean" of the Jewish medical group, Leon Judah Solway graduated from the University of Toronto medical faculty in 1909. Russian-born, Solway studied at a rabbinical seminary in New York before undertaking his medical education. He did postgraduate work at Johns Hopkins Hospital in Baltimore and in New York before setting up practice in Toronto, where he had a minor appointment at the Faculty of Medicine in 1917–18. Continuing his postgraduate training in England in 1921, Solway earned an MRCP (Member of the Royal College of Physicians), a rare designation for the times, and subsequently devoted his large practice to internal medicine, especially cardiology. Like Willinsky, he was

Dr. Leon Judah Solway, regarded as "dean" of the Jewish medical group in the early years, was the first president of the Toronto Jewish Medical Association and co-chief of Medicine at Yorkville Mount Sinai. (Hart, The Jew in Canada*)*

appointed to the indoor staff of the Toronto Western Hospital, and, in 1938, the two were elected Fellows of the Royal College of Physicians and Surgeons of Canada.[20]

Another Mount Sinai doctor to make a significant mark in the early days was Louis J. Breslin. Arriving in Canada from Russia as an infant in 1893, Breslin became the first Jewish medallist in medicine at the University of Toronto, winning the silver prize in his class of 1912. Trained in internal medicine in Baltimore, New York, and Philadelphia, Breslin was recognized as a brilliant diagnostician and clinician who also possessed a much-sought-after expertise in the medical-legal field. For many years he was a coroner, as well as being on the out-patient staff of the Toronto General Hospital, and he ultimately earned the distinction of being the first Jewish doctor to become a Fellow of the Royal College of Physicians and Surgeons by examination.[21]

Among the early Jewish doctors in Toronto, Abraham Brodey was distinguished by his significant academic achievements. A gifted student, Brodey had already earned an MA prior to beginning his medical studies at the University of Toronto; he subsequently won the silver medal upon graduation from the medical faculty in 1913. Following postgraduate study in England and France, he became a Fellow in Physiology at U of T, and spent one year in research under the

Dr. Louis J. Breslin, the first Jewish doctor to become a Fellow of the Royal College of Physicians and Surgeons by examination, practised at 405 Dundas Street West from 1914 until his death in 1952. (Hart, The Jew in Canada*)*

celebrated Professor T. G. Brodie on the glomerular function of the kidney. He then became a demonstrator in applied chemistry, before he went to New York for further postgraduate training. From 1916 to 1919, Brodey was named acting professor of pharmacology and materia medica at the University of Toronto during the military service of Professor B. Henderson. In 1919, he was appointed demonstrator in physiology at the Royal College of Dental Surgeons, Toronto. Along with Breslin, Brodey took charge of the early pathology service at Mount Sinai Hospital, assisted by a lone laboratory technician, eighteen-year-old Fanny Ziskin.[22]

Dr. Bernard Willinsky, known as "Bunny," worked closely with his older brother A. I. and, in 1945, would follow him as chief of Surgery at Yorkville Mount Sinai. When he graduated from the U of T's Faculty of Medicine as the gold medallist in 1928, the younger Willinsky had already completed dental school. After postgraduate study at several institutions in England, he returned to Toronto, where he shared an office with his brother on Spadina Avenue. A keen yachtsman, Willinsky trailed Marilyn Bell as official physician during her historic 1954 swim across Lake Ontario. A lifejacket of his design that held a wearer's head above water became the prototype for one approved by the Department of Transport. Both Willinsky brothers were widely esteemed in the community, and remembered as much for the sheer

Dorothy Dworkin and the ladies of the Auxiliary (Ezras Noshem *society) of Mount Sinai Hospital in the 1920s. (The Ontario Jewish Archives)*

One of the many fund-raising events to support Yorkville Mount Sinai. From left: Mrs. E. F. Singer, Mrs. Simon Fines, Dorothy Dworkin. (Courtesy Joyce Fines Dain)

force of their personalities and their eclectic non-medical interests as for their surgical skill.[23]

In 1925, Mount Sinai received its first provincial grant, a princely $1,300, and plans were made to add an Out-Patient department, provide better facilities for the medical staff, and take on interns. The latter project, of course, had a high priority, given the experience of the hospital's current doctors. Still, in order to finance these modest improvements, a great deal more money was needed than the hospital received from its three main sources of income: patient fees, subscribers' dues, and an allowance from the Federation of Jewish Philanthropies. To supplement these, Dorothy Dworkin launched a Ladies' Auxiliary, which promptly set to work organizing bazaars, teas, and other events, including a hugely successful baby contest, judged by Dr. Alan Brown, who, as chief pediatrician at the Hospital for Sick Children and one of the inventors of the baby cereal Pablum, was Toronto's celebrity pediatrician. In their zeal for the cause, Dworkin and her cohorts would often station themselves outside synagogues following services, "when [their] co-religionists were in a mellow mood," and solicit funds for the hospital.[24] Unfortunately, the federation, whose mandate was to allot funds to Jewish organizations in lieu of individual appeals to the financially beleaguered community, took a dim view of this freelance effort to enhance the treasury, and it complained of Mount Sinai's violation in executive director Joseph B. Woolf's report of 1925.[25]

By early 1929, the hospital had become so overcrowded that the board and medical staff jointly decided to launch a campaign to build a new hospital. The site of the Grace Hospital, then at College and Huron streets, was seriously considered for the relocation. But when the stock market crashed in October, all plans had to be scuttled in favour of augmenting the present building with a small addition and much-needed equipment. Architect Benjamin Swartz coordinated the former, extending the basement of the hospital. The interior of the building was spruced up at a cost of $2,500, and minutes of the board that autumn record other expenditures: a new case-room table, $125; two hospital desks, $250; an operating-room lamp, $125; a suction machine, $350; a

Belle Sadowski as a young graduate nurse, 1916. (Courtesy Allen Taradash)

larger water heater, $100; and a new heating system in the sun parlour, necessary to provide additional bed space, $250. The minutes also proudly inform members that Dr. David Perlman had donated a gas and oxygen machine, valued at $350, and that the Ladies' Auxiliary had raised enough money to discharge one of the hospital's $6,000 outstanding mortgages, saving $420 a year in interest.[26] That same year, Mount Sinai took on its first intern, Milton Raymers, and employed six Jewish nurses, duly noting that these women were "enabled to obtain positions they could not have done at a non-Jewish hospital." (One of those nurses was Belle Sadowski, who became a superintendent of nurses during the latter 1920s and whose brother Ben would come to play a monumental role in the hospital's future.) Daily rates in 1931 were as follows: private room, $3.50 to $5.00; semi-private, $2.80; ward, $1.75; operating-room fee $5.00 to $10.00; delivery-room fee, $3.00 to $5.00.[27]

The desperate need for additional space was to persist for the rest of Mount Sinai's tenure on Yorkville Avenue. In the deputy provincial secretary's report following a 1929 inspection of the hospital, he remarked, "The condition is satisfactory, much better than could be expected under the circumstances. This hospital has outgrown its usefulness and serious consideration should be given to the construction of a new building with ample capacity for the needs of the Jewish population of Toronto. At present, the hospital is very crowded and the staff

 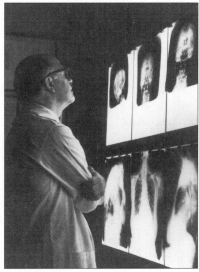

Left: Dr. David Perlman, a U of T Faculty of Medicine graduate of 1918, was a general practitioner who became an anesthetist at Yorkville Mount Sinai in 1926. (Courtesy Geraldine Perlman Shapiro) Right: Radiologist and history buff Dr. David Eisen recorded the early history of Toronto's Jewish doctors. (Courtesy Joy Eisen Wolfson)

members are badly handicapped on this account. I would respectfully request that immediate steps be taken to relieve this situation."[28]

The Great Depression, however, put all thoughts of expansion on hold. With fully a third of Toronto's population unemployed and widespread economic despair, many people were unable to pay for their hospitalization; with no government subsidy for indigent patients, debts quickly mounted. As secretary of the board of directors at this time, Dorothy Dworkin frantically scrambled to hold off creditors without unduly alarming the rest of the board, whose moral and financial support was so desperately needed. Occasionally she would dispatch the hospital bookkeeper, Rubye Orlinsky, to the bank with a bottle of *schnapps* for the manager, then turn up herself with a promissory note and a persuasive appeal for credit.[29] More often, she had to hold signed cheques in her office safe until the hospital account could cover them.

But if the hospital's finances were in jeopardy during the Depression, its professional fortunes were beginning to improve with

Dr. Harold Pritzker in his tiny "pathology lab" at Yorkville Mount Sinai in 1938. (Courtesy Dr. Kenneth Pritzker)

the addition to its staff of a number of specialists. Dr. David Perlman had become anesthetist to Mount Sinai in 1926, while retaining his general practice. During the late 1920s and early 1930s, several more Jewish specialists[*] had joined the group: Drs. Bernard "Bunny" Willinsky, Adolph Appell, and Abraham "Al" Track, Surgery; Dr. David Eisen, Radiology; Drs. Maxwell K. Bochner and Louis Kazdan, Ophthalmology; and Dr. Gordon Manace, Pediatrics. The latter's brother, Dr. Bernard Manace, returned to Toronto from studies in Ann Arbor, Michigan, and New York to promote the teaching and study of allergy as a specialty in Canada. The allergy clinic Manace established at Yorkville Mount Sinai in 1934 was Toronto's first. In 1935, Dr. Israel Shapiro became the first surgeon in the city of Toronto specializing exclusively in orthopedics, following his training at the Hospital for Joint Diseases in New York. In 1938, Dr. Harold G. Pritzker returned from Cleveland, where he had trained extensively in pathology, to complete Mount Sinai's coverage of major specialties.

---

[*] The term specialist was often loosely applied at this time, since no recognized standard for qualifications yet existed in Canada. G. Harvey Agnew, *Canadian Hospitals, 1920-1970: A Dramatic Half-Century* (Toronto: University of Toronto Press, 1974), p. 28.

Dr. Simon Fines, right, with an unidentified nurse on the grounds of Yorkville Mount Sinai. (Courtesy Joyce Fines Dain)

As an in-hospital medical specialty, Pathology was in its infancy, and Pritzker, who was employed only part time while maintaining a general practice out of his home, was given the grand sum of $50, most of which he spent at Woolworth's buying suitable glassware to outfit a broom-closet-size laboratory. Still, he was likely one of the most highly trained specialists at Yorkville when he arrived, held a non-clinical appointment as demonstrator at the University of Toronto in the late 1940s, and subsequently became the only chief of service to retain the title once the hospital was fully established on University Avenue.

It was also during the Depression that the hospital employed Dr. Simon Fines as administrator. Born in Byelorussia, Fines had been Mount Sinai's second intern in 1930. As a freshly licensed doctor, he had struggled to set up a general practice in rural Ontario, commuting to Toronto and his pregnant wife on weekends. But with chickens and eggs his only payment during those troubled times, he soon had to find a more reliable source of income. Like many hospital administrators in those days who had no real training for their supervisory roles, Fines took on a vast, undefined job, which likely included being director of nursing services, purchasing agent, personnel officer, public-relations official, board liaison, receiver of doctors' messages, enforcer of visiting regulations, and opener of the morning mail.[30] A central figure during the Yorkville years, Fines remained as administrator from 1932 to 1954, when he returned to general practice.

One cannot ignore the extraordinary personal bond that drew these early Mount Sinai physicians together, even as their professional relationships became cemented. In 1929, in recognition of its close alliance with the hospital, the Toronto Jewish Medical Association changed its name to the Mount Sinai Medical Society. Regular meetings of the society were held at members' homes until membership increased to the point where larger premises had to be secured. In addition to its medical agenda, the society organized annual fishing trips and established a weekly bowling league, which continued for decades. It also united the Jewish medical profession in its concern regarding the rising Nazi power in Germany. During the early 1930s, the group passed resolutions advising medical-supply houses not to solicit its members to purchase or use German-made products. Jewish pharmacists and dentists were instructed to follow suit. Through the Canadian Jewish Congress, the Mount Sinai Medical Society also rendered free medical and surgical services to "British War Guests" and applicants for enlistment in the Canadian Armed Forces.[31]

Certainly a powerful link between all the Yorkville doctors was their near-total isolation from a hidebound medical establishment, both in Toronto and beyond. So entrenched was the antipathy toward Jewish physicians, and indeed any "outsiders," that most of them simply endured their professional invisibility as inevitable. (A black doctor named Morrison, who practised on Bathurst Street, was similarly ostracized from the medical mainstream and was subsequently granted admitting privileges at Yorkville Mount Sinai in the 1930s.)[32]

Regrettably, there was no shortage of evidence to reinforce this general atmosphere of animosity, a truth brought home by an odious incident in Montreal in the late spring of 1934. On June 15 of that year, a day that has since been labelled Canadian medicine's "day of shame,"[33] seventy-five French-Canadian interns from Notre Dame, St. Jean de Dieu, Ste. Justine, Hôtel Dieu, and Miséricorde hospitals went on strike. The issue precipitating the action didn't involve a boost in pay or better working conditions; the principle that ignited these young doctors to abandon their sick charges and take to the streets in protest was their refusal to work alongside Dr. Samuel Rabinovitch, a Jew born in Palestine, who had graduated at the top of his medical class from the Université de Montréal. As the xenophobia escalated in the ensuing days, two more French-speaking hospitals considered joining the strike, while senior doctors at a third signed the petition requesting termination of Rabinovitch's contract. Meanwhile, the Quebec newspaper, *Le Devoir*, reported that supporters and "well-wishers" of the striking interns, including a veritable Who's Who of French-Canadian nationalist organizations and Catholic clergy, promised each one a strike fund of $500 and "many gifts of cigarettes." The paper also interviewed strike leaders on the subject of an already-existing committee headed by the Archbishop of Montreal to investigate "the Jewish question" at the Université de Montréal. One strike leader remarked, "The university authorities are the first to want to know if the university must receive Jews and why it is accepting them in such large numbers."[34] Only when Rabinovitch withdrew from the ugly fray, expressing deep regret in his letter of resignation that "the French interns have taken up the racial question in a hospital where the care of the sick should be their first and only consideration," did the strike finally come to an end.

Another incident closer to home was related years later by Mount Sinai's Dr. Israel Shapiro to a younger colleague, orthopedic surgeon Dr. Fred Langer, and neatly illustrates the prevailing atmosphere that contributed so substantially to the siege mentality adopted by many of the pioneer Yorkville doctors. In the early years of the Second World War, Shapiro was approached by a salesman of orthopedic appliances about a complicated spinal brace that had just come on the market. The salesman would be giving a presentation about the new brace during rounds at the Toronto General Hospital the following Saturday and invited Shapiro to attend. "I can't say I'll be there, but I'll try," responded Shapiro guardedly, sensing a possible roadblock. His instincts were right on the mark. When he called Dr. R. I. Harris, the General's respected orthopedic man, requesting permission to attend, Harris said

Dr. Israel Shapiro was ignominiously excluded from many professional events despite his status as Toronto's first orthopedic surgeon. (Courtesy Ruth Shapiro)

no, even though, according to Langer, Shapiro promised to not ask any questions and to leave immediately following the presentation.[35]

Within the hospital itself, a little cloakroom just off the main entrance served as the social and medical nerve centre where doctors met daily to exchange views on any subject. That cloakroom, Mount Sinai's safe harbour in every storm, attained mythic proportions in early hospital lore. Wrote Dr. Aaron Volpé of the place: "The entire business and policy of the hospital was settled there – with everyone pitching in. . . . There was so much eagerness and vitality and enthusiasm there. It was our own hospital. We were the pioneers and we had a fierce pride in this, our little hospital. . . . Every doctor gave of his best to the hospital and worked with the thrilling enthusiasm which only pioneers can feel."[36]

Overfilled to 140 per cent of its capacity during the Depression, the hospital was severely handicapped by lack of patient beds. It wasn't unusual in the early 1930s for doctors to come into the cloakroom and find their leather couch had vanished and was doubling somewhere as a confinement bed, or that all the chairs had been requisitioned for some higher purpose than a doctor's repose. Often the entire cloakroom was transformed into a circumcision room and the doctors drafted into a *minyan* (quorum of ten men required for religious

Mount Sinai Hospital on Yorkville Avenue following renovation by architects Richmond and Kaminker in 1935. (Mount Sinai Hospital)

rituals).[37] By 1933, plans were in motion to erect a modest annex to the building at a cost of $50,000.

The hospital already had $10,000 set aside for this purpose, thanks in large measure to a bequest from the estate of Dr. Israel Lavine, a 1923 medical graduate who had been forced to seek an internship in Detroit and had died tragically in an automobile accident while returning for a visit to Toronto. Using his connections with the Ontario government, board president E. Fred Singer was then able to obtain an additional $10,000 from the province and $5,000 from the city, the latter grant given on the condition that union rates be paid throughout the building project. Turned down by every loan company in the city for the remaining funds, the hospital next turned to a plan devised by Henry Dworkin, Dorothy's late husband, whereby individuals would purchase life-insurance policies as an additional guarantee on the mortgage. When the hat was passed, those who put up $1,000 each for the policies were Drs. M. Bochner, G. Manace, I. Vaile, S. Leslie, D. Esser, M. Kohan, D. Perlman, N. Shaul, S. Shaul, S. Fines, and D. Eisen, as well as the architects engaged for the project, Benjamin Kaminker and Edward Richmond, and hospital board leaders Fred Singer and Dorothy Dworkin.[38]

In the end, that expansion, too, was deemed insufficient, and a committee of doctors was appointed to consider alternative locations as possible sites for an enlarged hospital, though ultimately, this idea was abandoned in favour of a complete modernization. An English Jew, Otto B. Roger, who had recently arrived in Toronto to take up an executive position with Shell Oil, took charge of the fund-raising effort, and in 1934 a two-storey-and-basement addition was constructed at the rear of the hospital and a Georgian revival façade appended to the front. The double doors of the brick building, now framed with Corinthian pilasters, featured the Star of David incorporated into the capitals. Steam heat was also installed at this time and plumbing was extended and upgraded.[39]

A Social Services department associated with the *Folks Farein* became the newest hospital division, and the extremely popular out-patient clinics were expanded and placed under the supervision of Dr. William Harris. Interns, who previously had received only board and lodging in exchange for their services, would now collect $10 a month, plus a $60 bonus at the conclusion of their terms.

For the first time, the hospital's kosher kitchen came under the watchful eye of a trained dietitian, Ida Yudashkin. A dental out-patient clinic opened under the direction of Dr. Saul Simon, bringing the Jewish Dental Society into close association with the medical society. As well, there were now two new surgical suites, and bed capacity increased from thirty-five to eighty-six. With the purchase of an electrocardiograph machine in May 1935, Mount Sinai Hospital, though still a small institution, was now completely modern and up-to-date.

3

Ben Sadowski's Dream

Although the improvements following the addition of 1934 were significant, a multitude of problems arose that no amount of renovation or updating could alleviate in such a small hospital. Because virtually every Jewish doctor in Toronto was allied with Mount Sinai and, for the most part, shunned everywhere else, the competition among them for patients and for the hospital's very few beds was relentless. The situation was demoralizing, and led to a certain degree of jealousy among the medical staff and unseemly jockeying for influence with the chiefs of departments.

Serious overcrowding also continued to be a chronic obstacle at Mount Sinai on Yorkville, to the point where a private room there could legitimately be defined as a cot in the hallway surrounded by a screen. So, in the late 1930s, there was one final attempt to expand when the hospital offered to purchase the adjoining property.[1] However, when the owners declined to sell, the conclusion was finally reached to rebuild on another site. Ben Sadowski, president of National Motors and a dynamic, successful community leader, was appointed head of the expansion campaign.

By all accounts, Sadowski was a tough but brilliant individual, who "thought big" in everything he undertook. He was born in 1894 in

Ben Sadowski's vision and formidable influence shaped the future of Mount Sinai Hospital. (Courtesy Yvonne Sadowski Davies)

Massey, Ontario, a rugged frontier town, where his father, the resident postmaster, regularly dealt with the local native people in their own language. As a youth, Sadowski was sent to Minneapolis to study for the rabbinate, a calling for which he quickly determined he was unsuited. Returning to Toronto, he studied maths and physics at the University of Toronto, teaching there briefly following his graduation. But eking out a living as a poorly paid university instructor had little long-term appeal, and Sadowski decided to pursue another of his great interests: automobiles. After a brief stint as a mechanic in a Parkdale garage, Sadowski opened a Willys-Knight dealership before expanding into the highly successful National Motors.

Sadowski's communal accomplishments were vast, and paralleled his corporate ones. He was part of a group of men who were at the very centre of Jewish philanthropy in Toronto. Organizations such as the United Jewish Welfare Fund, Toronto Hebrew Free Loan Society, Canadian Jewish Congress, Jewish Immigrant Aid Society, and Jewish Family and Child Service were all products of his prodigious energy and largesse. Within the wider Toronto community, Sadowski also commanded a great deal of respect. He maintained close ties with the University of Toronto, for which he acted as a "dollar-a-year" consultant throughout the Second World War. He was also a capable leader of the city's Red Cross and Red Feather (a forerunner of the United Appeal) organizations, as well as being a founder of the Canadian Council of Christians and Jews. But among all his various charitable endeavours, Sadowski's greatest love was Mount Sinai Hospital.

Like a parent anguished on account of an underachieving child, Sadowski believed that Mount Sinai was destined to become much more than a narrowly defined and community-rooted hospital. Utterly convinced of the great potential within the Jewish community, he resolved that the hospital's medical staff, many of whom were highly experienced yet inadequately trained specialists, would eventually rank among the finest in the profession. He envisioned acceptance and respect from the medical establishment and from the broader community. And, most of all, he dreamed that, one day, Mount Sinai would become affiliated with the University of Toronto, as one of the Faculty of Medicine's teaching hospitals.

To even entertain, let alone propose, such a grandiose notion in 1942 was audacious, but Sadowski was nothing if not a persuasive and steadfast visionary, long accustomed to having the upper hand. He assembled a group of close friends and business associates with whom he had frequently worked for charitable causes. These individuals, including Samuel Godfrey, Jacob Davis, Henry Rosenberg, Louis Posluns, Reuben Rosefield, Percy Hermant, Charles Foster, J. Charles Epstein, Arthur Cohen, Jack Granatstein, Morris Till, Sam Zacks, Irving Oelbaum, Jule Allen, and Samuel Lunenfeld began to meet regularly in Sadowski's home to plan the institution that would fulfil his dream. It was to be called, appropriately, *New* Mount Sinai Hospital.

Although he remained obstinate and aggressive, never wavering from his course, Sadowski encountered considerable opposition to his plan. Certainly Jews outside the hospital "family" did not universally embrace such an exalted vision of the future. For one thing, many people, including his close associate, Samuel Lunenfeld, expressed concern that a hospital in the Sadowski mould would lose its vital connection to the Jewish community, which, after all, had provided its original reason for existence.[2] Others felt the most appropriate move for Mount Sinai would be into the north suburban neighbourhoods, where Jewish families were beginning to relocate and where the new Jewish

Home for the Aged was soon to be built. Even among the Yorkville doctors, serious fault lines were forming, as many of them came to realize that the limitations of their training would likely reduce, if not eliminate, their influence at a new hospital. What's more, having endured humiliating treatment at the hands of the medical establishment, many Jewish doctors were understandably reluctant to turn over the hard-won independence they enjoyed on Yorkville to authorities at the University of Toronto's Faculty of Medicine.

An irascible Ben Sadowski was completely unmoved by these arguments, all of which he dismissed as short-sighted. New Mount Sinai Hospital, he firmly believed, would become the *pride* of the Jewish community. And in order to rise to the highest level of medicine, to prove how good it could be, it was imperative for the hospital to situate at the very heart of medical activity in Toronto, not on its periphery. That heart, Sadowski knew unequivocally, was University Avenue, the location of the Toronto General, which was the university's dominant teaching hospital. The conflict played out with a good deal of resentment at the time, but was ultimately resolved in Sadowski's favour.

In December 1942, the board obtained an option on a block of land on the east side of University Avenue between Gerrard and Elm streets, owned by one of its members, Samuel Lunenfeld. Lunenfeld was a wealthy steel magnate and real-estate developer from Galt, Ontario, who had an abiding concern for medical research and who had contributed generously for that purpose to the Hospital for Sick Children. The land Lunenfeld acquired at a cost of $140,000, an amount he then offered to donate for the purpose of a new Jewish hospital, was just south of both the University of Toronto and the Toronto General Hospital. Without question, Sadowski thought, it was the perfect location for New Mount Sinai.

Unfortunately, not everyone agreed with that assessment. Considering that Toronto was still in the midst of a sorry era in which both written and unwritten restrictive covenants existed forbidding the sale of certain property to Jews, it wasn't entirely unexpected when some of the occupants along University Avenue were less than delighted with their proposed new neighbours. Those who were involved at the time say the Toronto General was particularly appalled that a Jewish hospital should establish itself next door, and threw up roadblocks to impede such an eventuality.[3] The Hospital for Sick Children, meanwhile, announced that it had planned to purchase that parcel of land for its own expansion, but had been compelled to drop negotiations when the war situation worsened.

In 1944, when the Hospital for Sick Children proposed that New Mount Sinai consider another piece of land on the northwest corner of University at Elm, Ben Sadowski recognized a golden opportunity. In a bold move, he agreed to accept the alternate property and to hand over the east University Avenue land to Sick Kids for the sum of one dollar – with certain conditions. There would have to be a commitment from the University of Toronto (whose medical faculty was virtually synonymous with the mighty Toronto General) that, once specific requirements were fulfilled, New Mount Sinai would be permitted to become an accepted teaching hospital. Furthermore, the Hospital for Sick Children, a rigidly WASP bastion of medical élite, was to begin accepting Jewish interns and residents.[4]

It is likely that the provincial government had a hand in bringing pressure to bear on the General and Sick Children's hospitals, since the Ministry of Labour at Queen's Park was already moving toward the human rights legislation that would begin toppling barriers against minorities and introduce much-needed changes to Toronto. In any event, a satisfactory agreement was eventually reached. And although the board of New Mount Sinai expressed some last-minute apprehension about the size of the second plot of land, which wouldn't hold as large a structure as the first due to its configuration, and about the "odour of beer" wafting across the street from a brewery on the southwest corner, it promptly saw the wisdom of accepting such a deal.[5]

It would be twelve long years from the birth of the idea of New Mount Sinai to the day when its doors would finally open in the summer of 1953. Much of the fund-raising had to be put on hold until after the war, as did serious planning for the actual construction. In the meantime, the hectic pace and chaotic conditions persisted at 100 Yorkville.

Notes from Yorkville

To help finance the major expansion of 1934, Dorothy Dworkin's Ladies' Auxiliary had moved into high gear. By that time, the organization had split into several units: the Sinais composed the largest group. Medical and dental wives each maintained their own auxiliaries. The Twigs were unmarried women, in many instances daughters of the Sinais. Later, the Cradle Club formed, a group of young mothers who focused on the maternity needs of the hospital. Then there were external organizations, such as the group of teenage girls calling themselves Club Alexis, who donated their time and talent to the hospital. This hodgepodge of auxiliaries usually functioned independently, raising funds for specific projects that each group identified as worthy of attention. In 1931, for example, the Sinais presented the hospital with its first refrigerator, and also used the proceeds from a gala theatre night at the Standard Theatre to pay off the hospital's mortgage, which was ceremoniously burned on stage by president E. Fred Singer following the performance.[6] But once a year, beginning in 1940, all the auxiliaries combined their efforts to produce a giant three-day street fair held at Alexandra Park. The event, which featured games, food, amusement rides, and sales of merchandise either made by the women themselves or contributed by companies they solicited, attracted twenty thousand people annually and brought

F1405-23-81 #17 MSR 6871

Preparing for the annual Alexandra Park outdoor fundraiser in aid of Yorkville Mount Sinai. (Archives of Ontario – Dorothy Dworkin Collection)

Club Alexis members gathered on the front steps of Yorkville Mount Sinai, 1940.
(Courtesy Faye Corbin)

F1405-23-81 MSR 6871-18

"The Sinais" led by Dorothy Dworkin, second row, fifth from left, circa 1940.
(Archives of Ontario)

in so much money that Dr. Simon Fines required a police escort several times a day when he shuttled deposits to the bank.[7] In 1940, the auxiliaries together raised $11,000.

Dr. Maurice W. Selznick became the first Toronto Jewish doctor to enlist in the military in 1939. He was followed by twenty-nine members of the Mount Sinai Medical Society and approximately one hundred more young Jewish medical graduates who signed up prior to going into practice. Drs. Charles Krakauer and I. P. Weingarten were killed in action.[8]

As early as 1934, the Medical Advisory Council began considering the plight of refugee Jewish doctors, bringing several who managed to escape the horrors in Germany to Yorkville to serve as interns. Dr. Abraham Brodey was especially involved in this work.[9]

Records show that two women physicians, Bertha Wilensky and Rose Abron, were appointed to the associate staff in the Department of Obstetrics and Gynecology in the mid-1930s. In addition to the pair, the only other Jewish women practising medicine in Toronto during this decade were Drs. Cecile Markowitz, Anna Gelber, and Dora Borsook.[10] In 1940, the intern committee hired Frances "Fanny" Gula as the first and only woman intern at Yorkville Mount Sinai. This was undoubtedly a courageous initiative, since all women medical graduates in those early years endured blatant gender discrimination and had considerable difficulty securing internships. Needless to say, being Jewish compounded those problems. As a result, many women doctors practised only briefly or not at all. Dr. Gula (later Dr. Frances Levy) defied that pattern, however, and after being singled out by the Medical Advisory Council as the best intern of the year,[11] carried on a busy family practice in Hamilton, Ontario, until her death in 1984.[12]

In 1938, a committee that called itself the Central Medical Bureau was convened to put an end to the exploitation of the lodge doctors. Dr. John Soboloff, president of the Lodge Doctors' Association, and Dr. Coleman Solursh, along with accountant Charles Sanders, called a meeting of the lodge representatives to summarily advise them that the member physicians would no longer endure the conditions under which they worked. The custom was ripe for abuse, since, as mentioned, a tiny membership fee gave a lodge member and his entire family unrestricted access to the doctor's services and menacing powers over him. If the doctor didn't arrive quickly enough after being summoned, for example, he risked being hauled before the executive of the lodge and accused of poor practice. (One doctor told the Central Medical Bureau of being called on a rainy weekend to examine a woman who complained of stomach pains. When the condition was pronounced minor, the woman then insisted the doctor take her to Eaton's, since it was on the way back to his office.) Paradoxically, the fact that they tolerated such exploitative conditions meant that Jewish doctors often didn't inspire much confidence in their patients.

With the full cooperation of the Mount Sinai board and the Medical Advisory Council of the hospital, who collectively pressured the doctors to end the current practice, Soboloff and Solursh issued an ultimatum to the lodges. Election of doctors, which was demeaning and fostered unethical practices, was to be suspended. Lodges would henceforth be provided with a list of practitioners, from which members could select their own physician. Furthermore, the doctors demanded a proper professional accounting of the fees they would receive relative to the number of patients served.

It wasn't without spirited protest that the lodge representatives finally relinquished their unreasonable control over the doctors. (The largest of the mutual-benefit societies, Pride of Israel, refused to yield at all.) But in the end, most of the organizations capitulated to the Central Medical Bureau's demands. Lodge doctoring continued under the modified rules until 1947, at which point economic conditions had improved and new forms of insurance had become available. Essentially, however, its disappearance immediately elevated the stature of the Jewish doctors, both within their own community and beyond it.[13]

In November 1941, to help alleviate the space shortage, the Mount Sinai Medical Society, in the name of seven trustees, purchased a small house

Laboratory facilities improved at Yorkville Mount Sinai following major renovations. (Courtesy Dr. Kenneth Pritzker)

at 101 Yorkville, diagonally across from the hospital. The building, which they named Dorothy Dworkin House, was used chiefly for meetings, library facilities, and lectures. Several years later, when the building was sold, the doctors turned over the proceeds to New Mount Sinai Hospital.

It seems that not every crisis on Yorkville Avenue could be averted by acquiring additional space. A report of the Hospital Practice Committee in the autumn of 1941 noted several intolerable situations needing attention and, at the same time, provided a snapshot of daily life at the hospital. From the X-ray department, for example, there was an urgent request "that the drain of the hospital be repaired in order that the X-ray room may not be flooded out every time it rains." The report went on to disclose: "This water also reaches into the out-patient office and the girl there complains she is unable to work when it rains." Under the reproachful rubric, "Re Patients Clogging Up the Hospital," the following sensible solution was offered: "Any patient staying more than three weeks should be re-examined by the chief of service with a view to discharge." The same communication took a hard line against doctors who eroded decorum by their habit of "tickling nurses in the ribs," and admonished others who persisted in "settling their political differences in vigorous voices" outside the operating rooms.[14] Other disciplinary action focused on the overly aggressive tactics of the competing "circumcising solicitors," which evidently had gotten so far out of hand that Dr. Simon Fines had to bar the *mohelim* from canvassing new mothers or entering the nursery.[15]

The introduction of antibiotics to the civilian population in 1945 had an immense impact on the practice of medicine at the hospital. Among other benefits, mastoid disease, one of the foremost reasons for surgery, especially on children and young adults, was virtually wiped out. In those days, penicillin was given by intramuscular injection every three hours around the clock, and the few interns billeted on the third floor of the hospital were awakened accordingly to administer the drug throughout the night. It was considered a major victory by the young interns when they prevailed upon the administration to allow the night-shift nurses to give the penicillin shots.[16]

Another mission assigned to the long-suffering interns was obtaining permission from family members when post-mortem examinations became necessary. Since Orthodox Judaism expressly forbids autopsies, their enthusiasm for this task, not to mention their success rate in gaining authorization, was abysmally low, only to rise, according to one account, when the mostly impecunious interns were offered the incentive of a pastrami sandwich for each permission obtained.[17]

Most patients of Yorkville physicians were Yiddish-speaking Jews, many of them working-class people employed in the garment trade. As a result, the busiest office day was Saturday, when factories were closed and the workers free to come. In 1946, Ruth Mather was secretary/medical assistant in the mornings to gastro-enterologist Dr. Louis Cole and in the afternoons to cardiologist Dr. Sidney Carlen in the small office they shared at 116 College Street. Her memoir of those days includes the following accounts of the communication barriers that continued to plague immigrant patients and their doctors:

> [Dr. Cole's] practice involved a lot of messy lab work as well as
> the office routine. Periodically, gastric analyses were performed in

Dr. Sidney Carlen led the cardiology service at New Mount Sinai Hospital for many years. (Courtesy Dr. Peter Carlen)

the office. He would pass the tubes and then go off to the hospital. I picture him in his white coat, standing over some poor unlucky soul, pushing the tube down through a nostril and urgently repeating the Yiddish word for swallow – it sounded like "*shlingin, shlingin.*" The patients would sit in the waiting room like penitents, having eaten a meal of white bread and water. While I typed, I could keep my eye on them through the little opening.

Dr. Carlen was a third-generation Canadian, so Yiddish had not been used in his home, although his father spoke it well. This posed a problem. Usually, the older people brought a member of the family to interpret. The doctor made an effort to learn Yiddish and took some lessons from an old rabbi, but, due to the pressure of practice, these had to be discontinued, and he never achieved his goal. When someone came without an interpreter, both the doctor and the patient would communicate with whatever words they knew, filling in the gaps by gesticulating with hands and face.[18]

With so few fully qualified, accredited Jewish specialists in those days, patients who were given a distressing diagnosis or advised they needed major surgery would often appeal to their Yorkville practitioners to send them to a "big-shot Gentile doctor" for a second opinion.

One of the surgical greats in Toronto, Dr. Roscoe Graham, was every-thing his Jewish contemporaries were not: renowned in his field, uni-versally respected, tall, elegant, with a rose in his lapel. All the Yorkville specialists understood immediately when their patients, fracturing the famous man's name, insisted, "Get me Oscar!"[19]

Building New Mount Sinai

As the war came to an end, plans began in earnest for the new hospital. Ben Sadowski was now president of the hospital, and Arthur Cohen was named chairman of the Building Committee. The first subscribers' meeting of the New Mount Sinai Hospital Building Fund was held on February 9, 1944, and, later that spring, Dr. J. J. Golub, director of the New York City Hospital for Joint Diseases, was hired as consultant to plan for the new hospital. Mindful of the mandate to heed all require-ments necessary for a teaching hospital, the board asked University of Toronto professor of hospital administration Dr. G. Harvey Agnew to recommend architects, and the firm of Govan, Ferguson, and Lindsay was contracted. It must have been considered appropriate to appoint a Jewish firm as well, because the firm of Kaplan and Sprachman was named as co-architects. The exchange of property with the Hospital for Sick Children, under discussion for several months, was finally con-cluded on February 3, 1945.

Golub's original report called for an 8-storey, 200-bed hospital plus 40 bassinets, with provision for expansion to 400 beds. It was fully equipped for teaching purposes, with out-patient departments, confer-ence and demonstration rooms, and suitable laboratories, and the cost was projected at $3 million.[20] During the next few years, both the design and the construction costs were to undergo many revisions. But what was evident from the outset was that a great deal of money had to be raised. Even though New Mount Sinai, like its predecessor on Yorkville, would be a non-denominational hospital serving more non-Jewish patients than Jewish ones – facts noted in a newspaper editorial about the building campaign[21] – the burden of the expense would be borne by

New Mount Sinai Hospital at 550 University Avenue, under construction in 1951, would incorporate some of the latest technological advances in hospital equipment. (Courtesy Dr. Kenneth Pritzker)

the Jewish community. The board hired Sol Grand, former director of Winnipeg's United Jewish Welfare Fund, to become executive director of the New Mount Sinai Building Fund Campaign. His Welfare Fund counterpart in Toronto, Florence Hutner, one of the community's most knowledgeable and capable executives, was also recruited to organize and direct building-fund activities.

By the time Toronto Mayor Hiram McCallum turned the first sod on September 30, 1948, the estimated cost had risen to $4,250,000, considered a "huge sum" for a hospital, according to the *Globe and Mail.*[22] What would be unique about the New Mount Sinai, aside from its state-of-the-art equipment, was that it was to have no public ward with more than four beds, a feature quite unheard-of in Toronto's existing general hospitals. As construction progressed, plans and costs escalated even further, evolving finally into a 12-storey, 350-bed hospital, plus 86 bassinets, with a price tag of $7,300,000. Public grants toward the eventual cost amounted to only a fraction of the total, with the city allotting $300,000, the province, $380,000, and the federal government, $379,600.

Kenneth Pritzker, son of New Mount Sinai's pathologist-in-chief Harold Pritzker, and Mount Sinai's current pathologist-in-chief, is the young boy admiring the soon-to-be-opened hospital in the summer of 1953. (Courtesy Dr. Kenneth Pritzker)

In three renewed campaigns under Ben Sadowski's stewardship, almost all of the remaining $6 million was raised within the Jewish community.

One significant conflict arose in 1951 concerning the issue of *kashruth*, or kosher, food services for the new hospital. Although there was never a question of not providing strictly supervised kosher food for those Jewish patients desiring it, the dilemma involved having additional non-kosher food services available for those patients and staff not restricted by religious dietary laws. The hospital was urged by the Council for Religious Affairs of the Canadian Jewish Congress to follow the example of the Jewish General Hospital in Montreal, founded in 1934, which maintained a strictly all-kosher operation. Private citizens representing the Orthodox community also wrote to the board, one warning ominously that "if the news that the Jewish Hospital was not going to be a truly Jewish Hospital were to leak out, so to speak, there would be some very grave repercussions indeed." But, in the end, it was decided to introduce the dual kitchen service, in the manner of some of the newer hospitals under Jewish auspices in the United States. In defence of this decision, it was noted that an all-kosher set-up would entail a 15-to-20-per-cent higher food cost.[23]

Lawyer Rose Torno's professional overhaul of the various Auxiliary groups produced an efficient, focused organization that henceforth would play a major role in hospital affairs. (Courtesy the MSH Auxiliary)

Even before the move to University Avenue, one of Ben Sadowski's highest priorities had been to establish a fresh, invigorated Women's Auxiliary. Since the hospital's inception by the *Ezras Noshem* in 1922, women had been at the forefront of all its important activities. Certainly Dorothy Dworkin and her brigade of hardworking supporters had saved the day on more than one occasion, by filling in on wards during wartime staff shortages and by faithful fund-raising. But the sheer number of splinter volunteer groups at the Yorkville hospital was unwieldy, creating too much unnecessary competition for scarce dollars and services. In the new, modern hospital, reasoned Sadowski, there ought to be a single cohesive auxiliary, as efficient and contemporary as the sleek, buff-coloured building.

To fashion such an organization, Sadowski called upon Rose Torno, a graduate lawyer and volunteer for the Red Cross, who had been sent to England by the Department of National War Services during the Blitz to make a study of women's war work in Great Britain. Torno's government report outlined in great detail how the British had harnessed their volunteer women's skills, experience, and dedication in aid of the war effort. In another context, this information would now help provide a vision for the New Mount Sinai Auxiliary.

At her own expense, Torno travelled to major hospitals across North America in order to study volunteer organizations and devise an appro-

priate model for New Mount Sinai. With ideas plucked from several of
these, combined with her own considerable experience, she devised a
plan enunciating her concept of Volunteer Services, and proceeded to
write a constitution for the proposed Auxiliary. The emphasis was to be
on producing highly trained volunteers for service within the hospital.
Orientation, dress code, and training were to be rigidly controlled.
Fund-raising would take a secondary role.

It wouldn't have been unusual if the leaders of the Yorkville women's
groups had felt threatened by this takeover, orchestrated as it was by
someone entirely new to Mount Sinai Auxiliary affairs who, moreover,
didn't speak a single word of Yiddish, yet managed to successfully and
diplomatically conduct meetings of non-English-speaking volunteers.[24]
But so awed were the majority by Torno's abundant capabilities, intelligent vision, and lofty standards for the hospital, along with her obvious
commitment and drive, that most of the women were just anxious to
sign on and help carry it out. Through presentations to various service
groups in the city, efforts were made to recruit new members. Any costs
incurred in administering the Auxiliary were either underwritten by
members themselves or kept to the barest minimum, with the result
that the original stake of $10,000 that the board allotted for start-up
costs was never touched.[25]

Within a year after it was launched, in November 1953, Torno's
Auxiliary had assembled a corps of 3,244 members. In addition, 375 volunteers dedicated 27,000 hours of service to the hospital in 24 departments. A gift shop, well stocked with items hand-crafted by talented
members, was introduced by Alice Herman and Anne Cowan in a small
corner of New Mount Sinai's front lobby and would prove to be one of
the most successful of the Auxiliary's ventures. The group's publication,
Highlights, originally a hand-typed bulletin sent quarterly to all
members, first rolled off the mimeograph machine in July 1954. At the
Auxiliary's first annual meeting, a luncheon held at the Royal York
Hotel for which tickets cost $1.75, the renowned Metropolitan Opera
star, tenor Richard Tucker, made a guest appearance to sing "God Save
the Queen," and it was announced that the Auxiliary membership drive
had brought in a staggering $82,000 at a time when annual dues were $5,

Premier Leslie Frost addresses the public at New Mount Sinai's official opening ceremony. Seated to the left of the premier is Ben Sadowski. (Courtesy Dr. Kenneth Pritzker)

with life membership $100, payable over three years. That event marked the beginning of countless achievements and milestones accomplished by an extraordinary hospital Auxiliary that ever since has been admired and emulated across Canada and around the world.

On August 18, 1953, in the presence of local dignitaries, a proud *paterfamilias* Ben Sadowski, and an appreciative Premier Leslie Frost, New Mount Sinai Hospital was ceremoniously opened. The following day, an editorial in the *Globe and Mail* accorded official congratulations and generously acknowledged responsibility for completion of the project:

> Chief credit for the tall, handsome building on University Avenue must go to Toronto's Jewish community, which labored for twelve years, and against many unforeseen difficulties, to raise the biggest part of the cost. Yet, gentile patients will make the biggest use of the hospital, for in its new home, as in the old one, it will treat ·all who come. And many of the nurses will be English and Scottish, brought here from principal hospitals of the United Kingdom. Viewed from this aspect, Mount Sinai symbolizes a kind of health that perhaps is even more important than the physical kind.[26]

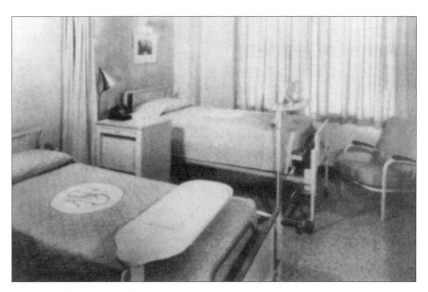

*The press made a great fuss over New Mount Sinai's high-tech hospital beds, which could be raised or lowered electronically. Note the monogrammed bedspreads. (*Highlights *magazine)*

City newspapers had a field day reporting the unusual "gimmicks" and "gewgaws" featured in the new hospital "to make the patient's day seem easier and the doctor's day seem shorter." One account, a humorous attempt to allay "fears of robots taking over our hospitals," described in minutest detail New Mount Sinai's whirring electric beds and revolutionary "telautograph system" to summon doctors. But surely readers were more comforted to learn that "in the operating room . . . the surgeon can work unworried about explosions from static electricity [since] special humidifying and air conditioning systems eliminate this peril completely." Or that "every last piece of equipment in the operating room is straight from the factory."[27] Hyperbole aside, there were indeed many innovations at New Mount Sinai, including five delivery rooms finished in sheet rubber, one of the first uses of this material in North America, and automated dumbwaiters to whisk food to patient floors.

Of those applauding the great achievement, none were more gratified than the doctors from Yorkville Avenue, many of whom had visited the construction site daily as New Mount Sinai was nearing com-

Moving day. Patients being loaded into ambulances for the trip from Yorkville Avenue to New Mount Sinai Hospital on University Avenue. (Courtesy Dr. Kenneth Pritzker)

pletion. Regrettably, three of the original pioneers from the early days, Drs. L. J. Solway, Benjamin Cohen, and Louis J. Breslin, did not live to see the new hospital open; nor did E. Fred Singer, the hospital's first president. But, for the rest of the staff, the most exciting consequence was that the facilities now at their disposal would place them on an equal professional plane with colleagues in the rest of the city. The future of New Mount Sinai Hospital appeared bright and full of promise.

4

Rx for Hospital Administration

❦

No sooner had Building Committee chairman Arthur Cohen tapped the final cornerstone into place than efforts got under way to realize the vision of New Mount Sinai first articulated by Ben Sadowski but now universally adopted by everyone associated with the hospital. At the time of the move, the medical staff was organized into twelve departments, each headed by one or, in some instances, two chiefs. They were: Medicine – Drs. Mitchell Kohan and Charles Markson; Surgery – Dr. Bernard "Bunny" Willinsky; Obstetrics and Gynecology – Dr. Louis J. Harris; Ophthalmology – Dr. Maxwell K. Bochner; Pediatrics – Dr. Gordon Manace; Anesthesia – Dr. David Perlman; Radiology – Drs. David Eisen and Cyril Rotenberg; Pathology – Dr. Harold Pritzker; Physical Medicine and Rehabilitation – Dr. Harry Silverstein; General Practice – Drs. Coleman Solursh and Ira Pollock; and Otolaryngology – Dr. Ivan Vaile. Although sporadic discussions about instituting a research department had been conducted since 1936, the first one now materialized under the direction of endocrinologist Dr. Bernard Leibel.

Following the war, the medical staff at Yorkville Mount Sinai had swelled rapidly, as several young Jewish doctors who had either just completed their training or had been recently discharged from the Armed Forces joined the various departments in preparation for the

When it opened in 1953, Toronto's New Mount Sinai Hospital was considered one of the most modern hospitals in North America. (Mount Sinai Hospital)

move to University Avenue. No one familiar with the first two decades of the new hospital will fail to recognize the names of these individuals, some of whom went on to devote their entire careers to the institution and were, for many years, the heart and soul of the hospital. Leaders of various divisions within the Department of Medicine in 1953 were Dr. Sidney Carlen, the first fully trained Jewish cardiologist in Toronto, and Dr. Harold Taube, directing Gastro-enterology. Other subchiefs in Medicine were Drs. Bernard Manace in Allergy and William Garbe in Dermatology. Junior men on the medical service would achieve prominence in the years to come: Drs. Joshua J. Chesnie, Irving Rother, Louis Cole, Henry Goldenberg, Oscar Kofman, Sidney Sharp, Isaac Shleser, S. Victor Feinman, Maurice Heller, and Allan Sharp. Important additions to the Department of Surgery were Drs. David Bohnen (General), Earl Myers (Colo-rectal), Leonard Davies (Orthopedics), and Irving Ritz and William Spring (Urology). Obstetrics and Gynecology added Drs. Jack Fedder, Bernard Ludwig, David Shaul, Roland Suran, Lionel Tanzer, and Jack Teichman.

*Thomas McNab directed pharmacy services at New Mount Sinai for more than two decades. (*Highlights *magazine)*

Change and reorganization were evident everywhere in the new hospital. Thomas McNab was appointed director of the modern pharmacy, a position he would retain for the next twenty-three years. A more comprehensive Social Services department than the one provided on an informal basis to Yorkville patients and their families by the *Folks Farein* mutual-aid society was now a necessity, and Margaret Brock arrived in the spring of 1954 to set one up. A graduate of the Montreal School of Social Work, she introduced a more-modern approach toward total patient care. Until well into the 1960s in most Toronto hospitals, social-work services were provided by volunteers, or, in some instances, by public-health nurses, and were not an integral part of hospital treatment. Establishing an independent professional Social Services department, therefore, put New Mount Sinai in the forefront of this area. The department was soon augmented by four medical social case workers and two student social workers.

Gradual movement was made toward another area of expansion when a brief was submitted to the Ministry of Health for authorization to establish a Neuro-Psychiatric Unit. Although at least three psychiatrists were associated with the hospital, this specialty area had not been an active service on Yorkville Avenue, and indeed, several years were to pass before this weak link would grow strong. Dr. Oscar Kofman became the lone neurologist in 1952, until the arrival of Dr. Sidney Starkman and neurosurgeon Dr. Irving Schacter a few years later. Until the acquisition of more-advanced radiological equipment in the next decade, many of their patients requiring extensive tests or hospitalization had to be admitted elsewhere. A spacious cardiac clinic, headed by Dr. Sidney Carlen, was an enormous luxury in the new accommodations, given the previous facility on Yorkville, which was described as "not much bigger than a bathroom."[1] In its newest incarnation, the clinic was connected to a fully equipped heart station for pre-consultation testing and was stocked with one of the earliest direct-writing electrocardiograph (ECG) machines.

One must remember, however, that a state-of-the-art physical plant, for the most part, benefited those patients who were ultimately admitted to the new hospital. It would be many more years before a reliable ambulance service, the 911 emergency number, and a qualified resident house staff, not to mention a whole variety of new drugs and surgical procedures, would relieve the pressure on some of the hospital's practitioners of bearing around-the-clock responsibility for their patients. Until then, urgent home visits and an almost uninterrupted stream of crises, especially cardiac emergencies, remained an integral part of doctors' daily lives. Every evening for years, for example, Mount Sinai cardiologist Sidney Carlen lugged home with him a cumbersome thirty-pound mahogany case containing a battery-powered Cambridge ECG machine, lest he be summoned to an emergency during the night. So sensitive and temperamental was this rudimentary instrument that simply wearing a wristwatch while operating it or playing a radio next door would render the record unreadable.[2]

A memorable incident from Dr. Carlen's practice captures this turbulent and still-primitive climate: One evening around 1950, Carlen received an emergency summons to the home of a man with severe coronary artery disease. The man was not much over forty, but diabetes and other complications had aged his arteries prematurely. When Carlen arrived, the man was suffering acute pulmonary edema, and desperate measures were needed to save his life. His wife, his teenage daughter, and a neighbour woman were all in despair, and, when Carlen asked for help, they were too stricken with fear to assist.[3] Then the man's son, a young boy about twelve, appeared in the doorway. He had just arrived home after riding his bicycle with friends and had come upon the terrible scene.[4] "Whatever you want me to do," the little boy told the doctor, "just let me know and I'll help." And the boy assisted as Carlen saved his father from certain death by the only means then at his disposal, a procedure known as venesection: letting a large volume of blood from a major vein in the man's arm, thereby immediately releasing pressure on his heart. Helping to carry out this ghastly task on anyone, let alone on his own father, would have been traumatic for any child, but the lad stood firm and never flinched.

Carlen was enormously impressed, and the next morning at the hospital he glowed with praise for the stout-hearted young boy who had assisted him so bravely. Today, that boy is well-known Canadian neurosurgeon Dr. Charles Tator, who on that occasion was perhaps performing the most difficult and courageous medical act of his life.

New Ventures

For the purpose of starting research at New Mount Sinai, a proper medical library had to be cobbled together from the old hospital's limited store of books and journals, and, in order to expand this collection and keep the hospital current, the Medical Advisory Council elected to assess each doctor $5 a year to supply and maintain the library.[5] It wasn't until 1956 that a proper library was stocked to serve the text and reference requirements of each department. To facilitate the many changes throughout the hospital, and to serve as a liaison between the board of directors and the Medical Advisory Council, the first Joint Conference Committee was convened.

An early new venture was the opening of a tumour registry, which permitted the classifying and close follow-up of all patients with tumours and cancer. To coordinate and support the service, a Cancer Committee was organized by Drs. George Goodman and Alan Bassett, and a tumour clinic was established in the Out-Patient department.[6] This made New Mount Sinai the first general hospital in Toronto not directly associated with a university to have a recognized tumour service. In a departure from standard procedure, the hospital's registry noted religion in its request for patient information, a factor considered significant considering the apparent higher incidence of certain diseases in Jewish populations. Some of the earliest statistical findings of the tumour service indicated that cancer of the breast was the commonest form of malignancy amongst New Mount Sinai patients, followed by that of the bowel and lung. Almost four decades later, the discovery of two breast-cancer genes and their higher incidence in Ashkenazi Jewish women would confirm these early observations. The tumour registry also noted a much higher occurrence of cancer of the ovary than in other statistical reviews, and a much lower occurrence of bladder cancer.[7] Another initiative in cancer treatment was the acquisition of radium to treat certain gynecological cancers. This took place in 1954 when the hospital purchased 100 mg with suitable applicators.[8]

Administration

But if the collective will for progress was present by the beginning of 1954, the administrative means to achieve it was not. Although for the time being, the frustrating matter of overcrowding had been eliminated, many of the internal problems that plagued the Yorkville hospital in its later years continued to rankle – only magnified in the larger premises. Tempests over medical specialization and qualifications swirled unabated, as did conflicts over allotment of beds, teaching goals and responsibilities, staff appointments, and the endlessly debated question of whether general practitioners should be permitted to administer anesthetics. (The ultimate decision was no.)[9] When the hospital first opened, Sol Grand was appointed executive director to deal with the non-medical affairs of the hospital. Dr. Simon Fines was now designated medical director, a title he would retain for a final year before returning to general practice. Frank Baird, a management consultant with a corporate background, had

Harvard-trained hospital admin-
istrator Sidney Liswood reorganized
the medical staff in 1954 and is
credited with putting New Mount
Sinai on a course leading to university
affiliation. (MSH Image Centre)

also been temporarily installed to help alleviate administrative headaches and stanch the rapidly increasing monthly deficit. But Grand died suddenly before the year was out, and Baird's expertise wasn't in hospital management, leaving Fines and the hardworking chief comptroller, Abe Bohnen, overwhelmed. It was evident to the board that the steady hand of a professionally trained hospital administrator was sorely needed at the helm.

Several candidates were interviewed for the job, but the eventual appointee became known to the board as a result of a chance encounter that had a coincidental connection to Mount Sinai. As a young doctor recently discharged from the Canadian Army, Leonard Davies had travelled down the eastern seaboard of the United States seeking a residency program in orthopedic surgery. Stopping at Beth Israel Hospital in Boston, he had a meeting with Sidney Liswood, an assistant administrator there. Upon his return home, Davies told his father-in-law about his trip and his conversations with Liswood. As it happened, Davies's father-in-law was New Mount Sinai board president Ben Sadowski.

A couple of visits to Toronto at Sadowski's invitation left Liswood impressed with the Jewish community, but reluctant to take on the fractious medical staff and the onerous task of putting the hospital into condition to seek university affiliation. Yet so forceful and mesmerizing was Sadowski's appeal, according to Liswood, that he eventually agreed,

The excellent reputation and strict discipline of Ella Mae Howard conferred distinction on New Mount Sinai's Nursing department. (MSH Image Centre)

taking office on November 1, 1954.[10] A native of Brooklyn, New York, Liswood had studied hospital administration at the University of Chicago, interning at the Yale University Hospital before going overseas as an assistant battalion aid surgeon during the Second World War. Following the war, he had completed a master's degree in public health at Harvard and had recently begun lecturing there. At thirty-eight, he was in line for advancement at Beth Israel. He would need all those credentials and more to pilot New Mount Sinai toward its lofty objective.

Upon his arrival, however, Liswood's first concern had little to do with the board's ultimate goal for the hospital, but rather with direct patient care. Discovering that some of the nurses at the new hospital had inadequate training, he set out to find a first-class director of Nursing. An appeal to Gladys Sharpe, then president of the Canadian Nurses Association, resulted in a meeting between Liswood and Ella Mae Howard, an assistant professor and clinical supervisor at the University of Toronto Faculty of Nursing. Trained at Royal University Hospital in Edmonton, McGill University in Montreal, and Western Reserve University in Cleveland, Howard immediately impressed Liswood as the quintessential nurse-administrator. Highly intelligent, authoritative, and unwaveringly committed to patient welfare, she was precisely the person needed to manage the Nursing department at New

Mount Sinai. The only difficulty was that Howard didn't want the job.[11] With a university appointment and a pension, she wasn't about to forfeit her benefits and return to the wards. But Liswood was undeterred, and persuaded the board to offer equal remuneration. More significant, he promised Ella Howard that, if she accepted an appointment as director of Nursing, she would be assured of his unqualified support.

The strong alliance forged between the two would stand Mount Sinai in good stead for many years. Until her retirement in 1970, Howard was recognized throughout the hospital and Toronto's medical community as a one-woman quality-assurance program. She oversaw the hiring of new nurses, many of them her former students at the university, and, in doing so, maintained the highest possible standards while attracting a strong cadre of nurse-leaders. Jean Campbell, brought in as assistant director of Nursing Service, and Marie Sewell, assistant director of Nursing Education, were two of Howard's first appointees who went on to have long and distinguished careers at Mount Sinai. Marie Sewell Rice, in fact, became director of Nursing following Howard's tenure.

Doctors, too, came under her careful scrutiny, and she had no hesitation in instituting changes in their operating-room procedures that she deemed necessary. Another top priority was to stimulate in-service as well as postgraduate training for all nursing staff.[*] One obstetrical nurse from the Yorkville hospital who was encouraged by Howard to acquire university training in administration was Aina Zulis, and, when New Mount Sinai was on the threshold of becoming the first Toronto hospital to hire a clinical teacher to instruct new mothers in infant care, Howard consulted her about the appropriate individual to employ. Like her director, Zulis was convinced that well-educated individuals made the best teachers. But as a young mother herself, she had one reservation about this appointment. "Most of the clinical teachers were fresh from school and very bright and hardworking. But I told Miss Howard

---

[*] In 1955, the Women's Auxiliary began assisting this effort by providing annual bursaries.

that, in addition to finding someone who could answer a broad range of questions from patients, we needed someone who was a mother herself, and who could understand the difficulties these women faced when they went home with their babies."

"In that case," replied Howard crisply, "you'd better take the job yourself." Zulis taught the postnatal course for three years, and, in 1970, became assistant director of Nursing Education.[12]

To further cement Howard's authority, Liswood later lobbied to have her made a full voting member of the Medical Advisory Council, which probably made her the first director of Nursing in the city to achieve that status. A tall, regal woman, whose very appearance commanded respect, Howard was regarded as tough, but fair and humane, the only staff person who, as one doctor fondly remembered, "caused everyone in a room to rise to their feet when she came through the door."[13]

Because she was exceptionally well connected in both nursing circles and at the University of Toronto, Howard determined that New Mount Sinai should become more widely known on the nursing front and take its rightful place in the broader hospital community. To hasten this goal, she held several teas in her home, to which she invited head nurses who were registered with their provincial nursing associations. She introduced Liswood to the Canadian Nurses Association executive, of which she would soon become president, and to administrators at the Faculty of Nursing, promoting the hospital's innovative and progressive program for nurses all the while. As a result of her networking, Liswood was subsequently invited to address several annual meetings of the Canadian Nurses Association.[14]

On July 1, 1955, the same day that Ella Mae Howard joined New Mount Sinai, Sidney Liswood gained an assistant in Gerald P. Turner, who in years to come would achieve his own eminence as chief administrator at Mount Sinai. Only twenty-six years old, Turner experienced something of a baptism by fire when, shortly after his arrival, he had to take over the administrative reins for several months while Liswood convalesced from a serious heart attack. A graduate in pharmacy from the University of Manitoba, Turner had received a diploma in hospital administration

*Manitoba-born Gerald Turner got his
first job in hospital administration at
New Mount Sinai in 1954 and stayed
for forty years. (*Highlights *magazine)*

from the University of Toronto and interned at St. Boniface Hospital in
Winnipeg. The strong tradition of mentoring, teamwork, and management leadership that began with the partnership of Liswood and Turner
continues at Mount Sinai to this day.

Baycrest

Almost the first order of business on the hospital's agenda was the for-
malization of its relationship with the combined Baycrest Hospital and
Jewish Home for the Aged, opened on north Bathurst Street in
November 1954. (Sam Ruth, a student and colleague of Sidney Liswood
from Boston, would soon arrive in Toronto to become administrator at
Baycrest.) Even before the founding of the Yorkville hospital, there had
always been a close association between the Jewish doctors and *Moshav
Zekanim*, the Cecil Street Home for the Aged. Moreover, many of the
community leaders responsible for building New Mount Sinai, including the ubiquitous Ben Sadowski, were equally involved with Baycrest.
Now, with the establishment of two entirely new institutions, it was
time to clarify and entrench that relationship in the hospital by-laws.

The agreement reached by the boards obliged every doctor on the
staff of New Mount Sinai to become part of the staff at Baycrest, and to
provide medical services there as necessary. Assignments to Baycrest

were to be for a period of three months annually, a term that could be extended any time at the request of the serving physician or the chief of service at Baycrest. Interns were also assigned for a term of one month per year.[15] In addition to administering general medical care, Mount Sinai doctors were also required to perform all admission examinations. Medical care in both the hospital and the home for the aged was coordinated by Dr. Henry Himel.

For the next few years, the issue of staff doctors' service to Baycrest was the subject of many discussions at both board of directors and Medical Advisory Council meetings. There is no question that, for some medical staff, this agreement represented a burdensome additional responsibility (for which there was no added compensation), and consequently there was the occasional dereliction of duty. Nevertheless, the penalty for this – suspension from New Mount Sinai – remained severe, and the policy was strictly maintained. The inviolable pledge to fulfil obligations to Baycrest, coming at a time when practising medicine in a chronic-care institution was unpopular, was New Mount Sinai's means of proclaiming to its supporters that it would never lose sight of its continuing responsibility to the Jewish community.

Out-Patient Care

A further demonstration of this commitment was the establishment of a large Out-Patient department in the new hospital, the one area of the modern building that, in principle at least, was based closely on the Yorkville model. At the old location, a large Jewish immigrant population had faithfully attended clinics, primarily to receive free care and drugs, but also to visit and connect with other immigrants within a caring and familiar environment. With the postwar arrival of even more European refugees, the need for such a facility became greater than ever. Sarah Cherniak, Yorkville's popular out-patient nurse-cum-social-director, took over where she left off at the old hospital. Doctors contributed their services, and the hospital underwrote the cost of drugs, staff, and equipment. In 1954, $123,000 worth of free care was dispensed in the Out-Patient department. By the following year, the volume

Allergist Dr. Bernard Manace, seen here in New Mount Sinai's Out-Patient department, was one of the first physicians in Canada to practise this specialty. (Highlights *magazine*)

*Dr. Wulf Grobin's "school" for diabetic care was a much-heralded innovation of New Mount Sinai's Out-Patient department. (*Highlights *magazine*)

Dr. Mitchell Kohan, New Mount Sinai's first chief of Medicine, was a consummate teacher who spoke several languages learned from his many ethnic patients. (MSH Image Centre)

increased to \$158,000,[16] a large portion of which was donated to the hospital by the Auxiliary.

Aside from its provision of free care, the Out-Patient department became a crucible of innovation. Dr. Wulf Grobin introduced classes at which diabetic patients learned, from a series of one-hour lectures, how to deal with the many complicated aspects of their care. Instruction was given in as many as four languages to ensure that all patients understood the information. So unique was this public-health venture that it became the subject of an editorial in the *Journal of the Canadian Medical Association*.[17] Until 1960, New Mount Sinai also served as the only centre in Toronto that offered prenatal instruction in its out-patient clinic.[18]

One major issue during these early days on University Avenue proved somewhat troublesome, and provided Liswood with some of his most difficult moments at New Mount Sinai: the bureaucratic tangle caused by having co-chiefs in certain departments. It was a problem that had to be addressed. The practice was a holdover from Yorkville days, when it seemed to be a politically expedient solution for dealing with professional rivalries. But a policy of sharing the top job also led to inevitable confusion and conflict, neither of which was tolerable in a major community hospital, let alone a progressive teaching environment. In a few instances, departments were headed by individuals whose specialty

Dr. Bernard Shapiro led the Department of Radiology for twenty-five years. (MSH Image Centre)

training wouldn't pass muster at the university. The board, now single-minded in its pursuit of ultimate affiliation, concurred, and the some-times-delicate job of replacing some of the department chiefs with others of the calibre to teach students at all levels had to begin.[19]

With the establishment of Baycrest Hospital, there was an opening for chief of Medicine at that location. Dr. Charles Markson received the appointment at Baycrest, leaving Dr. Mitchell Kohan to independently fill the spot at New Mount Sinai. Kohan would play an important role in the developments of the decade to follow. In great measure, it would be through his tireless efforts that New Mount Sinai's Department of Medicine would become the first department to affiliate with the University of Toronto.

Radiology was the next department to undergo scrutiny. The co-chiefs each worked half time, a situation that, wherever it existed in the hospital, compromised the continuity of care. A full-time chief was urgently needed, and Dr. Bernard Shapiro, a native Montrealer and McGill graduate, was recruited from the Westminster Hospital in London, Ontario, where he had been chief of Radiology. In the critical years to follow, the very affable Shapiro would assume a leadership role that extended far beyond his own specialty.

Dr. Harold Pritzker, who had also functioned part time since his assignment to the Pathology department, now became full-time chief of

Obstetrician and gynecologist-in-chief
Louis J. Harris and his partner,
Dr. Bernard Ludwig, had a huge
following in the Jewish community.
(MSH Image Centre)

that service, as well as director of Laboratories. Dr. Joseph Gollom stepped in as head of Otolaryngology, while Dr. Bernard Laski took over as chief of Pediatrics. This group would provide robust leadership in the busy postwar years.

While overseeing the twenty-two-bed Pediatric department, Laski maintained his long-standing relationship with the Hospital for Sick Children, where he had served since 1948. Two other pediatricians associated with Yorkville Mount Sinai, Drs. Gordon Manace and Jack Slavens, had appointments at Sick Children's Out-Patient department, but Laski had been the only Jew to receive an indoor appointment at the famous children's hospital. As well, he now had the distinction of being the only New Mount Sinai doctor to have a clinical teaching appointment at the University of Toronto.

Another part-timer, Dr. David Perlman, who was approaching retirement, announced that he would hand over the reins of the Department of Anesthesia as soon as a suitable replacement could be found. In 1956, Dr. Saul Eisen assumed that position. Dr. Louis J. Harris, who had succeeded the late Benjamin Cohen just prior to the hospital opening, was chief of Obstetrics and Gynecology. Dr. Coleman Solursh took over General Practice and Dr. Harry Silverstein led Physical Medicine and Rehabilitation. Dr. Maxwell Bochner, an original Yorkville pioneer and long-time chief of Ophthalmology, also continued

Chiefs of service at New Mount Sinai and Baycrest in 1960. Second row, from left: Drs. Harry Silverstein, Charles Markson, Coleman Solursh, Bernard Shapiro, Bernard Laski, "Bunny" Willinsky, David Bohnen, Louis Harris, Charles Moses, Barnet Berris, Henry Himel. Front row, from left: Dr. Nathan Levinne, Sidney Liswood, Drs. Maxwell Bochner, Mitchell Kohan. (Courtesy Sidney Liswood)

as head of the Medical Advisory Council and chief of staff. Dentistry, which was designated an independent department at the hospital, came under the leadership of Dr. John Sherman.

Accreditation

In preparation for developing a teaching program, Liswood instituted several additional changes. First, he requested an official survey by both the Royal College of Physicians and Surgeons and the Joint Commission on the Accreditation of Hospitals. The approval of these bodies was a crucial prerequisite for initiating both undergraduate and postgraduate training. (The Joint Commission, a Chicago-based inspection organization, predated the 1959 launch of the Canadian Council on Hospital Accreditation.) A date for inspection by Dr. Karl Hollis was scheduled for March 1955. The hospital then appealed to the

Canadian Medical Association for an increased allotment of interns, subsequently receiving approval for fifteen.[20] To date, the hospital had accepted only a handful of interns, many of them refugees from Europe whose command of English was limited. In a brief crisis of confidence, however, it decided to defer an application permitting residency training in specialty departments until after the accreditation survey.[21]

The task of readying the hospital for the first accreditation was a monumental one that kept staff working day and night. Despite the postwar reduction of ethnic tensions in an increasingly multicultural city, it was abundantly clear to the new administrators that, in order to officially advance its reputation, the Jewish hospital would have to follow regulations to the letter. No qualifying elements necessary for accreditation could be left open to question. Compliance would have to be absolute. As a result, procedures such as the collection and completion of medical records, previously carried out in a comparatively lax manner, now had to meticulously conform to standards and deadlines. New communications methods had to be implemented to expedite lab results to doctors and permit easier dictation, systematization, and retrieval of records. And there were other organizational skills that New Mount Sinai's staff had to learn in a hurry. Accredited hospitals were expected to adopt certain particulars in their constitutions; they had to organize a whole variety of committees to oversee different aspects of patient care and hospital management, all of which required precise documentation of their membership, attendance, and activities.

For the first time, elaborate emergency procedures were devised to handle potential disasters both large and small, and regular rehearsals of those scenarios were instituted. During the 1950s, at the height of the Cold War, the government assisted all hospitals in preparation for the possibility of an atomic-bomb attack, and, at New Mount Sinai, miltary-style teams were appointed for this purpose. The hospital devised intricate plans, including the scooping up of critical personnel for evacuation by helicopter and the storage of Army-issue stretchers and emergency drug stock within the hospital. Obviously, with the spectre of nuclear warfare very vivid in those days, the accompanying drills were vital, even if a few individuals did express bewilderment about how

Eager to begin a teaching program, New Mount Sinai offered a year of residency in Surgery, Medicine, and Obstetrics and Gynecology in 1953–54, prior to official approval from the Royal College of Physicians and Surgeons in 1955. (LeRoy Toll)

logical it was to have staff from all the University Avenue hospitals simultaneously wending their way to their mutual evacuation spot – a high school in Orangeville.[22] Worthiness of the scheme aside, this frenzy of organization did ensure that the days of *laissez-faire* operation of the hospital were finally and forever over.

The favourable results of the accreditation process in the spring of 1955 delivered a much-needed boost to morale. Having passed inspection by the official governing bodies, New Mount Sinai for the first time became fully accredited for one year of residency training in Medicine, Surgery, Obstetrics and Gynecology, Pathology, and Anesthesia, and subsequently, eight residents were assigned to these specialties. Heartened by this tangible expression of approval, Liswood still reminded the board in his annual report that continuation of that endorsement would be partly dependent on "the calibre of the doctors who comprise our medical staff; their preparation, their training and the status they have achieved in the medical community."[23] In other words, the message was clear that certification and fellowship designations for specialist doctors would be desirable, if not mandatory, in the very near future. Accordingly, a flurry of academic activity ensued, and, by 1959, twenty-two physicians obtained fellowships and thirty-one were certified in their specialties.* Among them was chief of Medicine Dr. Mitchell Kohan, who, anticipating affiliation with the university, returned to academic study, then wrote and passed his fellowship examinations at the age of fifty-three.

One thorny question facing the Medical Advisory Council during the first years on University Avenue concerned the Pediatrics department. After dealing with intractable overcrowding on Yorkville, the group now had to consider the improbable dilemma of the new pediatric ward, which from the outset was only half full. In part, this situation was attributed to the fact that general practitioners who were not permitted to administer anesthetic in the hospital chose to perform tonsillectomies in their private offices rather than admit children to the pediatric ward. The council was loathe to reduce the number of beds, even though these could easily have been filled by other departments, since it was deemed crucial to maintain Pediatrics in order to facilitate staff appointments at the Hospital for Sick Children. In 1955, the occupancy rate did rise to 72 per cent from 49 per cent the previous year, but the viability of the Pediatrics department remained tenuous.

Education

Even without affiliation with a school of medicine, New Mount Sinai plunged headlong into education. Almost immediately, the University

---

* At that time, there were two tiers of specialists designated by the Royal College of Physicians and Surgeons. Certification required three years of postgraduate specialty training, followed by an examination. Fellowship added an extra year of training and a much more rigorous set of examinations. Certification was abandoned in 1967, and fellowship became mandatory for specialists. Report of the Administrator, 1959, p. 4.

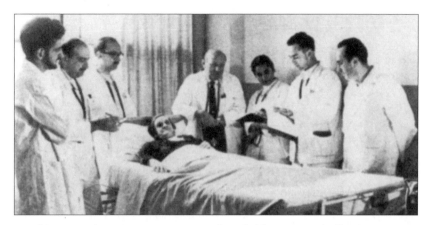

*Teaching rounds at New Mount Sinai, here led by Dr. Mitchell Kohan
(centre), were well established long before affiliation with the University
of Toronto. (*Highlights *magazine)*

of Toronto began using New Mount Sinai as a training centre for its
schools of social work, pharmacy, and hospital administration. X-ray
and laboratory technicians, physical and occupational therapists, and
dietitians also began doing field work at the hospital.[24] By 1956, with
Ella Mae Howard on board, the hospital was approved for the clinical
training of nurses from the university's Faculty of Nursing.

In 1955, clinical pathological conferences were regular occurrences,
as were bedside ward rounds. A curriculum for postgraduate training of
general practitioners, developed jointly by the Department of General
Practice and various specialty departments, was extended to doctors in
the community as well as to hospital staff. Lectures were frequently
delivered on such topics as "Electrocardiography" or "Office Surgery,"
and, to broaden experience, the staff of ninety to a hundred family
doctors was assigned on a rotating basis to the specialty out-patient
clinics in addition to maintaining the department's own clinic. The
Department of General Practice, in fact, was in the vanguard of educational programming in the early years. As it evolved into the first Family
Practice Unit in a large city hospital in Canada, this unit, under the
original direction of Dr. Coleman Solursh, became the model used by
the Canadian College of Family Practice to encourage other hospitals to
follow suit in subsequent years.[25] Solursh was also responsible for

organizing New Mount Sinai's first Annual Clinical Day, held on September 18, 1957, in cooperation with the local chapter of the Academy of General Practice.

For their part, staff doctors began inviting Jewish medical students to tour the new facility. After plying them with corned-beef sandwiches, the doctors managed to convince many potential junior interns and residents that a modern community hospital was an attractive place to learn, arguing that, without the hierarchical system of a university teaching hospital, the students would acquire extra experience and authority.[26] A preceptorship program was instituted, pairing each intern with a member of the medical staff for the purpose of obtaining more personalized guidance and advice. And as an added incentive, the Spadina Avenue YMHA threw in a free membership for each intern and resident.

Eagerness to begin teaching was felt keenly among the medical staff. In the early days at New Mount Sinai prior to university affiliation, a few doctors, including radiologist Dr. Bernard Shapiro, surgeon Dr. David Bohnen, and pathologist Dr. Harold Pritzker, held informal classes in their offices or even at their homes on weekends to discuss with interns the management of unusual cases. Very early on, a small group of specialists in internal medicine who had trained and taught at the Toronto General after the war started teaching informally at New Mount Sinai. Drs. Irving Rother and Henry Goldenberg, for instance,

An unsolicited donation by Holt Renfrew of a mink coat and six $50 gift certificates in 1955 spawned the tradition of an annual Mount Sinai fundraiser Ball, being planned here by Auxiliary members. (Highlights *magazine*)

New Mount Sinai Hospital Ball 1957 attended by Mr. and Mrs. Ben
Sadowski, left, and Mr. and Mrs. Noah Torno, right. (Courtesy Yvonne
Sadowski Davies)

commandeered a room in the hospital's basement and conducted
classes in hematology.[27]

Even the Auxiliary became involved in the enthusiasm for educational
programming, approaching the board with a proposal for public-health
lectures to be given by staff physicians. Although common enough
today, such programs represented a unique undertaking for an
Auxiliary, but Rose Torno's group received full cooperation for the
venture. Some of the earliest public lectures given in the hospital were
"Diet Fads" by Dr. Harold Taube, "Three Stages in Every Woman's Life"
by Dr. Louis J. Harris, and "The Tensions and Pressures of Daily Living"
by a panel made up of Drs. Jacob Goldstein, Sidney Carlen, Louis Cole,
and Henry Sager. A panel presentation that seems particularly prescient
in this age of antibiotic-resistant bacteria was given in March 1957 by
Drs. Pritzker, Bohnen, and Rother, along with bacteriologist Dr. T. E.
Roy of the Hospital for Sick Children. The topic, "The Magic of Wonder

Drugs – Their Use and Abuse," alerted the audience to the possible consequences of indiscriminate use of these powerful new drugs.[28]

By 1956, the Women's Auxiliary welcomed men as volunteers within the hospital, and, shortly thereafter, a group of high-school students and "business girls" formed a Junior Auxiliary. A feature about auxiliaries in the journal *Canadian Hospitals* reported on the work of the powerful New Mount Sinai organization, calling its accomplishments "a stupendous achievement." It was a fitting tribute to the Herculean efforts of Rose Torno, who concluded her term as president in 1958 and was succeeded by Ruth Brown.

Research at New Mount Sinai got off to a slow start, but was stimulated by the involvement of board member Samuel Lunenfeld, for whom medical research was a lifelong passion. In addition to his own substantial pledge to the new hospital, Lunenfeld was committed to generating outside support and had a penchant for dreaming up schemes that would accomplish this goal. On one occasion he bid for a gold golf

The earliest support for research at Mount Sinai came from the City of Hope Leukemia Fighters, seen here presenting a cheque to Sidney Liswood. (Highlights *magazine*)

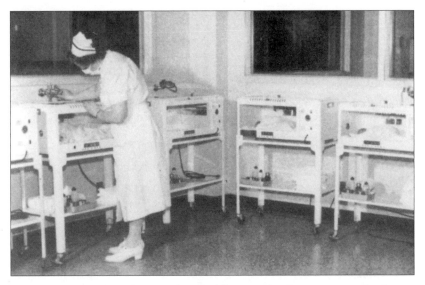

A five-cent dose of antibiotics identified by a group of New Mount Sinai physicians in 1958 saved many Toronto newborns from infection with thrush. (Highlights *magazine*)

putter at a charity auction, with the proviso that the Damon Runyon Research Fund donate a like amount to New Mount Sinai.[29] The special donation was forthcoming, and supplemented a generous joint research grant to the hospital and Baycrest by the Atkinson Foundation and regular contributions after 1957 from a group founded by Anne Finkle and called the City of Hope Leukemia Fighters, later renamed the Leukemia Research Fund.

Efforts in research, though modest at first, were pursued intensively and productively. Some of the first individuals involved were: Dr. Norman Green, who set up a Radioactive Isotope Laboratory to study thyroid uptake; Dr. David Bohnen, who worked on a heart-lung apparatus for use in surgery; Dr. Henry Goldenberg, who investigated highly complicated procedures for diagnosing blood diseases; and Dr. Harold Pritzker, who conducted studies to establish the cause of a rare type of pneumonia.[30] It would not be long before research at New Mount Sinai would have a significant impact on other Toronto hospitals, when Drs. L. J. Harris, B. Laski, H. Pritzker, A. Eisen, J. W. Steiner, and L. Shack determined that giving a few drops of the antibiotic Mycostatin to infants after birth virtually eliminated the incidence of thrush in the newborn. Reported in the *Canadian Medical Journal* and locally in the *Toronto Star*, the group's findings had an immediate effect, as intensive-care nurseries at the Hospital for Sick Children and other newborn nurseries in the city quickly moved to implement the procedure.[31]

In 1956, the hospital submitted a brief to the Ministry of Health, requesting that it be placed in the Group A category of hospitals, a rank usually reserved for teaching hospitals affiliated with a faculty of medicine. After intensive review, an order-in-council was passed, placing New Mount Sinai in Group A, making it the first hospital not affiliated with a university to be so designated.[32]

Government Matters

No issue had greater consequence for hospitals in the latter part of this decade than the introduction of hospital insurance to the province. In 1956, Premier Leslie Frost created the Ontario Hospital Services Commission (OHSC) to design a concept of universal provincial hospital insurance. Although proposals for such a policy had been put forward since 1945, the financial foundation necessary to put one into place did not exist.[33] Once that situation changed, the three-man commission, consisting of Arthur J. Swanson, Msgr. John G. Fullerton, and Dr. John B. Neilson, undertook to develop a comprehensive plan whose foremost task was to assess appropriate payments to hospitals for approved services. Various interested groups contributed to the debate, leading to passage of the Hospital Services Commission Act. The Ontario Medical Association, for example, was largely in favour of the legislation that assigned these wide powers to the OHSC, but balked at insuring "medical services in the diagnostic field" for both in- and out-patients.[34] The eventual compromise covered only in-patient diagnostic services as a benefit of the plan. It would take almost another decade before coverage became complete with the introduction of compulsory prepaid insurance for medical services, initially called OMSIP, now known as OHIP, the Ontario Health Insurance Plan.

In addition to patient services, the provincial and federal govern-

ments each allocated capital grants for expansions, new treatment programs, special equipment, and additional active-treatment beds. This
windfall immediately gave hospitals the wherewithal to upgrade staff and
services, as well as to implement such increasingly standard policies as a
staff pension plan. (One became effective at New Mount Sinai on July 1,
1958.) All expenditures, of course, were subject to government approval.

It took two years for the government-led insurance plan to come
into effect, during which time hospitals were required to submit
detailed budgets and proposed funding requirements for analysis by the
OHSC. On the basis of these forecasts, the commission drafted a
formula that determined the rate at which the hospital would receive
funding from the provincial government. For New Mount Sinai, this
worked out to a *per diem* rate of $20.10 per patient. By the time the
complex plan went into operation on January 1, 1959, all bugs had been
carefully worked out and the system worked effortlessly.

One cannot overestimate how profoundly hospital insurance
affected the efficient operation of New Mount Sinai and every other
hospital in Ontario. But the principal impact of this milestone, the
patient's relief from the fear of pauperization, was underscored by Otto
B. Roger, the board's budget chairman, in his annual report for 1959: "It
is no exaggeration to state that when a patient leaves our hospital he is
relieved of the great financial anxieties that used to accompany hospitalization in the past. His only concern is that of effecting a complete
recovery. His attitude to the hospital is one of relief and thankfulness
for the services that have been rendered to him."[35]

Expansion

In some measure, the new partnership with the government spurred
thoughts of expansion, although incipient ones had already been
brewing since the mid-1950s, as the medical staff swelled into the
hundreds and the 350-bed hospital became patently inadequate.
Furthermore, very early in the life of New Mount Sinai, the initial burst
of enthusiasm for the modern premises on University Avenue had given
way to a painful reality. Despite meticulous attention to detail in the

original plans, there were serious design flaws in the hospital that would necessitate a considerable overhaul to the building. One of the most difficult to contend with was the physical relationship between certain departments. The operating rooms, for example, were on the eleventh floor, while the laboratories were nine floors below, on the second. What immediately became clear was that the necessity for quick test results during surgery made the contiguous placement of these departments essential.

At the height of the postwar baby boom, the obstetrical department was one of the busiest services. Yet at a time when women remained in the hospital for at least a week following childbirth, there were only seventy-four adult beds on the seventh-floor obstetrical service, and the number of labour rooms was insufficient to fill the growing demand. The layout of the Radiology department inherited by Dr. Bernard Shapiro on his arrival in 1955 provided one of the most glaring examples of how the hospital's architectural plan fell woefully short of its goals. Years later, Shapiro liked to tell the story of how he and his wife had been driving through Toronto to Montreal on the day that New Mount Sinai opened. Seeing the official ceremonies taking place on University Avenue, the pair stopped so that Shapiro could join the public tour and check out the Radiology department. "It's terribly designed," Shapiro reported back to his wife. "I'd hate to have to work there."

A short year later, as chief of the department, Shapiro found that two cystoscopic rooms were taking up premium space right in the centre of the department, where consultation and viewing areas should have been, while a radiographic room, housing equipment used for two highly specialized tests, as well as for a whole variety of common skull X-rays, was situated outside the department entirely. Because of the distance, that equipment was being used only for the rarely required tests and not for the more frequently ordered skull X-rays. In explaining the gravity of this problem to the board, Shapiro pointed out that the mistake in location and consequent underuse of the costly machine was resulting in a $44-per-examination depreciation. Additional errors in this department typified the confusing and unworkable arrangements in several others. A room authorized as a doctors' dressing room was used only occasionally, while staff went without daily office space; a crucial darkroom was too small and improperly shaped for necessary equipment; filing space was inadequate for storing films.[36]

An even-more-serious problem existed in the Emergency department, which was so small that patients frequently had to be rerouted to other hospitals. Within each department, beds had been incorrectly allocated, but reorganization after the fact proved to be nearly impossible. The bed shortage meant certain departments were quickly taxed to the limit. In only four months following the introduction of the OHSC program, for instance, waiting lists for beds in the medical and surgical departments actually doubled.[37] Perhaps most troubling of all, the eventual bed requirements for university affiliation had been miscalculated, an error that would lead to a good deal of troublesome dislocation in years to come.[38]

In 1956, a Health Survey Committee chaired by board member Gurston Allen was assembled to study these problems in conjunction with New Mount Sinai's long-term goals. It commissioned a report from the firm of Agnew Peckham and Associates, Hospital Consultants. The initial recommendations proposed a 208-bed expansion on the existing foundation. Plans provided for a Psychiatric Unit for inpatients, plus increased X-ray, Laboratory, and Physical Medicine departments. The Agnew Report also maintained that an apartment-type residence should be built as soon as possible on one of several properties, bounded by Elm and Murray streets and University Avenue, that the hospital had begun to acquire as early as 1954. Reasonable rents, it was hoped, would attract nurses and hence help alleviate the severe shortage of nursing personnel. It was further suggested that possibilities be explored for building such a structure without any public campaign or financial outlay by the hospital.

Nursing Education

It had been a dream since Yorkville days to establish a school of nursing at Mount Sinai that functioned in the same manner as other hospital-linked schools such as those at the Wellesley or the Toronto General.

Not only were those nursing schools privately owned by the hospitals, but they fostered a sense of tradition in their graduates that kept the hospitals consistently well staffed and furnished with lifelong loyal supporters. Only vague notions of starting a similar school for New Mount Sinai had been in the air during the period when so many more pressing issues had to be addressed. But, in 1958, the director of Nursing, Ella Howard, came across a report written by nursing educator Dr. A. R. Lord concerning the Metropolitan Demonstration School, which had been set up as a pilot program for the training of nurses in Windsor, Ontario, between 1948 and 1952.

Although the program had been discontinued, the theory behind it intrigued Howard. It was based on the principle that, if a school of nursing had a known source of income, its own governing body, a well-prepared teaching staff, adequate facilities, and full control of the students' time and educational experiences in both the classroom and clinical fields, then that school could produce a well-trained nurse in two years instead of the usual three subscribed to by the traditional hospital schools.[39] As unfamiliar as this concept seemed, none of the essential ingredients for producing graduate nurses at the Windsor school was new. All of them, in fact, had been embodied in the first organized school of nursing founded by Florence Nightingale. Yet what set this program apart was the stringent focus on curriculum and the time-saving elimination of extra ward duties not directly linked to it. Impressed, Howard left the report on Sidney Liswood's desk and awaited his reaction.

It was swift in coming. Pronouncing the concept intelligent and workable, Liswood, along with Howard and their ally in the project, Gladys Sharpe, president of the Canadian Nurses Association, prepared a brief for submission to the Ontario Hospital Services Commission (OHSC). In it, New Mount Sinai proposed to donate land for the building at the corner of Elm and Murray streets as its contribution to the school and to provide clinical experience within the hospital. Howard then recruited Blanche Duncanson, former director of the Toronto Western Hospital School of Nursing and a nurse-administrator at the University of Toronto, to be principal of the school if it was approved. In the early

Blanche Duncanson was recruited by Director of Nursing Ella Mae Howard to be principal of the innovative Nightingale School of Nursing. (Highlights *magazine)*

months of organization, the two women remained somewhat secretive about their dealings with the commission, keeping the plans from their staffs and also, for a time, from the provincial nurses' association executive, of which they were both officers. There was some concern that other nursing schools might attempt to sabotage the idea before it was fully developed, since an independent two-year course would most certainly drain part of their potential student populations, not to mention the student nurses on the wards of their affiliated hospitals.[40]

Many details remained to be worked out. Students at the new school, it was decided, would have to be exceptionally well prepared academically prior to admission. Entrance requirements included an Honours Secondary School Graduation Diploma, with nine papers in Grade 13 plus a science option. When the blueprint was complete, all of the participants agreed that this carefully directed and controlled system of training was an efficient method of producing well-trained nurses. Still, in a profession whose prevailing education was hallmarked by the long-standing tradition of apprenticeship on hospital wards, the new school's guiding philosophy – a focus on academic study – was a complete and radical departure, and as such, it was subjected to a great deal of criticism.

In remarkably short order, however, in October 1959, the Nightingale School of Nursing was approved by the OHSC, in collaboration with the provincial and federal governments as the financing authorities, along with the Department of Health and the Registered Nurses Association, which had statutory responsibility for nurses. The school was to be owned by the Province of Ontario and operated by a board of trustees, consisting of A. J. Swanson and Msgr. John Fullerton of the OHSC, Dr. C. C. Goldring, former Toronto director of education, and Otto B. Roger and Gurston Allen, treasurer and vice-president respectively of the New Mount Sinai Hospital board. Sidney Liswood and Ella Howard were on the advisory committee.

Prior to the opening of the new Nightingale School of Nursing by Premier John Robarts on December 3, 1962, the classes were held for a time in quarters provided by the Hospital for Sick Children at 221 Elizabeth Street. Twenty-three students making up the first graduating class of the two-year program became eligible to write the registered nursing examinations; all of them passed. New Mount Sinai continued to have a close and proprietary interest in the school until 1974, when nursing schools in Ontario were transferred to the Ministry of Colleges and Universities, and the Nightingale School of Nursing became part of George Brown College.

Striving for University Affiliation

In 1957, armed with the recommendations of the Agnew Report for expanded departments and more beds, Ben Sadowski and Sidney Liswood had both begun making tentative approaches to the University of Toronto regarding affiliation between the hospital and the Faculty of Medicine. On the advice of U of T president Sidney Smith, it was decided to initiate very preliminary, exploratory discussions with the dean, Dr. J. A. MacFarlane. Dr. Mitchell Kohan also opened dialogue with his counterpart, Dr. R. F. Farquharson, then head of the university's Department of Medicine. Records of these early conferences are sketchy; however, following his meeting with Kohan on December 27, 1957, Farquharson prepared a memorandum to be passed on to the dean, entitled, "The Possibility and Problems of Establishing a University Teaching Medical Service at the New Mount Sinai Hospital."

In it, he expressed the opinion that the institution of such a service at the present time would be "fraught with many difficulties." Not the least among these, suggested Farquharson quite legitimately, was the fact that the large staff of well-qualified doctors who had already been in private practice for ten to fifteen years would find it difficult to adjust to university teaching regulations that required teachers to go on salary and restrict their private practices. "Establishment of a university service would hurt many of them greatly," wrote Farquharson, "no matter how carefully it is done or how understanding and tactful the University staff might be. If there were enough public beds to allow two services, it would be easier, but actually there are not now quite enough beds for a university service alone."[41]

The only reference in the minutes of the hospital's executive to these early meetings indicates that "the greatest progress had been made with Dr. Farquharson who manifested a genuine desire to see our negotiations in this matter go forward."[42] But Liswood's personal recollections suggest that a wide chasm still remained to be breached before New Mount Sinai would be welcomed into the university fold.

As Liswood tells it, he once arrived for an appointment at the university only to be greeted by Dean MacFarlane, legs crossed atop his desk, his body language loudly proclaiming his attitude toward New Mount Sinai. "Tell me, Mr. Liswood," asked the dean, "where do you think *Jewish medicine* is heading in the next century?" The usually avuncular Liswood was stricken by what he clearly discerned to be a slur, and he countered with a blistering rejoinder: "I don't really understand your question, Dean, but I think I *do* know what you're implying." Then Liswood added, "If New Mount Sinai becomes a teaching hospital at the University of Toronto Faculty of Medicine, you will have the best teaching and the best medical care in the city of Toronto. If New Mount Sinai *doesn't* become a teaching hospital, then we will still provide the best medical care. So do you want the best care affiliated with the University of Toronto, or do you want to see it provided at an [unaffiliated] hospital on University Avenue that will always be like a sore thumb in your eye?"

And he turned on his heels and walked out.[43]

5

Growing Pains

The 1960s was a decade of rapid growth, exploding knowledge, and unbridled optimism for Canadian hospitals, and New Mount Sinai certainly basked in that general climate of hope and expansion. But more than any other factor, it was the fresh and welcoming breeze blowing southward from the University of Toronto that ushered in the most far-reaching consequences for the hospital and its future.

In 1962, Dr. John Hamilton was appointed the new dean of the University of Toronto Faculty of Medicine. A pathologist by training, Hamilton was a friend of New Mount Sinai chief of Pathology Dr. Harold Pritzker, who had been a past president of both the Toronto Academy of Medicine and the Canadian Association of Pathologists. Early in 1962, on his own initiative, Hamilton requested a meeting with board president Ben Sadowski. The tenor of the discussion, during which the dean expressed the university's desire to affiliate with New Mount Sinai, starting a teaching program within the departments of Medicine and Pathology, was entirely amiable. In fact, Sadowski jubilantly reported to the board that greater progress had been made in the few short months leading up to that eventful meeting than in all the previous years of the hospital's existence.[1]

Following that occasion, the momentum toward the long-awaited goal gathered speed. On May 1, 1962, Dean Hamilton met with Sidney Liswood to begin hammering out the details and timetable for affiliation. It was agreed that the university's present chief of Medicine, Dr. K. J. R. Wightman, and his counterpart at the hospital, Dr. Mitchell Kohan, would strike the first deal for a teaching unit that would begin operation in September 1962. Initially, third- and fourth-year students would train at the hospital. The two men also held a frank exchange about the unique nature of New Mount Sinai, which Liswood recorded in a memorandum:

> I then said that we hoped that not all or only Jewish medical students would be assigned to our hospital. Dr. Hamilton replied that he would be distressed if this were the case, and in fact, he hoped the day would come when non-Jewish men would be appointed to our staff. I told him that in the years that I had been at the hospital, no outstanding non-Jewish physician had applied to our staff. However, since staff appointments for Jewish physicians at other hospitals were not generally available, and since we were the only public general hospital under Jewish auspices in Metropolitan Toronto, the pressure on us for staff appointments of Jewish physicians was extremely great, and in fact, greater than we had room for on our staff. . . . He replied that he felt the situation with respect to the availability of staff appointments at other hospitals for Jewish physicians had improved, and that this would improve further as Mount Sinai became a teaching hospital. He said that he recognized our unique problems and was sympathetic to them. Insofar as future staff appointments on the teaching unit were concerned, this would be made jointly by the University and the hospital and would be acceptable to both groups.[2]

Almost miraculously, barriers that, to the previous university administration, had loomed like icebergs in the path of an ocean liner began to melt away. As Wightman noted without any apparent alarm in a letter to Hamilton the week prior to the crucial meeting, "The

*Dr. John D. Hamilton, dean of the
Faculty of Medicine, was considered a
great friend of Mount Sinai Hospital.
(University of Toronto Archives)*

difficulties of grafting an academic program into a situation where
there is rather keen competition among a large number of qualified
staff men has been pointed out to them. I think they have discussed this
problem among themselves, and feel prepared to make whatever
sacrifices are indicated. If this proves to be the case, I am in favour of
seeing what can be done."[3]

Indeed, something *was* done about a long-standing university regulation regarding rank of the medical staff, which was unacceptable to
the hospital. In previous agreements with other institutions, the university had always stipulated that only a teacher could be on the active staff
with authority to admit patients. At New Mount Sinai, a core group of
very senior doctors, who were central to its functioning, were unable to
commit to university teaching at this stage of their careers, and it
seemed unjust, in light of their collective contributions, to abruptly rel-
egate them to secondary status. Hamilton agreed, and determined
that the rank of these individuals would be preserved and that they
could participate in teaching as "clinical consultants" or "volunteers."
Subsequently, this new ruling was extended to other teaching hospitals
in Toronto as well.

But it was Hamilton's gracious parting remarks to Liswood as that
May 1 meeting concluded that served as the soothing balm after years of
bruised professional sensibilities and painful struggle for acceptance by

the university and the Toronto medical establishment. "The members of the senior faculty," acknowledged Hamilton, "are fully aware of what Mount Sinai has gone through in reaching [its] present position and what you have accomplished, and I want you to know that you have our admiration and respect."[4] Obviously moved, Liswood wrote to the dean later that day:

> I find it difficult to adequately express the emotion I am experiencing as a result of our meeting this morning. It is a feeling of accomplishment, pride and satisfaction for our hospital mingled with one of humility when I realize how serious is the responsibility of participating in the training of the doctors of tomorrow. May I express my personal gratitude for the cordiality with which you received me, and my personal assurance that we shall do everything in our power to adequately meet this responsibility and add to the reputation of the Faculty of Medicine.[5]

As much as this heartfelt exchange registered a clear signal that a new era had finally begun, that individuals with tolerance and vision had begun to assume positions of power, and that stubborn prejudices were at last dissipating, it would be incorrect to suggest that anti-semitism within the medical profession evaporated overnight or that bastions of bigotry had suddenly been transformed into oases of equal opportunity. The following excerpt from the minutes of the Medical Advisory Council of the Toronto General Hospital concerning the application of a certain Dr. Horowitz for courtesy privileges demonstrates that, in 1963, subtle discrimination against Jewish doctors was still alive and flourishing:

> Dr. C. explained that Dr. Horowitz is a fully qualified Obstetrician and Gynecologist who has come here from South Africa and has not been allowed to receive an appointment in any other hospital in Toronto. He felt that certain other hospitals might have more obligation to a person like Dr. Horowitz than the Toronto General Hospital but recommended an appointment with the expectation

that it would be temporary. The hospital in the area in which Dr. Horowitz practices is undergoing enlargement and Dr. C. antici- pates that he will obtain privileges there.[6]

Nor was that 1963 incident an isolated one. As a resident in Internal Medicine at the Toronto General in 1967, Dr. Michael Sole, now head of the Division of Cardiology at that institution and holder of the Searle Chair in Cardiovascular Research at the University of Toronto, was invited by Drs. K. J. R. Wightman and Douglas Wigle to return to a staff position in Cardiology following additional postgraduate training in the United States. The news of that offer prompted telephone calls from three senior members of the hospital's Department of Medicine, all inquiring whether Sole didn't think he'd be "happier" practising across the street at Mount Sinai. "No, I wouldn't," Sole recalls his calm but firm reply. "I see my future here."[7] Still, the tide had clearly turned, for, once Sole affirmed this position, he encountered neither opposition to his presence at the General nor obstruction to his rise through the ranks.[8]

Staff Residence

With the Nightingale School of Nursing in full swing and the prospect of attracting much-needed graduate nurses within reach, the pressure to provide residential accommodation for them and for interns close to the hospital began to mount. Furthermore, space at New Mount Sinai was now at a premium, and rooms on the second floor, which had originally been assigned as living quarters for interns, were more urgently required for expanding departments. In an effort to finance this residence project, the hospital had applied for a grant to the Ontario Hospital Services Commission (OHSC). But, in June 1961, that request was denied. The commission ruled that the proposed thirteen-storey residence, to be built on the north side of Elm Street between Murray and McCaul, did not merit a claim on its increasingly limited funds, and that, in any event, an urban area such as downtown Toronto should supply ample housing for hospital personnel. Although board members grumbled that the OHSC had dealt cavalierly with the hospital during the previous two years, when it had repeatedly conveyed the impression that a grant for this purpose would be forthcoming, it was nevertheless decided to proceed to erect the staff residence and finance it with the hospital's own resources.[9] Almost immediately, the Women's Auxiliary, now headed by Tannis Silverstein, pledged $500,000 over eight to ten years toward the construction. Since the group had been raising more than $50,000 a year for free care prior to the introduction of hospital insurance, this amount could now be redirected to other important endeavours.

When the Bank of Nova Scotia agreed to provide a loan, plans for constructing the estimated $1.4-million building got under way. A series of properties on McCaul Street was expropriated and demolished for the apartment-type residence, which would house interns and other house staff as well as nurses. The concept was something entirely new in hospital accommodation and actually provoked quite a stir when it was first conceived. For one thing, unlike nurses' residences associated with other hospitals, which, for the most part, functioned as dormitories, this one provided self-contained apartments that were not restricted to female occupants – nor indeed to nurses. More than a few eyebrows were raised around town at the propriety of such an avant-garde mixed style of residence. But the board persisted, and must be credited with helping to eradicate the long-held perception of graduate nurses as vulnerable girls requiring protection rather than as adult professional women entitled to privacy and independence.

Plans called for a variety of accommodations – thirty-one bachelor, ninety one-bedroom, and six two-bedroom apartments – and rents were well below the market rate in order to attract and retain hospital staff as tenants. When the apartment opened in October 1962, it was an immediate success. Sixty per cent of nurses and interns new to the hospital that year rented apartments at the 200 Elm Street residence, which would soon be connected to the hospital by an underground tunnel.[10]

Psychiatry

Psychiatry has been described as the weak link in the early days of New Mount Sinai, and moreover the service was, for several years, a source of great turmoil and distress to the Medical Advisory Council and the administration. An interim head of Psychiatry had been appointed to organize what, at the time, was a division of the Department of Medicine, but the results proved unsatisfactory. In the plans for future expansion, provision had been made for in-patient service, yet the only treatment currently available was the free service in the out-patient clinic, which was provided by a rotating roster of volunteer psychiatrists. So, at the same time that other large general hospitals in Toronto were busily adding in-patient psychiatric beds and expanding their services, New Mount Sinai was contending with a lack of continuity of care, a group of disgruntled psychiatrists, and a recognized lack of leadership. It was plain that significant changes had to be made.

One of the part-time psychiatrists in the Out-Patient department was Dr. Stanley Greben, who, following training in psychiatry at Maudsley Hospital in London, England, and at Johns Hopkins in Baltimore, returned to Toronto, where he had an appointment at the Toronto Psychiatric Hospital. In 1958, in deference to his "community feeling," Greben had become one of the volunteer psychiatrists in the Out-Patient department at New Mount Sinai, but periodically over the next four years he had requested and received leaves of absence from this minor staff appointment due to the frustrating inadequacies of the service. It came as a complete surprise, therefore, when, in 1962, he was invited by chief of Medicine Dr. Mitchell Kohan to consider becoming head of Psychiatry at New Mount Sinai. Despite the unfortunate beginnings for psychiatry at the hospital, the opportunity to build something entirely new was compelling, and, in the nine months that it took Greben to decide to accept the offer, he made a study of several hospitals in the United States whose psychiatry services he admired. He also paid a visit to Dr. Aldwyn Stokes, chairman of the Division of Psychiatry at the University of Toronto, whom he had known since his student days, seeking and ultimately receiving a commitment that New Mount Sinai would become part of the university in psychiatry.[11]

The conditions on which Greben finally accepted the appointment as director of Psychiatric Service in July 1963 would completely revamp the hospital's ability to deliver psychiatric care. As head of the new unit, his

Dr. Stanley Greben developed Psychiatry at New Mount Sinai as an independent department rather than a division of Medicine. (Highlights magazine)

ultimate goal was to construct an entirely independent Department of Psychiatry, on a par with other full departments rather than merely a division of the Department of Medicine. As benign as this change in status sounds today, it was utterly contrary to the prevailing view of psychiatry at other teaching hospitals and at the university's Faculty of Medicine (where psychiatry was not a separate department), and hence would require strong leadership and considerable influence and authority to put into effect. A movement toward psychotherapy, notably a form of intensive treatment known as psychoanalytically oriented psychotherapy, or dynamic psychotherapy,[12] which was not a particularly favoured treatment mode in Toronto psychiatric circles at the time, was another Greben innovation. The backbone of the teaching program in psychiatry at New Mount Sinai was to be a concentrated program of supervision and seminars, and a determination to set the highest standard for education that would attract the best residents and produce superior specialists.[13]

The first residents, Drs. Harvey Maldofsky and Alfred Margulies, arrived in 1964 to launch the teaching program, and a clinical psychologist, Dr. W. H. Otto, also joined the section. In addition, the group set up a consultation-liaison service with other departments, as well as an emergency service. In 1967, Greben was named chief of a separate and independent Department of Psychiatry, but it wasn't until 1974 that in-service beds were first installed.

New Mount Sinai's first chief of Surgery, Dr. Bernard "Bunny" Willinsky, ruled the department with an iron hand. (MSH Image Centre)

Surgery

Ever since the opening of New Mount Sinai in 1953, Dr. Bernard "Bunny" Willinsky had ruled the Department of Surgery with an iron hand. Under relentless pressure to appoint some deserving and talented young Jewish surgeons to the hospital staff (even Toronto Mayor Nathan Phillips sought Willinsky's favour by promoting a candidate at one time), he was chronically unable to satisfy the constant demands for beds made upon him. As a result, in the early years of New Mount Sinai, the Department of Surgery was always larger than it should have been for the capacity of the institution. Once the hospital was approved to train one resident, the rivalry was extended to another echelon. Dr. Abraham Eisen landed the first Royal College–approved surgical residency in 1956, and Willinsky promised Dr. Irving Koven that, providing he stuck around and did a year of pathology under Dr. Harold Pritzker while waiting his turn, he would be awarded the surgical residency the following year. Though Willinsky was called on to be Solomon-like and hard-nosed in these situations, he also displayed a legendary capacity for kindness and generosity. In 1958, after Koven, a native Maritimer, completed his specialty training, Willinsky provided him with a rent-free office for the first year and even paid his telephone bill.[14]

Once it became apparent that university affiliation was on the

Left: Dr. David Bohnen was the first Jew to study surgery in the prestigious Gallie course at the Toronto General Hospital in 1943. (MSH Image Centre) Right: A highly respected executive at Mount Sinai for thirty-seven years, Abe Bohnen began his career as comptroller in 1953. (Randy Bulmer)

horizon, however, Willinsky knew that his days as chief of Surgery were numbered. Among the younger surgeons on staff was Dr. David Bohnen, who possessed the unique distinction of having come through the Gallie Course in Surgery at the Toronto General Hospital in 1943, the first Jew to be awarded this prestigious training. Since all chiefs of teaching services had to be approved by the university, it was obvious to Willinsky, who was approaching retirement age, that Bohnen would get the nod. Accordingly, Willinsky resigned in June 1961, and Bohnen was immediately named his successor.

A superior surgeon, greatly respected by his staff, but a tense individual, as reserved in manner as his brother, Abe, the hospital comptroller, was warm and outgoing, David Bohnen soon began selecting appropriate teachers, which, in effect, meant those surgeons who had been awarded fellowships by examination. When affiliation of the Department of Surgery was achieved in 1964, Drs. Irving Koven, Milton Chris, Irving Rosen, and Bohnen himself were the only ones to initially get teaching appointments. The following year, Dr. Saul Sidlofsky, a former New Mount Sinai intern and, like Bohnen, a Gallie course graduate, joined the group in General Surgery after completing additional training at three leading cancer institutes in the United States.

As head of the Department of Surgery, chairman of the Medical Advisory Council, and a president of the Toronto Academy of Medicine, Bohnen wielded tremendous influence at New Mount Sinai. He remained as surgeon-in-chief until his untimely death from cancer in 1975.

Radiology

Radiology was one of the fastest-growing services at New Mount Sinai, and the development of the hospital department closely parallelled the development of the clinical science itself. After his appointment as chief, Dr. Bernard Shapiro hired Drs. Imre Simor in 1956 and Marvin Steinhardt in 1962, and the three proceeded to energetically build the service. Until then, the department had concentrated on simple diagnostic radiology, but the new team was interested in more-progressive procedures, including neuroradiology and angiography (X-rays associated with the nervous and vascular systems respectively), and it soon built an excellent reputation in these areas.

Before long, the volume of work increased to four times what it had been before the trio arrived. Not always flush with funds for the latest equipment, they did have the enthusiasm and resourcefulness of Irving "Bob" Fisher, the chief radiographer, who cleverly managed to adapt or augment existing machines to enhance their function. Once, the enterprising Fisher rigged up a makeshift automatic film changer out of a manual one, a modification that permitted him to take several rapid films in succession. The ersatz machine worked satisfactorily until the hospital acquired the means to purchase the conventional automatic equipment.[15]

Under the guidance of Shapiro, the Radiology department was responsible for the introduction of several pioneering procedures. The first significant advance occurred in 1962 with the purchase of an image intensifier. This allowed doctors to take an actual movie strip of film, which was then projected onto a television monitor. After investigating

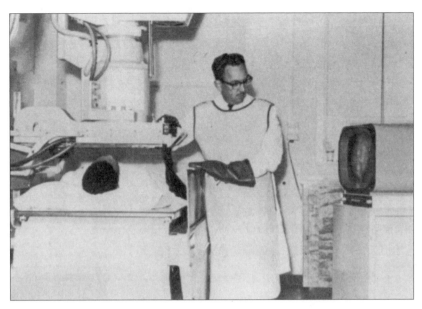

Dr. Bernard Shapiro demonstrates the Radiology department's new image intensifier in 1962. (Highlights *magazine*)

the new science of mammography, Dr. Simor travelled to the United States to train in the technique with its originator, Dr. R. L. Egan. In 1969, New Mount Sinai bought one of the first mammography machines in Toronto, acquiring a unit devoted exclusively to breast X-rays a year later, and confirming the hospital's strong interest in the study and treatment of breast disease.[16]

Forays into nuclear medicine, a special interest of Shapiro's since his involvement with Canada's first isotope lab at the Jewish General Hospital in Montreal, also began early. In 1964, in a small, rather primitive lab led by Dr. Paul Walfish, the group began taking static pictures of various organs following the injection of radioactive isotopes. Larger, more-detailed films became available when gamma cameras were purchased in 1967. Within a few years, Drs. N. David Grayson and Richard Holgate would arrive to oversee further exciting developments in nuclear medicine and neuroradiology respectively.

In 1969, Shapiro heard about a radiologist in Brooklyn, New York, who was doing echo studies on pregnant women to produce images of their fetuses. He set off to investigate the new imaging technique, and returned to New Mount Sinai with the city's first ultrasound equipment. Shapiro then persuaded Dr. Murray Miskin, who was just completing his training, to undertake this work. The young resident agreed to do so, albeit with great reluctance. It proved, however, to be an excellent decision, as Miskin's name later became virtually synonymous with ultrasound within Toronto radiology circles.

Appointments

During this decade, there were several important changes in the leadership of various departments. One of the hospital pioneers, Dr. Coleman Solursh, resigned in 1961 after a long career devoted not only to the well-being of his patients but to promoting the status of the general practitioner and the new concept of "family medicine." Dr. Nathan Levinne succeeded Solursh as chief of General Practice, injecting his predecessor's goal with fresh purpose. In 1970, the newly named Department of Family Practice would become affiliated with the university medical

In 1961, Dr. Coleman Solursh, left, was succeeded as chief of General Practice by Dr. Nathan Levinne, right. (Highlights *magazine*)

Pathologist-in-chief Dr. Harry Strawbridge was a pioneer in the technique of needle biopsy of the kidney. (MSH Image Centre)

school with Levinne as associate professor.[17] Another new chief to take office in 1961 was Dr. Charles Moses in the Department of Dentistry. He would be succeeded in 1965 by Dr. Harry Jolley.

In September 1963, the hospital suffered a grievous loss in the unexpected death of Dr. Harold Pritzker. A committee was immediately established to search for a new chief pathologist and director of Laboratories. In the interim, bacteriologist Dr. Kamil Gal and pathologist Dr. Segundo Mariz assumed internal responsibilities for the hospital, while pathologists from the other teaching hospitals generously rallied together to cover Pritzker's teaching functions for the pathology residents.[18] Following an exhaustive search that took more than a year to complete, Dr. Harry T. G. Strawbridge was appointed to the dual post on February 1, 1965. Trained at the University of Edinburgh, Strawbridge had previously served as pathologist at the Winnipeg General Hospital.

The appointment was a unique one, given that Strawbridge was the first non-Jewish chief in Mount Sinai Hospital's history. But pressed today about whether that fact had any impact, Strawbridge bristles at the suggestion, observing that he has never before been asked such a question, and that not being Jewish was "absolutely never an issue." "The boys were wonderful to me," he contends in a sweeping reference to administrators Liswood and Turner, board executives, and fellow staff, all of whom had been solely committed to finding the best person to fill the top job in Pathology.[19] Perhaps Faculty of Medicine dean Dr. John Hamilton, who not so many years before had commiserated with Sidney Liswood's confession that an outstanding non-Jewish physician had never applied to Mount Sinai's staff, would have better appreciated the historic nature of the occasion.

Strawbridge designed his department on the classic British model, establishing four separate divisions. He recruited Dr. Derrick Abbott to oversee Hematology, Dr. Alan Pollard for Clinical Biochemistry, and Dr. John Angus Smith for Medical Microbiology, retaining the portfolio of Surgical Pathology for himself. The group's arrival coincided with a period of tremendous technological advancement in hospital pathology departments worldwide, as automation provided the capacity for processing a large number of samples. In 1967, for example, New Mount Sinai purchased its first Technicon 12 Channel Analyzer, instantly improving its volume and diagnostic expertise in blood chemistry.[20] A specialist in electron microscopy, Dr. Yvan Bedard joined the group in 1972, and, within six months of his arrival, the department's first Philips 301 electron microscope was added to the equipment inventory, its vastly superior magnification now permitting identification of poorly differentiated tumours and improved diagnosis of renal diseases.

After shepherding New Mount Sinai into the halls of academe in 1962, Dr. Mitchell Kohan was invited by the university's Dr. K. J. R. Wightman to serve an extra year prior to his mandatory retirement as chief of Medicine. On July 1, 1964, Dr. Barnet Berris took over this crucial position. A highly respected specialist in internal medicine, trained at the University of Minnesota, in 1950 Berris had become the first Jewish physician ever to receive an indoor appointment at the Toronto General Hospital, and he had been associated with the University of Toronto since that year. Berris's journey to this unparalleled achievement included navigating the predictable shoals encountered by other Jewish medical graduates from the University of Toronto in the 1940s. Despite the fact that his academic performance at U of T was among the highest in the faculty, for example, he was denied internships at both the

Chief of Medicine Dr. Barnet Berris became Mount Sinai's first full professor at the Faculty of Medicine.
(MSH *Image Centre*)

Toronto General and St. Michael's. Later, following four years of specialty training in Minnesota, that university's professor of medicine personally recommended his protégé to his counterpart, Dr. R. F. Farquharson at the Toronto General. Farquharson agreed to take Berris on, but the General's board protested loudly, and it was only when Farquharson threatened to resign over the matter that the board succumbed. Even then, Berris was singled out to take an *extra* year of residency, so the home town Department of Medicine could "get to know him" before he was accepted on staff.[21]

The arbiters must have been well satisfied, however. So exalted was Berris's reputation when he arrived at New Mount Sinai in 1964, both as a consummate clinician and as a teacher, that, decades later, several long-time senior staff point to his appointment as chief of Medicine and his magnetic ability to attract the best and the brightest students and staff to work with him as watershed events in the hospital's history. Known around Mount Sinai as "the doctors' doctor," Berris was named chairman of the Medical Advisory Council in 1975 and honoured in 1979 when the Medical Group of the Canadian Society for the Weizmann Institute established the Dr. Barnet Berris Career Development Chair in Cancer Research at the Weizmann Institute of Science in Israel.

In 1964, Berris and Dr. David Bohnen became the first geographic full-time chiefs for their respective clinical services. A relatively new university concept, "geographic full time" denoted an office within the hospital, a limited private practice, and a salary from both the university and the hospital to permit the chief to devote most of his time to the supervision of patient care, research, and education. In 1968, the university named Berris full professor, the first New Mount Sinai doctor to be so honoured.

Other important appointments in the Department of Medicine at this time were Dr. Joseph Houpt, a specialist in rheumatology, and Dr. Paul Walfish, a former resident at New Mount Sinai who, with the help of a Medical Research Council Scholarship, returned following a post-graduate fellowship in Boston to begin trailblazing research in endocrinology that would soon bring him international renown. In 1969, the Department of Physical Medicine, thus far run single-handedly by Dr. Harry Silverstein, gained the additional expertise of Dr. Jose Jimenez, a graduate of the University of Madrid. A former associate professor at Queen's University and at the University of Alberta, Jimenez provided the necessary nucleus to expand this increasingly important area of medicine at New Mount Sinai.

Dr. Maxwell Bochner reached retirement age in 1966. His association with the hospital as chief of Ophthalmology dated from shortly after its inception on Yorkville Avenue, and he had been chairman of the Medical Advisory Council for an extraordinary span of thirty-eight years. A source of guidance and vision for the entire medical and nursing staff, Bochner and his opinions were widely revered. When he recommended that Dr. Bernard Teichman be named his successor as chief of Ophthalmology, the endorsement was immediately adopted by the Medical Advisory Council.[22]

Teichman, nevertheless, was a somewhat reluctant recruit. As one of the few Jewish specialists trained at the University of Toronto and the Toronto Western Hospital, he had returned from additional graduate studies in the United States in 1950 only to be informed by that hospital's chief of department, Dr. Clement McCullough, that there was no place for him at the Western and that his "destiny lay at Mount Sinai."[23] Bochner, as Yorkville's chief of staff, welcomed Teichman with open arms, noting, however, that Mount Sinai had only 88 beds, and that Teichman would have to line up with the rest of the 350 staff physicians for an opportunity to fill one of them. Incapable of conducting a practice in his sub-specialty of tear-duct surgery without hospital beds, Teichman beseeched his one-time mentor, Dr. McCullough, once again. This time McCullough relented, assigning Teichman partial privileges for admitting purposes at the Western, although he was not officially "on staff" there, as, ironically, he was at Mount Sinai.

After eight years in this state of professional limbo, Teichman was finally granted full-time staff status at the Western and given a coveted university appointment. So, in 1966, when Sidney Liswood approached him to take over as chief of Ophthalmology at New Mount Sinai with a view to bringing the hospital's division into the university, Teichman was initially hesitant. Moreover, the facilities at Sinai were lacking: there was only one refracting room and a single small treatment room in the entire hospital. But, from New Mount Sinai's perspective, Teichman was clearly the right person to pilot the important venture of departmental affiliation, since Clement McCullough was now the head of Ophthalmology at U of T. In the end, Teichman agreed, and the following year university affiliation was extended to the department at New Mount Sinai, as well as to Otolaryngology and Obstetrics and Gynecology. Still, there was penance to pay. Because Teichman had tweaked the nose of the Western by jumping ship, he was demoted for a time by the university.[24]

It was with a good deal of pride and fanfare that New Mount Sinai named Dr. Gerald Edelist to the position of anesthetist-in-chief in the summer of 1969. Fresh out of medical school, Edelist had served as a junior intern at New Mount Sinai prior to extensive specialty training in New York. As the Auxiliary publication, *Highlights*, trumpeted, his return to this illustrious position as chief of service and his associate professorship at the university marked the first demonstration that "the quality and scope of the medical programs at New Mount Sinai . . . [were] sufficient to reverse the brain drain to the U.S. . . . and attract such a qualified physician to come 'home.'"[25] Edelist's marked the first, but cer-

Dr. Gerald Edelist, anesthetist-in-chief, began his medical career as an intern at New Mount Sinai.
(Highlights *magazine*)

tainly not the last, of such "homecomings." He would later become professor and chairman of the university's Department of Anesthesia.

In 1969, someone who would be a veritable fixture at Mount Sinai first became associated with the hospital. Renee Fleishman became one of only four professional directors of Volunteer Services in Ontario hospitals, taking on the important function of assigning and training volunteers. Increasingly, the role of "coffee server" was being supplanted, as several hundred dedicated individuals received training from a highly skilled leadership group in order to become a vital part of the health-care team. Under Fleishman's management, the Department of Volunteer Services has evolved into a completely separate entity from the Auxiliary, focusing exclusively on patient care. So confident did the medical staff become in the selection and training process over the years, that, by 1997, volunteers were being carefully streamed into seventy-eight programs within the hospital, devoting almost a hundred thousand hours of service annually to patient care. This extraordinary record of continuing dedication has steered volunteerism professionals from all over the world to Mount Sinai's door in an effort to emulate its success.

Within a year after she succeeded Ella Mae Howard as director of Nursing in 1970, Marie Rice's title was changed to assistant administra-

Volunteers at Mount Sinai undergo rigorous training in order to effectively complement the professional staff. (Highlights *magazine*)

tor–Nursing, reflecting the increasingly complex managerial function she was already providing. Anne James was simultaneously appointed assistant director of Nursing, responsible for the direct-patient-care services of that department. Finally, two students in hospital administration, who would have significant impact on the future direction of the hospital, became administrative residents under the tutelage of Gerald Turner. Gordon M. Kerr arrived in 1964 and Theodore J. Freedman, today the president and CEO of Mount Sinai, followed in 1969.

New Programs and Other Changes

A progressive pilot program was initiated in late 1961 under the sponsorship of the city's Department of Health, with grants from the Department of National Health and Welfare. The Home Care program was the first of its kind to consider the ramifications – for both patient and hospital fiscal welfare – of early discharge of suitably selected patients. At home, with support provided through the coordinated Home Care program, such patients were followed to assess the results of this hitherto untested concept. New Mount Sinai was one of two hospitals selected to participate in the two-year study.

Marie Sewell Rice led nursing at Mount Sinai from 1970 to 1980. (MSH Image Centre)

Two new specialty units were added to New Mount Sinai in 1968 when a portion of the seventh floor was converted to provide space for a three-bed Coronary Care Unit and another three-bed general Intensive Care Unit. A team of specially trained nurses staffed both units. Clinical clerks first made an appearance at New Mount Sinai in 1969 as twenty final-year medical students were assigned on a full-time basis to begin their clinical training.

Almost immediately after his arrival in Toronto, Dr. Harry Strawbridge became heavily involved with an exciting new educational venture begun by colleagues across the street. Dr. Murray Young, director of Laboratories at the Toronto General Hospital, was the first to see a need to revise the training of medical technologists, which until 1958 consisted of an apprenticeship period with no formal classroom theory. Young resolved to upgrade this system, and, along with his colleague, biochemist Dr. Diana Schatz, proceeded to set up a ten-week concentrated course for training of their own students in the basement of Toronto General's Private Patients' Pavilion. The early participants were so much better prepared for clinical work that the two determined to extend the course to ten months and make it available to students at other hospitals. Additional teachers, including several from New Mount Sinai, were invited to conduct classes. This pilot program, known as the

Technician Training School and geared exclusively to medical laboratory students, carried on informally at the Toronto General for several
years.[26]

In 1965, the co-founders decided to organize an official regulatory
training school and also to amplify the curriculum to include radiology
training and inhalation therapy (now called respiratory therapy). By
this time, it was also becoming essential to provide continuing education for working technologists in order to cope with the rapidly emerging new techniques and data. New Mount Sinai's Dr. Harry
Strawbridge, an enthusiastic supporter of the concept, was elected executive director of the new institution, and became instrumental in developing its first curriculum. Sidney Liswood was named to the board of
directors. According to Dr. Schatz, the new school, to be called the
Toronto Institute of Medical Technology, fit in perfectly with Liswood's
well-known vision of a broad educational role for hospitals.[27] To reinforce that perspective and ensure that the institute would, to everyone's
mutual advantage, be part of a strong Toronto health-care community,
the board of New Mount Sinai generously offered to provide land for
the school at cost.

On the southwest corner of the designated property, located at Elm
and St. Patrick streets, was a small building scheduled to be demolished
prior to construction. In addition to his weighty advisory duties to the
new institute, Strawbridge found himself acting as custodian for this
building, a function that provided a colourful illustration of both the
literal and figurative role he assumed for the school in its early years.

Late one bitterly cold winter night, he was informed by the security
company that an alarm indicated a pipe had burst. When Strawbridge
rushed to the site to repair the damage, he became locked into the
building from the inside. Needless to say, the police who arrived to
investigate wanted to know what he was doing on the premises with a
bag of suspicious-looking tools at two o'clock in the morning.[28]

Installed in temporary quarters, first on Resources Road and then in
a synagogue on St. Clair Avenue until a quagmire of funding and government ministry assignment problems could be cleared up, the
Toronto Institute of Medical Technology finally opened at its new site in

Dr. Alan Pollard was a founder of Hospitals In Common Laboratory, a non-profit corporation to facilitate work sharing between more than two hundred hospital laboratories in Ontario. (MSH Image Centre)

1972, sharing services and an underground tunnel with the Nightingale School of Nursing and New Mount Sinai Hospital. The school was renamed the Michener Institute for Applied Health Sciences in 1991 to indicate its expanded mandate as well as to recognize the previous governor general, Roland Michener, and, in no small measure, his daughter, institute co-founder Dr. Diana Schatz.

One of the more interesting "firsts" at New Mount Sinai toward the end of the decade was the establishment of the In Common Laboratory (ICL). For a long time, informal agreements had existed between hospitals, particularly those within close proximity, to support each other in conducting laboratory tests. These arrangements were all achieved on an *ad hoc* basis: if hospital A wanted a complicated test done and knew that hospital B was performing such a test, the former would arrange for some type of joint effort. New Mount Sinai had always processed whatever tests it could on site. What wasn't offered within its own laboratory was sent to the Toronto General, the Hospital for Sick Children, or occasionally to a specialized lab in the United States.

But in 1967, a group of scientists, including Dr. Alan Pollard and Dr. Harry Strawbridge, chiefs of Biochemistry and Pathology respectively at New Mount Sinai, and Drs. Murray Young and C. J. Porter of the Toronto General, decided there was a more efficient way to coordinate services, share hospital laboratory workloads, and, at the same time, provide competition for some private labs.

With a small government grant, they set up an experimental laboratory on the fourth floor of New Mount Sinai, next to the Biochemistry department. The idea was to specialize in one simple test and furnish all hospitals with access to it, thereby freeing up the hospitals' own labs to provide more difficult tests for other client hospitals.[29] With a single technologist and an Auto Analyzer, the lab selected one test (uric acid) to process on a large scale and quickly interested three or four hospitals in using the service. As a government-funded experiment, there was no charge for participating hospitals.

After the In Common Laboratory had operated for a year or two and had added several more tests to its inventory, it became apparent that what most hospitals really preferred was to continue to do the routine testing in their own labs and send the more complex work out. Gradually, thereafter, the function of the ICL reversed, and it developed into a reference centre to which hospitals sent tests that were too complex or expensive to handle themselves. In the process, the ICL obtained one of the first laboratory computers in Toronto and did pioneering research in automation, quality control, and in the development of communications systems for laboratories.[30]

In 1974, the Ministry of Health ceased financial support for the ICL, which henceforth began to charge for its services. Now the ICL would be responsible for identifying labs offering particular services and making them available to any other hospital in the province. Pickup and delivery was organized, as was data and funding exchange. In practice, a hospital in a remote region had only to send a test that was beyond its own capabilities to the ICL, which would then select the appropriate lab, deliver the test, get it done, pick it up, return it to the original hospital, and arrange all financial transactions. It evolved into an efficient, one-stop operation that consolidated many different services. Furthermore, because of the volume (twenty to twenty-five hospitals providing and three hundred hospitals receiving service), prices were at a bulk rate and therefore kept low.

In later years, the ICL encountered vigorous opposition from owners of private labs when it embarked on a third function: setting up within the community and near doctors' offices several "bleeding sta-tions," which offered the identical standard of laboratory service as the hospital and, at the same time, would funnel work into the hospital lab-oratory. The motives of ICL directors were questioned, as private lab owners bitterly resented the competition. Nevertheless, this community arm of the ICL has grown, largely because of continuity of results, and a billing rate that is only 75 per cent of private lab fees. A not-for-profit organization, subject to complete government scrutiny and audit, the ICL puts any money it makes into enhancing the service through improved technology.

Other joint hospital programs also got under way during this period to take advantage of the opportunity to plan together, avoid unnecessary duplication, and cut costs. In addition to enrolling along with other downtown hospitals in two major enterprises, a communal steam plant and the centralized Booth Avenue Laundry, New Mount Sinai initiated a cost-sharing plan of its own. In 1968, administrator Gerald Turner, a pharmacist by training, began investigating the feasibility of joint pur-chasing of hospital pharmaceuticals. A committee of representatives from participating institutions undertook the very difficult task of establishing mutually acceptable standards. It then negotiated for the best drug prices, beginning with the most expensive category at the time – antibiotics. A critical element of the plan was that, despite group pricing, contracts would provide for drop shipments to individual hos-pitals instead of to a central warehouse. Surprisingly, prior to the for-mation of Hospital Purchasing Incorporated (HPI), which soon expanded into food and medical and surgical supplies and equipment, there had been no coherent joint-purchasing program for Toronto hos-pitals. HPI quickly proved to be a boon to participants. In 1968, it saved New Mount Sinai $190,000 on $600,000 worth of drug purchases.[31]

A constitutional change was instituted in 1961 as Ben Sadowski began his final term as president. Realizing that a strenuous campaign lay ahead for the expansion of the hospital, a campaign that would now be beyond the stamina of an aging Sadowski, the board introduced a new category of officer, "Chairman of the Board," which would be more cer-

Bertrand Gerstein represented a new generation of Mount Sinai supporters when he succeeded Ben Sadowski as president of the hospital board in 1966. (MSH Image Centre)

emonial than the executive position of president, although the chairman would still be an *ex officio* member of every committee of the hospital. The position of president was similarly amended to be restricted to a five-year term. In 1966, Bertrand Gerstein, head of a family-owned jewellery chain, assumed the presidency, and Sadowski became chairman of the board. Titles would change again a decade later, whereupon the outgoing president was deemed chairman emeritus, the new chief officer, chairman.

Within the hospital administration, similar changes transpired in 1966 as responsibilities became more complex. Gerald Turner was appointed the new chief administrator, handling day-to-day affairs of the hospital, while Sidney Liswood assumed the title of executive director, concentrating on external relations and overall operations. All of these manoeuvres were in anticipation of one of the most significant events of the decade – the expansion of the hospital. The organizational scheme commenced by the Health Survey Committee years earlier had finally been approved in principle by the Ontario Hospital Services Commission (OHSC) in 1964, and, thereafter, working drawings were developed in conjunction with consultants, architects, and relevant departments of the university.

One critical decision made by the OHSC in early 1967 in response to a study of the requirements for downtown Toronto was to exclude medical pediatrics from the expansion. Unsuccessful in securing a teaching affiliation with the Hospital for Sick Children, which would have enabled that institution's residents to rotate through New Mount Sinai's service, the hospital had no option but to begin to phase out the specialty. When the Royal College of Physicians and Surgeons announced that one-year approvals for residencies in non-teaching-affiliated specialties were being terminated as of July 1, 1970, New Mount Sinai's Pediatrics department ground to an abrupt halt, since it was impossible to function adequately without intern and resident coverage.[32]

Another reversal from the preliminary expansion proposal was the elimination of provision for open-heart surgery. Despite these two modifications, the original blueprint, which added 391,500 square feet, was maintained. The proposal called for an increase to 650 beds from the present 337, more than double the physical facilities for Laboratories, X-ray, and Physical Medicine, a 24-bed in-patient Psychiatric Unit, enlarged Intensive Care and Coronary Care units, a 12-bed Clinical Investigation Unit, an expanded teaching and research program, and larger facilities for the Auxiliary and volunteer corps.[33]

Chosen to superintend the expansion was a second-generation member of the original Mount Sinai "family," Monty Simmonds. Simmonds, the son-in-law of Sam Godfrey, one of the hospital founders, was, in addition to being a lawyer, president of Paramount Construction, and possessed an intimate knowledge of the building industry. A fund-raising campaign led by John D. Feinberg to raise the necessary $8 million of the $38-million anticipated cost of the expanded hospital was launched in September 1966, and, within seven months, $6 million had already been pledged. Various levels of government were committed to funding the rest.

Phase one of the program, completed in the spring of 1967, con-sisted of an addition to the fourth floor of the Elm Street wing, provid-ing essential laboratory and office space. Major renovations to other wings were scheduled to follow, but these appeared harder to imple-ment. A critical snag resulted from the fact that New Mount Sinai, like other structures on the west side of University Avenue, was built above

Taddle Creek, the underground waterway running south through the University of Toronto campus. To contend with this complicating factor, the hospital had been erected on a state-of-the-art concrete raft. When it came to expanding the building, however, difficulties arose from the inability of the foundation to sustain much additional weight, so that no more than a few extra floors could be added.[34] Other construction limitations included a radiant heating system that proved troublesome in a hospital environment, lack of freedom of design, restricted floor-to-floor ceiling heights, and the necessity for awkward ramps to overcome level differences.[35] By the time phase one of the expansion was complete, more than $1 million had been spent on consultant and architect fees in a valiant effort to overcome these obstacles and still integrate all the obligatory changes into the existing hospital. But, as compromises compounded, it was becoming increasingly obvious that the end product would be a jerry-built renovation.

In July, Liswood, Simmonds, and architect Sidney Bregman met for a sound and sober review of the situation.[36] Aside from the mounting physical obstacles to renovation, the recent announcement of the Faculty of Medicine that it was substantially increasing student enrolment and completely revising its teaching format meant that teaching hospitals would be expected to accommodate far more students at both the graduate and undergraduate levels. Might it not be a far better solution, they pondered, if the entire expansion project were scrapped before it went any further and replaced with an entirely new hospital just to the north of the existing one? Preliminary calculations suggested that such a scheme could be accomplished for approximately the same cost, additional benefits being that it would leave the present hospital intact for another use and eliminate all the disruption and dislocation that expansion entailed.

Understandably, such a sudden and dramatic proposal at first caused shock, given that so much time and energy, not to mention a considerable amount of money, had already been consigned to expansion. What's more, fund-raising activity was now virtually wrapped up. But the logic of the idea was indisputable, and, in a matter of weeks, the

Constructed in the 1920s, the Alexandra Palace Hotel at 600 University Avenue was demolished to build the present Mount Sinai Hospital. (City of Toronto Archives)

board wholeheartedly approved it. With its early foresight, the hospital had already acquired most of the necessary land just north of the building. Still, one additional property at 600 University Avenue was essential to complete the parcel. On that site stood a seven-storey office block, converted from the old Alexandra Palace Hotel, built in the 1920s. The owners were reluctant to sell, having just applied for rezoning in order to expand the building into a twenty-five-storey office tower, and they commanded a price far beyond the hospital's means. The ensuing expropriation resulted in a major arbitration. Even though counsel for the hospital, Alvin Rosenberg, and building chairman Monty Simmonds were ultimately successful in buying the property, the legal process sparked concern that the hospital might be perceived as intent on "empire building." "Sidney [Liswood] was terribly worried about that," Simmonds recalls, "and as part of our presentation to government we wanted to make it abundantly clear that we were not."[37]

In placing the proposal before the OHSC, therefore, New Mount Sinai advanced the suggestion that the original institution be shared by all the downtown hospitals as a hostel for non-active-treatment patients, a notion that held enormous appeal. When one of the consultants, Arthur Peckham, learned of the proposition, he wrote, "This is a sound, logical, economical and advantageous approach which will result in a decidedly superior solution for enlarging the New Mount Sinai Hospital and, at the same time, offer the downtown metropolitan hospitals a long-needed short term extended care facility."[38] Stanley Martin, head of the OHSC, and provincial Health Minister Dr. Matthew Dymond obviously agreed, because government approval to proceed was granted forthwith. Having already donated land to the government for the Nightingale School of Nursing and the Toronto Institute of Medical Technology, New Mount Sinai now offered to do the same with its original hospital for the purpose of some form of chronic-care facility still to be determined.

To celebrate the widely praised decision, the hospital mounted a special event on August 15, 1968, to commence demolition of the buildings on the new site and, at the same time, to recognize three groups of individuals whose contributions made possible the beginning of construction of the new hospital: some original *Ezras Noshem* founders of the Yorkville Mount Sinai, the charter membership of the hospital's 25-Year Club, and the dedicated fund-raisers for the $8-million building campaign.[*] The ceremony began at 100 Yorkville Avenue with the assembly of hospital matriarch Dorothy Dworkin and a group of escorts, who then paraded to the new location in antique automobiles and period costumes. Participating in the festivities were Women's Auxiliary president Selma Eisen and several members of her board, who had committed their organization to a $500,000 pledge to the campaign.[39]

---

[*] Charter Members of the 25-Year Club: Phyllis Anderson, R.N.; Jessie Cameron, R.N.; Marjorie Cook, R.N.A.; Jean Cousins; Minnie Hall, R.N.; Rubye Halpern; Clara Hunt, R.N.; Marion Jacob, R.N.; and Helen Widgett, R.N.A.

*Studying plans of the new hospital are, front row, from left: Walter Zwig, Arthur Cohen, Sidney Liswood, Ben Sadowski, Monty Simmonds, Gerald Turner, Arthur Peckham, and Sidney Bregman; back row, from left: Harold Green, Bill Cameron, and Paul Krober. (*Highlights *magazine)*

By fall, plans were accelerating for the new hospital, which, it was unanimously decided, would drop the redundant "New" from its title and revert to the original name "Mount Sinai." Almost immediately, architects and consultants began conferring with administrator Gerald Turner and the Users' Committee to produce working drawings. The estimated total cost was determined to be higher than first expected – the OHSC projected $43 million as opposed to $38 million for the expansion – sending an intrepid John Feinberg back to the community to raise an additional $2 million.[40] Tendering, it was anticipated, would begin some time in 1968.[41] In October, an artist's sketch of the brand-new hospital appeared in the Toronto *Telegram*,[42] and other local newspapers heralded the potential boon for the city of the revised plan. "The proposal would have the effect," declared the *Globe and Mail* just prior to final approval being nailed down, "of providing Metro Toronto with a $10 million to $15 million facility for almost nothing."[43]

The euphoria was short-lived. On January 9, 1969, only days before Mount Sinai was to begin calling for tenders, the hospital was informed in a perfunctory telephone call from the Health Ministry that building projects for teaching hospitals would be immediately frozen. Days later, this was confirmed when the OHSC publicly directed all active-treatment hospitals to put the brakes on construction. With an orgy of building going on in the province – almost a hundred new projects were under way at the start of the year, many of them at teaching hospitals preparing for the Faculty of Medicine's shift in curriculum – the commission's Stanley Martin decreed that "enough was enough." Martin pointed the finger of responsibility for the financial excesses at the federal government. In November, Ottawa had warned the provinces that, due to consistently heavy demands since 1966 on its National Health Resources Fund, the annual federal funding limit was only $37.5 million. Ontario's share was $12 million, which, even after being matched by provincial and municipal contributions, was wholly inadequate to underwrite all these ventures.

Hardest hit by the cutbacks were the Mount Sinai Hospital, the Toronto Institute for Medical Technology, and a regional school of nursing planned for Belleville, all of which were in the process of calling for tenders but had not yet committed a shovel to the ground. A limited number of projects nearing completion was permitted to go ahead, including the conversion of the Sunnybrook Veterans' Hospital into a major acute-care teaching facility. The latter hospital had been given to the University of Toronto by the federal government in 1966. "I am sure our program merits commencement, and I'm hopeful there will be a reassessment," a crestfallen Gerald Turner told the *Toronto Star*.[44]

For the Mount Sinai medical and nursing staffs, the news amounted to a catastrophe. Struggling with unacceptably long waiting lists for admission and the highest physician-to-patient ratio in Metro Toronto, they were desperate for the added space and resources. Within a few weeks, an accreditation survey would focus prominently on the hospital's potentially hazardous space limitations. The accreditation council's Dr. W. I. Taylor reported, "Extreme examples noted are the department of radiology and the emergency service, although many other services, including laboratories, medical records, medical library, physical medicine, outpatient clinics etc. are also embarrassed by space deficiencies."[45] In a last-ditch plea for help, Liswood appealed to Health

Minister Matthew Dymond: "A day spent here would prove that our facilities are taxed to their utmost extent and that important programs are being held back because of the lack of space in which to initiate them," he wrote.[46] But no reprieve was forthcoming. Assured that the OHSC decision amounted to a deferral of indeterminate length rather than an outright cancellation, Mount Sinai would nevertheless receive no funding for the time being.

It is a curious footnote that, while the commission's funding reversal constituted front-page news in Toronto newspapers for days and triggered howls of public protest, the written accounts in Mount Sinai's own hospital publications and various committee minutes do not adequately convey the hand-wringing and depth of despair recounted years later by those most intimately involved. It may well be that a resilient board of directors, accustomed to dealing with impediments to the hospital's progress in the past, by now possessed an almost-instinctive impulse to stoically weather all storms and come up with a workable solution.

In fact, this is precisely what happened. Within days after Dr. Dymond ostensibly closed the book on the issue, Simmonds dispatched his friend and fellow board member, lawyer and government-insider Edwin Goodman, to Provincial Treasurer Charles S. MacNaughton with a simple-but-creative proposition. If Mount Sinai Hospital were permitted to proceed with construction without delay, it would agree to *privately* arrange all financing and make no claims for public grants during the fiscal years 1969–70 and 1970–71, on the understanding that the province would, at some future date, be able to honour its original capital-funding commitment. The suggested arrangement was "technically possible," MacNaughton acknowledged, and would be given further consideration.[47]

Meanwhile, influential board treasurer Noah Torno, chairman of Jordan Wines, approached the president of the Bank of Nova Scotia, with whom he did a considerable amount of business, to arrange a line of credit for the entire $43-million cost of the hospital, based solely on his personal undertaking that Mount Sinai's board would come up with the money if it became necessary.[48] "This was no ordinary business deal," explains Torno. "The bank felt it was dealing with the entire

Jewish community, and it had no reservations whatsoever about extending the credit. Besides, we both knew the government would come through with most, if not all, of the funds in due course."

Delighted with the financing compromise, the OHSC officially accepted the proposal on April 29, 1969.[49] Not only would the construction of Mount Sinai proceed on schedule, thus avoiding inevitable cost increases associated with postponement, but, because the OHSC wouldn't be required to lay out any money for some time, it thereby escaped substantial interest charges. (Once news of the deal became public, the board of the new University of Western Ontario hospital in London engineered a similar plan in order to get the green light to proceed with its own construction.)

When the OHSC's director of hospital planning indicated that future funding approval would total only $31.2 million, a figure approximately $3 million less than anticipated by Mount Sinai's board, the first order of business was to eliminate that amount from the proposed budget. Early contractual problems yielded another unexpected cost increase, and, by the time an agreement was signed with the British firm Laing Construction on January 30, 1970, building chairman Monty Simmonds vowed to take a hard line with regard to containing further unscheduled costs. He hired project manager Bill Cameron, whom he describes as "a rough, tough Irishman," to supervise the supervisors and be accountable exclusively to the hospital and its building committee.[50] Cameron issued an absolute rule that no change orders would be permitted, unless for every order that *cost* money there was a similar one that *saved* money. While this uncompromising attitude rendered Cameron somewhat unpopular on the job site, it characterized the rest of the building project, and resulted in a final tally that, unlike the simultaneously constructed London hospital, remained strictly within budget.[51]

6

Coming of Age

❧

Construction woes consumed a considerable portion of Mount Sinai's energies in the early 1970s. The new hospital, at last begun on February 2, 1970, was scheduled for completion by September 1972. But a crane strike and delays involving excavation and the installation of underground caissons to overcome the knotty Taddle Creek problem halted progress at several junctures, postponing that completion date numerous times. In the meantime, the board quickly conceived, planned, and authorized the building of a second non-profit staff residence adjacent to the first on the hospital's McCaul Street land to accommodate the anticipated doubling of personnel. As an "innovative low cost housing project," the 235-suite residence, the undertaking of a committee headed by the board's resident expert in building and renovation technology, Harold Green, qualified for a Central Mortgage and Housing Corporation loan of $2.4 million. Plans included a gymnasium, a daycare centre, and outdoor tennis courts for use by tenants.

A third project that quickly became imbued with tremendous symbolic significance was the construction of an underground pedestrian tunnel running from McCaul and Elm streets beneath University Avenue as far north as College Street. This subterranean umbilical cord linking the two staff residences, the Nightingale School of Nursing, and both the present and the "newest" Mount Sinai hospitals to the Hospital for Sick Children and the Toronto General would permit the easy flow of patients, doctors, nurses, professors, and students from one institution to another. It would also transport steam lines from the new Central Steam Plant on Walton Street behind the Hospital for Sick Children.

The completion of the tunnel in the fall of 1971 was a momentous occasion, rendered even more so because it coincided with the successful campaign to raise the $10 million that the board had assured the OHSC it would contribute to the cost of the new hospital. On November 30, Monty Simmonds, now the president of the board as well as the building chairman, invited Premier William Davis, several members of the provincial cabinet, representatives of Metro council, and a group of honoured guests to tour the tunnel and participate in a dedication ceremony. "When you create that freedom of movement, you have greatly eliminated not only the physical barriers to an interchange of facilities, personnel, and ideas for the public good, but also the psychological ones," Simmonds solemnly remarked to the assembled well-wishers on the subject of the tunnel.[1]

But Simmonds, who possesses a lambent wit, had a second agenda, which he was determined to cover that day. It seems that all contractual negotiations between the government and Mount Sinai Hospital regarding payment of construction costs had been based on either private conversations, personal correspondence, or verbal agreements between the principals. To the periodic discomfort of hospital accountants, no formal document existed outlining the official understanding, which was that the board would raise $10 million from community sources while the government would fund the balance of the $43-million cost of the hospital. As matters eventually unfolded, the government actually began issuing cheques well before the interval elapsed during which the hospital assumed responsibility for private financing, with the result that Mount Sinai never had to draw on its bank line of credit. Nevertheless, Simmonds decided the moment was right for reaffirming the terms of the deal.

With flashbulbs popping, he unrolled a scroll, hand-painted in lavish calligraphy, to be signed by the premier. "On this day, in the presence of

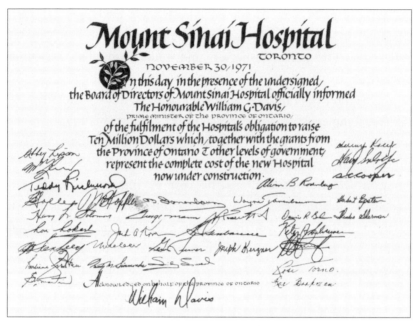

Mount Sinai president Monty Simmonds commissioned this scroll to remind the provincial government of its promise to fund the new hospital. (Highlights *magazine*)

From left: Monty Simmonds, Sidney Liswood, and Bertrand Gerstein look on as Premier Bill Davis signs the "acknowledgement" of the agreement to fund construction of Mount Sinai Hospital. (Highlights *magazine*)

the undersigned," it read, "the Board of Directors of Mount Sinai Hospital officially informed the Honourable William G. Davis, Prime Minister of the Province of Ontario, of the fulfillment of the Hospital's obligation to raise ten million dollars, which together with the grants from the Province of Ontario and other levels of government represent the complete cost of the new hospital under construction."[2]

"I don't know if I should sign this, Monty," hissed the premier through clenched teeth, smiling for the cameras. But sign it he did, and, according to Simmonds, the scroll remains the only written and signed confirmation of the agreement to fund Mount Sinai Hospital.[3]

When Laing Construction predicted that the hospital would be ready for occupancy early in 1973, consideration began to be given to an appropriate opening ceremony. The Queen was scheduled to visit Canada in the summer of 1973, and soon letters began to wend their way through bureaucratic channels toward Buckingham Palace, requesting that the opening of Mount Sinai Hospital be placed on Her Majesty's official schedule. The news that Queen Elizabeth and Prince Philip would indeed participate in the grand event and appear at Mount Sinai on the afternoon of June 26 following a visit to the Hospital for Sick Children across the street was greeted with uncommon joy and excitement. To anyone who had ever been closely associated with the hospital, the royal presence represented a degree of recognition and public acceptance that would have been utterly inconceivable to the immigrant founders and the beleaguered Jewish physicians of Yorkville Mount Sinai, for whom Buckingham Palace was as distant as the moon. Yet, as winter approached and further construction delays followed by an elevator strike made it evident that the hospital would most definitely not be finished in time for the royal visit, the triumphant mood came perilously close to being shattered. Administration briefly contemplated cancelling the historic appearance of the Queen, but opted instead to hurriedly furnish the main lobby, banish all obvious traces of construction, and erect an elaborate exterior dais for a "pre-opening" ceremony.

Excitement and unalloyed pride were palpable as the resplendent receiving party greeted Her Majesty Queen Elizabeth and Prince Philip

Her Majesty the Queen
and
His Royal Highness the Duke of Edinburgh
will be present

The Chairman of the Board
of
Mount Sinai Hospital
takes pleasure in extending an invitation to

Dr and Mrs. Joshua J. Chesnie
to be present on the occasion of the
opening of the new hospital
Tuesday, the twenty-sixth of June
nineteen hundred and seventy-three
at two-fifteen o'clock
600 University Avenue
Toronto

The book signed by Her Majesty the Queen to commemorate the opening of
Mount Sinai Hospital on June 26, 1974, is displayed in a glass case in the
hospital lobby. (Highlights *magazine*) Top: Mount Sinai proudly issued
elaborate invitations to the opening. (*Courtesy Henrietta Chesnie*)

in front of the as-yet-incomplete third Mount Sinai Hospital on the magnificent cloudless afternoon of Tuesday, June 26, 1973.[*] In his remarks to the assembled guests, board chairman Bertrand Gerstein, whose father, Frank, had been associated with both previous Mount Sinai hospitals, spoke for many in attendance when he made poignant reference to the protracted struggle behind the achievement. "Many of us are immigrants," he pointed out, "the parents of most of us are immigrants, and it is important to us that in some tangible way we should have the opportunity to express our appreciation. And in no better way could this be done than by helping to provide needed health services and facilities for the total community."[4]

After the Queen exchanged pleasantries with the selected dignitaries from the hospital, unveiled the cornerstone plaque, and signed the commemorative book, Gerstein and president Monty Simmonds escorted the royal couple back to their limousine. En route, Prince Philip queried Simmonds about why they were not following the usual royal protocol on such occasions of going inside the hospital to visit patients. "I'm afraid the hospital's not finished yet," admitted Simmonds.

"Why not?" puzzled the Prince. Simmonds, an expatriate Englishman and an avid sailor, knew that Prince Philip was a personal friend and sailing companion of Sir Maurice Laing, the principal of the British-based construction firm that was building the hospital.

"A friend of yours is in charge of building it, and he is quite late," explained Simmonds, relating the connection.

"Then I suppose you'd like me to chilly him up a bit," suggested the Prince helpfully.

"I would consider it a personal favour, sir," replied Simmonds, who last saw Prince Philip removing a little notebook from his pocket and jotting down the reminder: "Mount Sinai Hospital/Maurice Laing/Monty Simmonds."[5]

---

[*] The only sad note was the absence, due to illness, of Ben Sadowski, who died a few months later.

Preparing to Move

On the patient-care front, New Mount Sinai pressed forward with several programs well before the phased move into the hospital next door, which began in October, when carpeting, furniture, and equipment began to arrive, and concluded with the transfer of patients on January 20, 1974. In the meantime, with the demise of the fifth-floor pediatric ward, space became available for a radically revised Ambulatory department to replace the old Out-Patient department. The premise for the latter had been provision of care for indigent patients, a significant population served by Mount Sinai since its inception. But the introduction of universal health insurance in 1969 had eliminated that category, along with its consequent stigma, and the whole concept of out-patient services was in line for an overhaul.

In August 1970, the former pediatric wing of the old hospital was renovated to house the Family Practice Unit of the Department of Family and Community Medicine,[*] the first in a spectrum of new comprehensive ambulatory services planned for the new building. Led by Dr. Nathan Levinne and supported by the Specialty Services and Paramedical departments, the unit provided generous 9 A.M. to 9 P.M. office hours, and began attracting a huge volume of patients. Home visits by one of the unit's twelve family-practice physicians was an especially popular feature.

At about the same time, Dr. Levinne and Sidney Liswood began meeting with Dr. Henry Himel and Sam Ruth, their counterparts at Baycrest Centre, to discuss setting up a satellite unit close to that institution on north Bathurst Street.[6] Aside from the desire to continually cement ties and foster cooperation with Baycrest, the plan was to target the heavily Jewish population within the district of Lawrence Heights, recently designated a medically underserviced area, and hence an obvious location for an extension of New Mount Sinai's Family Practice Unit. Operational in September 1972, the satellite unit was installed in a

---

[*] The Department of Family Medicine underwent a name change shortly after formal affiliation with the Faculty of Medicine, becoming the Department of Family and Community Medicine.

little house at 30 Baycrest Avenue,[*] launching a new and flexible team approach to community-based health care. The goal of the team, headed by family practitioner Dr. Samuel Ginsberg and nurse Betty Clarke and augmented by an array of medical and paramedical personnel from both New Mount Sinai and Baycrest, was to formulate a specific team plan to suit the treatment needs of each individual patient, instead of the other way round – a truly innovative concept for the day.

Not long after the opening of the hospital's Family Practice Unit at New Mount Sinai, an Inhalation Therapy Unit was established nearby on the fifth floor of the old hospital. Run by inhalation therapist Terrence Allen under the direction of anesthetist-in-chief Dr. Gerald Edelist, this service, later called "respiratory therapy," was designed to diagnose and treat lung diseases and obstructed breathing processes in both ambulatory and in-patients. Elective out-patient surgery also expanded into ambulatory care early in 1971, partly to reduce costs of more-expensive in-patient procedures, especially when local anesthetic was appropriate, but also to allow physicians to perform minor investigations that previously would have automatically required hospitalization.

Another initiative was begun by staff ophthalmologist Dr. Fred Feldman, who launched the Glaucoma Testing and Treatment Clinic, soon one of the busiest of the ambulatory centres. The Division of Otolaryngology was also eager to institute change. Only months after his installation as the new chief of Otolaryngology following the retirement of Dr. Joseph Gollom in July 1970, Dr. Peter Alberti created an Otological Function Unit for the diagnosis of hearing and balance disorders. Besides holding fellowships from both England and Canada, the new chief was an expert in audiology, with a Ph.D. in the specialty from Washington University in St. Louis, Missouri. In 1982, Dr. Alberti would be appointed professor and chairman of the university's Department of Otolaryngology.

---

[*] Now the site of the Competency Clinic for Baycrest's Department of Psychiatry.

By the time the 65,000-square-foot Koffler Ambulatory Care Centre opened for business next door on the fourth-floor mezzanine in the new hospital in December 1973, it housed the Department of Family and Community Medicine, the specialty departments of Medicine, Dentistry, Obstetrics and Gynecology, Ophthalmology, Otolaryngology, and Surgery. All geographic physicians associated with these areas were located permanently on the same floor and did not maintain offices outside the hospital. As well, each department included examination/consultation rooms for the use of house staff and non-geographic physicians. To ensure patients the most efficient access to complete care, this floor also provided critical support services such as social work, psychology, nutritional counselling, patient pharmacy, and laboratory services. Connected to the main floor by escalator, as well as an elevator, to facilitate movement of a large volume of patients, the Ambulatory Care Centre was conceived as a centrepiece of the building, reflecting the hospital's changing role from being merely a provider of in-house treatment to that of partner with its patients in disease prevention and rehabilitation. A unique experiment at the time, the Ambulatory Care Centre firmly established the direction of future outpatient care at the new hospital.

A handsome, modern structure with marble walls and a profusion of donated art, the eighteen-floor Mount Sinai Hospital soon earned the nickname "Mount Sinai Hilton." (Mount Sinai Hospital)

Left to right: Joseph Mapa, Janine Girard-Pearlman, Gerald Turner (seated), and Theodore Freedman assumed increasing executive responsibilities in the new hospital. (Randy Bulmer)

On January 20, 1974, Mount Sinai completed the last phase of the move next door to 600 University Avenue, finally vacating the building that had been its home since 1953 and beginning another chapter in the life of the hospital. In a manoeuvre planned with military precision by assistant administrator Theodore Freedman, who had coordinated the move, and nurse-administrator Marie Rice, 150 patients and 40 babies travelled through the connecting tunnel to the brand-new 608-bed hospital. Ministry approval had been deferred for more than a third of those beds for the short term as a result of a freeze on active treatment beds throughout the province, but the expectation was that, by April of the following year, at least 573 beds would be operational. For the present, 366 beds opened, including, for the first time, a 24-bed Psychiatric Unit. In anticipation of the next round of bed openings for Ministry-approved programs, notably a 30-bed Rheumatic-Disease Unit and a 72-bed short-term "active" Rehabilitation Unit, the first of its kind within a general treatment hospital, staff was increased from 850 to 1,200.[7]

As of January 1, 1974, moreover, Gerald Turner was promoted to the top job of executive director responsible for the day-to-day internal operation of the hospital, while Sidney Liswood began a term as executive vice-president with responsibility for external relations. New administrative colleagues in the executive wing who would join Turner's team were

With the move to 600 University Avenue in 1974, Alvin Rosenberg became the new president of the board, serving until 1979. (Highlights magazine)

Janine Girard-Pearlman, director of education, and Murray MacKenzie, appointed assistant executive director in 1976. The newest administrative resident, Joseph Mapa, joined this group in 1977. A close associate of Turner, he would eventually become chief operating officer in 1993.

An additional change in governance occurred in April 1976 when Alvin Rosenberg, QC, former honorary counsel to the hospital, was elected president of the board, succeeding Monty Simmonds. In the tradition of all of his predecessors, Rosenberg possessed a deeply rooted family link to the hospital. Since its inception, his father, Henry, also a lawyer, had served as both honorary counsel and executive committee member of New Mount Sinai.

Mount Sinai Hospital: 600 University Avenue

Painstakingly designed to avoid repeating the errors of the previous hospital, Mount Sinai now consisted of eighteen floors: eight in the base structure of the building and an upper ten composing the tower. All patient beds, with the exception of seventy-six obstetrical beds on Level 7, were on the tower floors.[*] Until 1976, when the concept was

---

[*] An eleven-bed clinical investigation unit planned for Level 6 never opened.

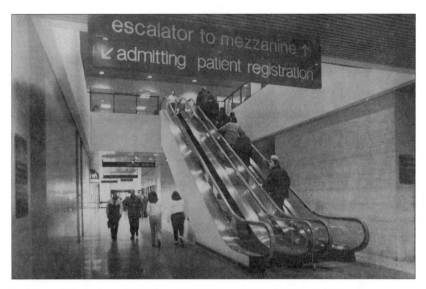

Bright public spaces give Mount Sinai Hospital an un-institutional ambiance. (Girish Ghatalia Architects)

terminated and private rooms redistributed to all services, a "private floor" of single rooms operated on Level 17. The Department of Laboratories and Pathology was established on Level 6, with radiological services and main operating rooms conveniently below on Level 5. Once again, both kosher and non-kosher kitchens would be available for patients and staff.

Esthetically, too, Mount Sinai was a triumph. With clean exterior lines and bronze windows, more reminiscent of a modern bank headquarters than a hospital, the building featured a gracious lobby, with walls of Italian marble and public elevators panelled in wood grain. A pair of majestic free-standing escalators leading to the mezzanine Ambulatory Care Centre wouldn't have been out of place in the most elegant hotel. Equally un-institutional was the mall slicing through the centre of the first level and connecting the two main entrances on University Avenue and Murray Street, a detail meant to eliminate congestion on the street floor while contributing a sense of community traffic flow. In total, floor space measured more than 900,000 square feet.

Enormously and justifiably proud of the result, the Toronto Jewish community began contributing gifts of paintings, sculptures, wall hangings, and other *objets d'art* to enhance the building and prevent the drab institutionalism characteristic of most hospitals. Counting design skills among her many talents, Valerie Fine, a key member of the board's executive committee as well as a future Auxiliary president and head of the Patient Care Committee, coordinated the decor. A small jewel of a synagogue, capable of seating forty, flanked by stained-glass panels and tucked into the southeast corner of the main floor, was dedicated in October 1975. Containing a holy ark whose magnificent bronze sculptured doors, executed by Sorel Etrog, bore the Hebrew inscription from Jeremiah, "Heal us, O Lord and We Will Be Healed," it was a gift of benefactors Joseph and Faye Tanenbaum.[8] Throughout the decade, the Auxiliary's publication, *Highlights*, reported similar dedication ceremonies for significant works of art generously bestowed on the hospital by individuals or art galleries. The moniker "Mount Sinai Hilton" was often heard during these years, usually in admiration or jest, but occasionally betraying scarcely concealed resentment. One particularly mean-spirited newspaper account provided a platform for several Toronto-area hospital executives to publicly expose their envy of Mount Sinai's "excessive lavishness," despite protests by executive director Gerald Turner that the illusion of affluence was the result of private donations, and that government-funded per-bed operating costs were no higher at Mount Sinai than at any other hospital in the city.[9]

After much debate on the appropriate use for the old hospital, the Ministry of Health designated it as a staging venue for the Queen Elizabeth Hospital for chronic and rehabilitative care, pending that institution's reconstruction on its Dunn Avenue site. When funding cutbacks later spelled the end of that major expansion project, however, the Queen Elizabeth Hospital renovated the building for its own purposes in order to set down roots permanently at 550 University Avenue.

By now fully affiliated with the university (the Department of Dentistry was the last to institute a teaching program in 1973), Mount Sinai united efforts with the other Queen's Park hospitals to develop additional joint programs that would eliminate wasteful duplication of services, personnel, and facilities and share expertise in designated areas.

The hospital had previously been invited to join the University Teaching Hospitals Association (UTHA), an organization established in 1971 for coordinating efforts within the university community of hospitals. Membership in both associations now encouraged the beginning of cross-appointments and joint programs, generally fostering closer ties between institutions. The placement of a Computerized Axial Tomography (CAT) scanner at the Toronto General in 1974, for example, a UTHA initiative, was coupled with a provision that access was to be shared with Mount Sinai Hospital's staff and patients. The revolutionary new scanner, invented in England in 1972, could assemble multiple X-ray images of the brain, creating far more detailed pictures than previously possible through conventional radiological techniques. This cooperative arrangement between hospitals, then unique in North America, was ideally suited to the cheek-by-jowl organization on University Avenue, and prefigured future joint efforts to share enormously expensive new technology.[10] (Mount Sinai got its own whole body CT scanner in 1981.) Certainly a healthy impetus to the spirit of cooperation was the fear, expressed at early UTHA meetings, that consensus on certain issues had better be achieved voluntarily before "outsiders" – likely one of the many commissions, special-report, or task-force consultants investigating hospital services in the early 1970s – *imposed* its decisions unilaterally.[11]

By the end of 1971, Mount Sinai had been participating in thirty joint programs with other teaching hospitals.[12] Some of the earliest included a Diabetic Day Care Centre at Women's College Hospital, a respiratory consultation service, a liver clinic at Mount Sinai, headed by Dr. Victor Feinman and Dr. J. C. Sinclair of the Toronto General, a dermapathology centre, and a counselling service for "unwed mothers." Joint security and disaster programs as a result of the connecting tunnel and joint bargaining with the Service Employees' Union on behalf of seven downtown hospitals also occurred for the first time. During the last year in the old hospital, two new tri-hospital programs had been successfully launched to serve Mount Sinai, Toronto General, and Women's College hospitals: a nephrology service to provide access to kidney-disease consultation and dialysis treatment and a Pulmonary Function Laboratory for sophisticated tests and research.

Aside from the proliferation of new patient services that accompanied Mount Sinai's opening, several non-clinical innovations took shape in the new hospital throughout the decade, spurred by the steadfast will of succeeding generations of trustees and administrators to provide the best possible care within a compassionate environment. The Nursing department, for example, launched a broad series of courses and sensitivity programs for its staff, reflecting a heightened awareness of the significance of nurse-patient relationships. Such courses as "Understanding Aging," "Perspectives on Dying," and "Non-Verbal Communication in Nursing" emphasized practices consistent with the hospital's philosophy of humane patient care.

A children's waiting room, equipped with toys, books, and craft supplies and staffed by volunteers, opened in September 1975, allowing patients to receive evening and weekend visitors who, without child care, would not be able to come to the hospital.

As a consequence of the findings of an Ad Hoc Committee for the Total Care of the Terminally Ill, established in 1975 to review the needs of patients, their families, and the staff who care for them, a consultation team composed of a physician, nurse, psychiatrist, social worker, rehabilitation therapist, dietitian, and clergyman was created to advise staff caring for terminally ill patients. As well, a group of volunteers trained by the Social Work department introduced a bereavement program to offer support for immediate relatives of recently deceased patients.

But in its diligent quest for high-quality patient care, Mount Sinai's creation of a patient representation program in 1974, the first of its kind in Canada, was surely the clearest demonstration of ideals put into action. Supplementing but in no way usurping the standard hospital peer-review mechanisms for evaluating medical care, a designated patient representative, Janine Girard-Pearlman (who added the role to her other administrative functions), fielded all non-medical complaints of patients, family members, and visitors. She soon began actively seeking comments from patients on such subjects as admission procedures, staff attitudes, and quality of meals in order to anticipate and prevent problems before they arose. So well received was the program that president Alvin Rosenberg and executive director Gerald Turner decided to involve the board in these issues. In 1977, the Patient Care Committee became a standing committee of the board, broadening hospital trustees' responsibilities from the traditional capital development and fiscal matters to include what is ultimately their primary commitment: the total welfare of patients.

Obstetrics and Gynecology

Early in March 1971, Dr. Frederick R. Papsin was appointed obstetrician and gynecologist-in-chief, taking over from Dr. Sidney Tobin, who had filled in as acting chief following the retirement of Dr. Louis J. Harris. Papsin had been a junior intern at New Mount Sinai back in 1958, prior to completing both his specialty training within the U of T program and a travelling fellowship in surgical gynecological oncology.[*] On staff since 1965 at the Toronto Western Hospital, where he established the first ovarian tumour clinic, and holding university teaching and research appointments, Papsin was eager for the challenge of the Mount Sinai position and honoured, at the relatively tender age of thirty-nine, to be invited to join the ranks of some of his former teachers. His decision to accept the post, nonetheless, was greeted by his university associates with general disapproval. As Papsin indelicately puts it, "They thought I was insane." The university's ill feeling toward Mount Sinai's Department of Obstetrics stemmed in part from some early members' reputation for fee-splitting, a common enough activity in the early decades of the twentieth-century, according to G. Harvey Agnew in *Canadian Hospitals, 1920–1970: A Dramatic Half-Century*. This practice, whereby doctors received "commissions" for referrals, was perhaps more widely pursued by Yorkville practitioners excluded from the mainstream medical market. In any event, Sidney Liswood had put a decisive end to fee-splitting by any New Mount Sinai staff member when he became administrator in 1954.

---

[*] In 1958, Dr. Frederick Papsin had been awarded the hospital's Harry Ely prize as "best intern of the year."

*Establishing a high-risk
Perinatal Unit at Mount
Sinai was top priority for
obstetrician and gynecolo-
gist-in-chief Frederick
Papsin. (Randy Bulmer)*

Although Mount Sinai's Department of Obstetrics and Gynecology
had affiliated officially with the university a few years earlier, there had
been precious little recognition from that quarter of the hospital's
strengths in the specialty. Yet from his own experience while interning
there, Papsin had an entirely different perspective. "Lou Harris was a
brilliant individual and an excellent gynecologist, as was his partner, Dr.
Bernard Ludwig, and they and others in the department had a huge following in the community," says Papsin.[*] (Both Harris and Ludwig were
gold medallists at the University of Toronto's Faculty of Medicine, in
1929 and 1956 respectively.) "Not only was the care given by Mount
Sinai's ob/gyn department superb, but several of its physicians were far
ahead of the literature, and doing cutting-edge things. No one could
touch them in terms of numbers and the quality of their work."

As an intern, Papsin had been impressed and intrigued by a young
Mount Sinai obstetrician, Dr. Ely Ravinsky, who had a keen interest in
the potential benefits of fetal monitoring. "Ravinsky had rigged up an

---

[*] Other influential members of the large Ob/Gyn department at the time
included Drs. A. Bernstein, A. Eiger, A. Eisen, J. Fedder, I. Goldman, S. Nash,
S. Norris, E. Ravinsky, M. Selznick, D. Shaul, J. Shuber, R. Suran, L. Tanzer,
S. Tobin, and G. Vozis.

apparatus almost the size of his desk that he had clipped to an ECG machine," Papsin recalls. "I knew of no other place where people were thinking so progressively." Another area in which former chief Lou Harris had been "pre-eminent," according to Papsin, was infertility, a sub-specialty that the university's department practically ignored at the time. Academic attention was more narrowly trained on cancer surgery – Papsin's own particular field of interest – while infertility and its treatment was, in the university's view, a poor cousin, all but dismissed as a mere profit-making sideline, of minimal significance.

With Papsin now installed as chief, Mount Sinai set about to bring legitimacy to this important, yet neglected, subject. The term "infertility," however, did not adequately convey the intended approach of Mount Sinai's department. For one thing, most infertility treatment available in Toronto, such as it was, focused almost exclusively on female reproductive problems. Mount Sinai had a much broader vision of a facility hitherto unavailable in Canada, if not North America. It would provide a service for both male and female patients with reproductive problems, and would encompass a patient-care facility, as well as a source for research, teaching, and training in reproductive medicine. Most important, the program would not be the sole domain of Obstetrics and Gynecology, but would encourage extensive involvement of other specialties.[13]

A key member and eager proponent of the resulting Reproductive Biology Unit at Mount Sinai was Dr. Jerald Bain, who had joined the hospital's Department of Medicine as an endocrinologist in 1972. A graduate in pharmacy as well as medicine, Bain had taken an early interest in male infertility during his postgraduate training in reproductive endocrinology at UCLA. But even in California, where research into male infertility was accessible, albeit limited, the existing treatment programs for all reproductive problems uniformly came under the rubric and management of Ob/Gyn departments.

With state-of-the-art laboratory facilities soon to be available in the new hospital next door, and temporary ones operating in the interim at Bain's research lab, Mount Sinai's innovative Reproductive Biology Unit opened in March 1973. Along with various problems related to female infertility and andrology (the study of male reproduction, a term unknown prior to the 1970s), the unit dealt with such conditions as menstrual irregularities, psycho-sexual problems, and numerous abnormalities related to the body's endocrine system. The treatment team, in addition to endocrinologist Dr. Bain, who was named director, included gynecologists Drs. Abraham Eisen, Jack Shuber, and David Shaul, the latter a specialist in the realm of human sexuality; urologists Drs. Martin Buckspan and Philip Klotz; psychiatrists Drs. Ed Browne and David Berger; psychologist Dr. Paul Lerner; social worker Renee Block; and nurses Marijean Major, Joan Gittens, and Marcia Wise.

The RBU was far from the only significant event for Mount Sinai's Department of Obstetrics and Gynecology during this period. Since its earliest days on Yorkville Avenue, the department had always been one of the hospital's busiest services, and, once undergraduate and post-graduate training became available, activity stepped up even further. A decision to abandon the distinction between "private" and "semi-private" or "standard ward" patients throughout the hospital and simply include everyone for teaching purposes was made very early. The concept was readily accepted by the public, and permitted a much larger teaching pool. Given the hospital's huge volume in this department, all the top graduates wanting to do obstetrics and gynecology made Mount Sinai their first choice for training.[14] Among those who began their association with Mount Sinai as ob/gyn students in the 1970s were current senior staff Drs. Paul Bernstein, Fred Engle, Fred Mandel, Elliott Lyons, Peter Hawrlyshyn, and Marshall Barkin.

Burgeoning new technology was revolutionizing the practice of obstetrics and contributing to safer deliveries and healthier babies. Mount Sinai was among the first hospitals in Toronto to provide expectant mothers with prenatal ultrasound and fetal monitoring. Following the early experiments in monitoring by Dr. Ely Ravinsky, Mount Sinai obstetrician Dr. Abraham Bernstein became deeply involved in this research. Along with a colleague, Dr. Leslie Organ, Bernstein developed the Owl monitor, one of the original such devices predating mass production by Hewlett-Packard. By the end of the decade, fetal monitoring and associated clinical research at Mount Sinai had permitted some of the earliest VBAC births in appropriate women, that is, vaginal birth after a Caesarean section. With the foresight that made him so success-ful in Mount Sinai's Department of Obstetrics and Gynecology, Papsin encouraged Dr. Harold Drutz, now the university division head and a renowned authority in the sub-specialty of uro-gynecology, to acquire training in that area.

Gynecology was also benefiting from a technological revolution. Papsin had introduced colposcopy to the Toronto Western Hospital in 1966 after learning the advanced technique for diagnosing cancer of the cervix in Austria during his postgraduate fellowship training. Now he began teaching it to residents at Mount Sinai. On one memorable occa-sion, those roles were reversed when Ob/Gyn resident Konstantin Valtchev announced, while assisting Papsin in a laparoscopic operation, that he had an idea for an instrument to move the uterus out of the way during certain of these surgeries. Within a month, Valtchev and a friend who was an engineer had created a prototype of the instrument, now known as the Valtchev mobilizer and used by gynecological surgeons the world over.[15]

Orthopedic Surgery

Major changes in the clinical science of orthopedic surgery began sim-mering in the 1960s, and percolated actively through the next decade, producing rapid growth, stellar accomplishments, and international recognition of Mount Sinai's contributions. When the university first affiliated with the hospital in 1962, orthopedics was part of the Department of Surgery rather than a separate division. Until this time, Dr. Israel Shapiro had headed up Mount Sinai's existing team of ortho-pedic surgeons, which comprised Drs. Leonard Davies, Maurice Charendoff, and John Zeldin, all of whom practised only part time at Mount Sinai, in large measure because chief of Surgery Dr. David Bohnen customarily allocated few beds to orthopedics.

But when the Department of Surgery signed on with the university,

Orthopedic surgeon Dr. Allan Gross began allograft surgery, the transplantation of bone cartilage, at Mount Sinai. (MSH Image Centre)

Dr. Ezra Silverstein, the first orthopedic surgeon with a university appointment, joined the staff. Even so, the university didn't immediately begin sending residents in orthopedics to Mount Sinai, and initially only general-surgery postgraduate training was offered there. The first orthopedic surgeon Silverstein recruited to expand the department was Dr. Allan E. Gross.

Gross had served as a junior intern at Mount Sinai in 1962, before training in orthopedic surgery at the Toronto General and then in England, where he researched an exciting new clinical field: the transplantation of bone and cartilage. In England, Gross met Dr. Frederick Langer, a Toronto-born, McGill-trained orthopedic surgeon with an extensive research background and a particular interest in bone tumours. Gross convinced Langer to come back with him to Mount Sinai and help Ezra Silverstein build a new division in orthopedic surgery.

In 1971, Gross returned to Mount Sinai to set up the first program in joint transplantation in Canada. Langer soon followed, establishing a lab for basic research at the hospital. At first, the services of an immunologist, necessary for this kind of procedure, were provided by the Toronto General,[16] but, before long, another orthopedic surgeon with a Ph.D. in immunology, Dr. Andrei Czitrom, joined the Mount Sinai group and assumed that function. In January 1972, the team, headed by Gross, performed Canada's first knee-joint transplant on a sixty-four-

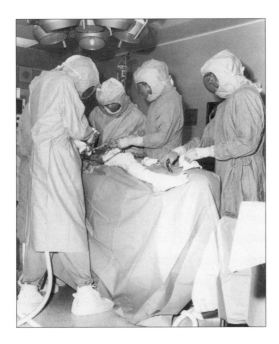

Patients travel from around the world for joint transplant surgery at Mount Sinai. Here Dr. Allan Gross performs the first living hip transplant, 1987. (MSH Image Centre)

year-old woman who received cartilage and a thin layer of underlying bone taken from a tissue-matched cadaver. Three months later, a second transplant followed.[17] With no indication of rejection or collapse of the grafts in their first patients, the team continued transplantation of joints with donated cadaver bone and cartilage in cases of severe osteoarthritis or trauma. The dramatic operations, called allograft surgery, attracted international media coverage, putting Mount Sinai and Dr. Allan Gross firmly on the map in this specialty.[*]

It was an extension of this early pioneering surgery that led to Mount Sinai's present status as a world centre for the treatment of sarcoma, musculoskeletal tumours of bone and soft tissue. In 1975, soon after adjuvant chemotherapy came into general use, Gross and Langer immediately saw another potential use for bone and cartilage transplantation. Prior to adjuvant chemotherapy, the standard treatment for cancerous bone tumours in limbs, one form of sarcoma, was amputation, a devastating consequence, particularly given that the disease

---

[*] In 1979, the American Hospital Association listed Dr. Gross's knee-transplantation surgery as one of the ten most important recent advances in medicine.

afflicts mainly children and young adults. But once shrinkage of the tumour was made possible by adjuvant chemotherapy or high-dose radiation, the surgeons determined that, if they could reconstruct around the defect, they could remove the cancer and still preserve the limb with a local resection and transplant. Whenever possible, the pair harvested bone the patient could live without, such as the fibula next to the shin; if not, they substituted donated bone.

At the same time that their "limb salvage" surgery was getting under way, Gross and Langer realized that, as a result of the publicity surrounding their successful operations, more bone and cartilage were being donated than they had immediate use for. So began in 1972 Mount Sinai's Bone and Tissue Bank, another resource then accessible at only a handful of major hospitals across North America.[18] Over the next decade, as the hospital developed the world's largest comprehensive orthopedic transplant program, the Bone Bank, later under the direction of hemopathologist Dr. Elizabeth Musclow, became linked with MORE (Multiple Organ and Retrieval Exchange), coordinating donations and screening for acceptability across Canada and abroad.

Among the early medical dramas encountered by the team of Gross and Langer was one that played out on a much larger stage than a Mount Sinai operating room. On October 22, 1973, days after the beginning of the Yom Kippur War, the two were summarily notified by the Israeli consul general that their services were urgently required on the battlefields of the Sinai desert. When the Middle East emergency arose, the orthopedic surgeons were among scores of Jewish doctors who had volunteered their assistance to an organization known as the American Physicians Fellowship. Within two hours of the appeal for help, Gross and Langer had joined one other Canadian and nine American orthopedic surgeons on a government flight to Israel, where they spent five weeks working frantically in Israeli field hospitals to save the lives and limbs of both Israeli soldiers and Egyptian and Syrian prisoners. Following their return to Toronto, accounts of their vivid experiences – both medical and personal – were in heavy demand, and for the next two years the two Mount Sinai surgeons found themselves on the speaking circuit at teaching hospitals, Armed Forces bases, and community group meetings across the province.

By 1974, in tandem with changes at the university, Mount Sinai established a separate Division of Orthopedic Surgery, naming Dr. Allan Gross as chief. The following year, upon Dr. David Bohnen's death, Gross was appointed surgeon-in-chief. Dr. Robert Stone soon relieved some of that responsibility when he came to Mount Sinai as head of the Division of General Surgery on July 1, 1976.

Mount Sinai surgeons leapt into the front ranks of sarcoma treatment when Langer was invited to become the surgical representative for the Princess Margaret Hospital in 1978, and subsequently opened a clinic there, bringing surgical cases from across the province to Mount Sinai. Micro-vascular surgeon Dr. Nancy McKee would join the team in 1979, and, in 1983, at the suggestion of the newly appointed chief of Surgery, Dr. Robert J. Ginsberg, Langer would move his clinic back to Mount Sinai. With all this expertise available, the orthopedic staff and CEO Gerald Turner determined that sarcoma would henceforth become a priority program at the hospital.

Yet before that decision could become a reality, there was a formidable hurdle to overcome. A smaller sarcoma program headed by Dr. Robert Bell existed at St. Michael's Hospital, whose administration had

Harvard-trained orthopedic surgeon Dr. Robert Bell now heads the world-famous sarcoma program at Mount Sinai. (Randy Bulmer)

petitioned the university to bring Mount Sinai's program over there. Turner vigorously objected, arguing that Mount Sinai had the city's only bone bank, as well as the surgical staff, and, most important, the will to make sarcoma one of its highest-priority programs, and therefore St. Michael's unit should amalgamate at 600 University Avenue.

Eventually Turner managed to persuade both university officials and St. Michael's administration that this was the more logical move, but it required a further arbitration to adequately fund the expanded unit. By 1989, however, the University Sarcoma Clinic at Mount Sinai, as it was called, would have one of the largest sarcoma practices in the world.[19] At that point, the highly complex Van Nes procedure, which the duo of Langer and Bell performed on patients with high-grade sarcomas of the knee and which was geared to salvage as much limb function as possible, had been carried out on only sixteen adults in the world, fifteen of them Mount Sinai patients.[20]

Oncology

In the impressive new approach to the treatment of sarcoma, however, surgery was only one-half of the equation. Equally important in this evolution was the ascendance of oncology at Mount Sinai. Until the arrival of Dr. Fred Langer in 1971, no specialist at the hospital had made cancer treatment a primary focus, although, as we shall see, senior general surgeon Dr. Alan Bassett had begun to acquire a large breast-surgery practice, and he had been providing some chemotherapy to breast-cancer patients and others with solid tumours, notably those referred to him by colo-rectal surgeon Dr. Earl Myers. A handful of staff physicians at Mount Sinai, including Drs. Joshua Chesnie, Irving Rother, and Henry Goldenberg, had also treated patients with lymphomas and other forms of cancer with oral and intravenous chemotherapy. Nevertheless, oncology as a medical specialty was still in its infancy, and none of these individuals had any formal training in the administration of cancer drugs. Chemotherapy, moreover, was still considered almost exclusively a measure to ameliorate symptoms or extend life and, for the majority of patients, was not expected to effect a cure.[*]

Bassett had long seen the need for chemotherapy for his own patients. Throughout the 1960s, he travelled frequently to the Leahy Clinic in Boston and the National Cancer Institute (NCI) in Bethesda, Maryland, to study what limited forms of chemotherapy were then available. Designated a principal investigator for the NCI in 1964, Bassett commenced clinical trials, which he brought back to Mount Sinai, frequently using new drugs then unavailable anywhere else in Canada, including at the Princess Margaret Hospital, which specializes in cancer treatment. Patients came from around the country seeking the scarce treatments, and, by 1977, with the establishment of breast- and colon-cancer units in the Ambulatory Care Centre, there was more chemotherapy being provided at Mount Sinai than at any other hospital in Toronto, with the exception of the Princess Margaret Hospital.[21] One revolutionary treatment Bassett introduced after seeing it in Boston was for treatment of metastasis to the liver. Aided by the mechanical talents of Helen Blue, director of Central Services, Bassett rigged up a small pump connected to a tiny catheter, which was capable of delivering a round-the-clock infusion of experimental drugs directly into the liver.

As chemotherapy research became more sophisticated beginning in the early 1970s, treatment grew considerably more complex and drugs far more toxic, requiring highly specialized management. The arrival of Dr. Martin Blackstein in the summer of 1973 made Mount Sinai only the second general hospital in Toronto to include a medical oncologist on staff.[†] Blackstein had solid credentials for the task. An MD with a fellowship in oncology and a recent Ph.D. in medical biophysics, the culmination of his research at Princess Margaret Hospital into DNA tumour viruses, he already held a research appointment at U of T and a clinical cross-appointment at the Toronto Western Hospital. But when

---

[*] The first cure for cancer (in Hodgkin's disease) wasn't reported in the medical literature until 1970.
[†] The first was St. Michael's Dr. James Goldie.

Nurse Eleanor Wasserman worked with Dr. Martin Blackstein to establish medical oncology at Mount Sinai in 1973. (Randy Bulmer)

U of T professor of medicine Charles Hollenberg suggested he pay a visit to Dr. Barnet Berris, Blackstein decamped for Mount Sinai.[22]

At first, oncology was relegated to one small room in the new hospital's fourth-floor Ambulatory Care Centre, where Blackstein and Eleanor Wasserman, the only nurse then willing to volunteer for what was in those days an extremely unpopular service, administered treatment and counselled patients. With the growing reputation of cancer surgery at Mount Sinai, the demand for adjuvant treatment mushroomed, and the pair was overwhelmed in the tiny quarters. Dr. Robert Stone, then chief of Surgery, soon recognized the necessity for a separate Division of Oncology, and he relocated cancer treatment to 12 North, a part of the hospital as yet unopened. For several years, Blackstein and Wasserman carried the huge clinical load alone, treating cancer in all sites, with an especially large case volume of sarcoma and breast cancer.

Until 1977, Mount Sinai was the only teaching hospital in Toronto with a fully coordinated oncology program.[23] Even when that was no longer the case, however, despite the small size of its staff, the oncology service at Mount Sinai quickly set itself apart from similar ones around the city. At other hospitals, especially in the early years of oncology treatment, a clinic concept prevailed, in which patients would be seen by one doctor on a particular visit, then by another on a follow-up appointment. As a result, patients often were confused about who was in a position of ultimate responsibility with respect to their treatment. More important, at a time of great anxiety they frequently felt adrift without a designated advocate concerned about their total care.

Originally through necessity (because he was the lone oncologist) but very soon through philosophy, Blackstein developed an individual treatment plan, as well as an individual relationship with each patient. In this course of action he had a strong ally in oncology nurse Eleanor Wasserman, who, during a visit to the Memorial Sloan Kettering Cancer Institute in New York, had observed patients taking numbers for treatment as if they were waiting to buy bread in a bakery.[24] Vowing that humane treatment of patients at Mount Sinai would be a hallmark of their care, a critical psycho-social tool and never a frill, the team established a policy of recognizing the emotional as well as the physical needs of cancer patients.[25] Even as the staff grew with the addition of a second oncologist (Dr. Ronald Burkes in 1985) and several highly trained specialist nurses, and even as Mount Sinai developed into a major centre for international drug trials, especially in lung cancer and sarcoma, this principle has been staunchly maintained.

Critical Care

Like oncology, critical care was first recognized as a specialized field of medicine in the early 1970s, and, with the opening of the new hospital, Mount Sinai's administration was anxious to avail itself of the new expertise for the much-expanded Intensive Care and Coronary Care units on the eighteenth floor.

In the course of correspondence throughout 1973, U of T professor of medicine Charles Hollenberg had recruited Dr. Arnold Aberman to the university's Division of Respirology. Aberman was a Montreal-born, McGill-educated respirologist, trained at Albert Einstein College in New York, with a specific proficiency in intensive-care medicine and shock research acquired at the University of California at San Francisco. As well as joining the Faculty of Medicine at the University of Toronto,

Four chiefs of service at Mount Sinai simultaneously led their respective departments at the University of Toronto. Clockwise from left: Drs. Gerald Edelist (Anesthesia), Allan Gross (Orthopedic Surgery), Peter Alberti (Otolaryngology), and Arnold Aberman (Medicine). (Randy Bulmer)

Hollenberg suggested that Aberman consider the new clinical post at Mount Sinai Hospital. With only three other critical-care specialists then working in Canada,[*] Aberman's skills were in high demand at six Toronto teaching hospitals. But two factors drew him to Mount Sinai: the opportunity to manage its brand-new ICU from the beginning rather than join another hospital's previously established unit and the outstanding reputation and personal qualities of chief of Medicine Dr. Barnet Berris.[26] The first demonstration of the latter occurred immediately following Aberman's arrival in July 1973, which coincided with that of oncologist Martin Blackstein, cardiologist Jack Colman, and gastroenterologist Alvin Newman. During the remaining months before the hospital relocated to the new building next door, Berris graciously shared his own office with the four young recruits to the growing Department of Medicine.

From 1973 to 1989, Aberman was co-director of Intensive Care at Mount Sinai, in association with staff anesthetist Dr. Leslie Bowers until

---

[*] They were Drs. Arthur Scott in Toronto, Brian Kirk in Winnipeg, and Garner King in Edmonton.

1977, and then with anesthetist Dr. Ernest Hew. An extremely high-
energy, stress-loving individual, whose rapid-fire speech has the ten-
dency to rattle those of a more taciturn nature, Aberman's personality
was uniquely suited to the pressure-driven climate of the ICU. A tightly
knit team of nurses, respiratory therapists, nutritionists, and ward
clerks working alongside the physicians was equally action-oriented,
and the group enjoyed a rare *esprit de corps*.

Among the estimable skills Aberman brought to the new hospital in
1973 was his affinity for computers. Monitoring of critical-care patients
via computer was already in place by this time, but the latest innovation
in ICU management was the use of computerized information for decision support, that is, instant aid in such things as tailoring appropriate
drug and fluid dosages or assistance in interpreting test results.
Although the technology was not yet in general use, Aberman simply
wrote his own programs for Mount Sinai's ICU.

In 1977, Dr. Berris stepped down as chief of Medicine, and the hospital's own search committee named Aberman as his successor. As was
mandatory for a dual university-hospital appointment, the university's
Department of Medicine was obliged to endorse the candidate. Never
before had a conflict arisen over an appointment of a new hospital chief
of service. But the brash thirty-three-year-old Aberman gave some university committee members pause. He clearly did not possess the years
of experience, let alone the *gravitas*, deemed appropriate for traditional
candidates. Neither were university officials accustomed to his
flamboyance, outspokenness, and decidedly entrepreneurial bent.[*]
Nevertheless, Mount Sinai persisted in its selection, and Aberman was
eventually named chief.

The unconventional qualities that initially alarmed the university
reaped benefits for Mount Sinai during Aberman's tenure as chief of

---

[*] From 1973 to 1984, Dr. Aberman and his wife, Janis, operated a lucrative business publishing cumulative five- and ten-year indexes to medical journals. In
1975, they won the Canada Enterprise Award for their ingenuity and success.
Dr. Aberman was also an occasional spokesperson for the National Citizens'
Coalition, an organization espousing free-enterprise principles.

Medicine when he introduced a Department Practice Plan to foster academic development in Medicine. The concept invited all solo practitioners in the department to pool all of their fees, enabling some to focus on research, some on teaching, and others on practice. The guiding principle behind the plan was not to equalize remuneration or discourage practice, but rather to provide sufficient and continuing support for research investigators.

Unlike more-rigid, top-down schemes that had incurred so much resistance when instituted elsewhere, Aberman's strategy was to encourage members of the department to willingly join the plan without any coercion other than professional peer pressure. "My position was to be like Tom Sawyer," he explains. "If you make it appear fun to paint the fence, then everyone wants to paint the fence." With the full support of executive director Gerald Turner, who provided financial backing until the plan was fully operational, the Department Practice Plan enticed the last sceptics into the fold. The plan was generally acknowledged to have been a factor in the acquisition of some of Mount Sinai's top researchers within the Department of Medicine, including nephrologist Dr. Alexander Logan, immunologist Dr. Philip Halloran, and respirologist Dr. Arthur Slutsky.

By the time Arnold Aberman stepped down as chief of Medicine at Mount Sinai Hospital in 1987, his professional star had risen to the point where he was named Sir John and Lady Eaton Professor and Chairman of the university's Department of Medicine. Following that appointment, the same university that had once disdained Aberman's bottom-line financial approach was mired in its own budget struggles, and only too eager to make use of his entrepreneurial gifts. In 1992, he was named dean of the University of Toronto's Faculty of Medicine.

Chaplaincy

For a hospital with a deeply rooted denominational history, it is perhaps surprising that Mount Sinai did not employ its own coordinating chaplain before 1976, when Rabbi Sheldon Steinberg assumed that function. Two years earlier, through funding provided by the

Rabbi Sheldon Steinberg strengthened multi-faith chaplaincy services throughout Ontario. (Highlights *magazine*)

Toronto Jewish Congress (now the Jewish Federation of Greater Toronto) and the Canadian Jewish Congress, a permanent chaplaincy service had been established for the region, and Rabbi Steinberg appointed director. Even though Mount Sinai had never had a patient population more than one-third Jewish, even when it was on Yorkville Avenue, the hospital had always welcomed rabbis and cantors from every Toronto congregation, who visited their own hospitalized congregants, as did clergy from other faiths, on a volunteer basis. From 1959 to 1964, for example, and again for sixteen years following retirement from his parish in 1975, Father Walter Mann, a member of the Order of St. Patrick, was a familiar and welcome figure on Mount Sinai's wards as he visited Catholic patients and families. Until the arrival of Betty Calvin, the ecumenical chaplain, in 1983, Father Mann visited all other Christian patients as well.

Since 1970, chaplaincy within hospitals had been undergoing a sea change as a result of a movement begun in Worcester, Massachusetts, toward professional clinical training for pastoral caregivers.[27] Central to the new approach was the notion of institutional chaplaincy as a ministry of presence and support rather than denominational instruction or advice. In the course of his postgraduate education in Boston, Rabbi Steinberg had undertaken this new training, and consequently he was much in demand throughout the province.

A Passover seder for patients and staff is led by volunteers. (MSH Image Centre)

Although he maintained a frantic pace, sharing his time with at least six other Toronto hospitals and provincial institutions, stretching from Whitby to Kingston, Rabbi Steinberg always occupied a vital niche at Mount Sinai. Known to virtually everyone within the hospital's walls and universally cherished as a rare and special individual, he was genuinely concerned about the welfare of all patients, families, and staff members. Stories abound about his caring: how he obtained a suit for an elderly Orthodox Jewish patient who felt uncomfortable attending hospital High Holy Day services in his bedclothes; how he arranged for Jewish patients from the Toronto General and Queen Elizabeth hospitals to come to Mount Sinai on holidays to participate in synagogue services; or how he visited every medical and surgical unit so that bedridden patients could hear the stirring sound of the *shofar*, the ram's horn blown on Rosh Hashanah, the Jewish New Year.[28]

Not only did Rabbi Steinberg ensure that all Jewish patients had the opportunity to fulfil their religious obligations and participate in Jewish holiday traditions, but he established a significant presence in the Ontario Multi-Faith Council, working tirelessly so that patients of other religions would also have access to pastoral care. Until Rabbi Steinberg's arrival in Toronto, chaplaincy services in city hospitals had

Social worker Maria Lee visited the streets of nearby Chinatown to encourage the Chinese community to use health services at Mount Sinai.
(Globe and Mail)

functioned from a strongly Christian base; one of his most enduring contributions was in locating representatives from Buddhist, Muslim, and Bahai communities, who would carry pagers for Mount Sinai and other Toronto hospitals, thereby filling the spiritual needs of all patients.[29] Although Rabbi Steinberg's untimely death in 1993 left a huge void in the hospital and chaplaincy communities, it is significant that, as a result of his initiatives, chaplaincy at Mount Sinai expanded into a department of four, coordinated in 1997 by Rabbi Bernard Schulman. The department has been responsible for some important and sensitive programs, including educational sessions for health-care workers on how to help ease the special fears of Holocaust survivors, for whom hospitalization evokes unique anxieties.

Chinese Outreach

Even as the new hospital was being planned and built, Mount Sinai identified a glaring gap that needed to be filled. Despite its location in the immediate vicinity of the city's main Chinatown, around Dundas Street and Spadina Avenue, the hospital was rarely patronized by Chinese patients. Aside from practitioners of traditional Chinese medicine, few community health facilities of any kind existed in Chinese languages. Not only did most Chinese immigrants fear hospitals intensely and avoid them even when they were seriously ill, but they also had little concept of preventative medicine and the contemporary role of hospitals in keeping people well.[30] Parallels with the experiences of Jewish immigrants before the existence of the Yorkville hospital were too obvious to ignore, and Mount Sinai determined to do something to alter the situation for its Chinese neighbours.

In casting about for an individual to help bridge this gap, the director of Social Work, Eva Kenyon, encountered Maria Lee, a recent graduate of McGill University, who combined a master's degree in social work with a proficiency in Mandarin, Cantonese, and Taisan, a widely used Canton dialect. When Lee joined Mount Sinai on May 1, 1974, she set in motion the largest and most-comprehensive outreach program for a specific cultural group that had ever been launched by a Toronto hospital.[31]

Full of enthusiasm for the project and culturally attuned to the downtown Chinese community, which was then composed mainly of elderly, non-English-speaking immigrants, Lee carefully planned her strategy. "I knew this wouldn't be a matter of simply handing out flyers in Chinese and waiting for the people to arrive at the hospital door," she remembers. "It was essential to first build trust within the community." Seeking out Chinese neighbourhood leaders, standing on street corners talking to passersby, and visiting local churches were only some of Lee's tactics for making herself familiar to the community. An indispensable ally was a Mrs. Chen, the owner of a Chinese travel agency on Dundas Street, who, as an unofficial community worker, cashed cheques, arranged funerals in the absence of next-of-kin, and transmitted news to and from home villages.

Frequently, the people Maria Lee met on the street would confide their medical problems, and she soon recognized a conspicuous need for preventative care and disease screening. This was especially evident within Tongs, the communal residences populated by culturally connected single individuals – mostly lonely old men without families. Her greatest triumph, however, was convincing Chinese immigrants that they indeed had friends at Mount Sinai.

Within the hospital, an equally concerted effort to welcome the

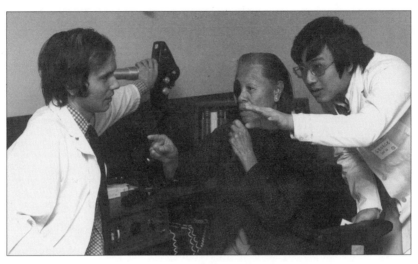

Student volunteers translated for non-English-speaking patients who flocked to the outreach eye-screening clinics. (MSH Image Centre)

Chinese community and provide appropriate services was being spear-headed by Dr. Nathan Levinne, a Yorkville veteran, who hired a Chinese-speaking doctor and nurse, Dr. Albert Choong and Janice Mark, to work in the Family Practice Unit. With the added zeal of the Department of Volunteers, several programs were launched over the next five years, beginning with conducted tours and installation of Chinese signs within the hospital and including Chinese-speaking translators to escort patients arriving for appointments. The heart of the program provided free glaucoma, hearing, hypertension, diabetes, and dental screening clinics, as well as opportunities for gynecological assessment and full physical examinations. Doctors, nurses, and an array of support personnel from Mount Sinai regularly contributed their time and services for these evening and weekend clinics, as did dozens of volunteer translators.[32] Medical staff even pitched in to supply staff and volunteers with Chinese meals on clinic days.[33]

The response of the Chinese community to the outreach was overwhelming. Hundreds of people attended each free screening clinic and, according to Maria Lee, the entire community soon identified Mount Sinai as "the Chinese hospital." With the full support of the hospital

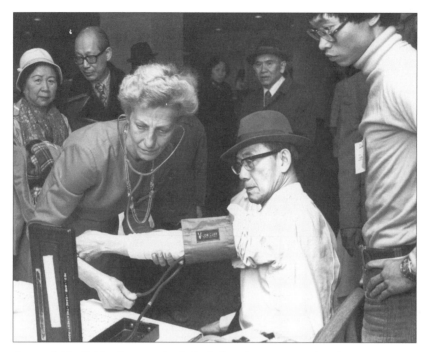

*Successful individual outreach clinics led to the creation of a Chinese
Community Health Centre at Mount Sinai. (MSH Image Centre)*

administration, the efforts of the Social Work department were then
extended into broader development of services for the Chinese community, including the Hong Fook Mental Health Services, the Chinese Legal
Aid Clinic, and an Association for Chinese Community Service Workers.
Before long, a close relationship blossomed between Mount Sinai and the
seventy-bed Mon Sheong Home for the Aged, which opened on D'Arcy
Street in 1974, with the result that the latter institution began supplying
Chinese meals-on-wheels for patients admitted to hospital, as well as for
homebound seniors. That shared concern for the needs of the elderly
soon led to the involvement of the Baycrest Centre for Geriatric Care,
whose chief executive, Sam Ruth, acted as adviser for the development of
the Chinese Community Nursing Home. Indeed, years later in 1988, when
Ruth was fêted at a tribute dinner marking his twenty-fifth anniversary
with Baycrest, the gala event at the Sheraton Centre's Grand Ballroom
was co-sponsored by the Chinese community and featured an unprecedented kosher–Chinese dinner of Szechuan beef and matzo-ball soup!

Over a thousand people attended the April 2, 1978, opening of Mount Sinai's innovative Chinese Community Health Centre, a culturally sensitive family-practice unit geared to the special needs of the downtown Chinese.[34] It was the difficulty experienced by so many workers employed in the restaurant, hotel, and garment industries of scheduling medical appointments during standard business hours that led Mount Sinai to establish this after-hours and weekend centre. Among the physicians Maria Lee recruited to staff it was Dr. Joseph Y. K. Wong, whom she had known at McGill when Wong was studying engineering. The likable Dr. Wong, a former intern at Mount Sinai, already had an enormous following in the Chinese community and was well on his way to becoming one of the most celebrated multicultural activists in Canada. The fourth-floor health centre was augmented by two storefront clinics, the Kensington Manor Clinic and the Beverley Manor Clinic, to attend to the needs of Chinese seniors.

By the time Lee left Mount Sinai in 1980 to be replaced by social worker Joseph Ng, the Chinese Outreach Program was firmly entrenched and serving as a model for many other institutions. Since then, the hospital's participation with the Chinese community has continued to flourish, with ongoing special screening clinics, expanded social work and community-development services, exchange of board members between Mount Sinai and several Chinese institutions, enthusiastic mutual fund-raising efforts, and, more recently, a Pacific Bridge Project to foster scientific, clinical, and academic links with universities and hospitals in Hong Kong, the People's Republic of China, and Taiwan. Since 1993 under the leadership of Dr. Warren Rubenstein, chief of Family and Community Medicine, an advisory committee has operated to advise Mount Sinai on how it can continue to serve the Chinese community in the areas of research, patient care, and education. One project to arise from that collaboration was the Chinese Seniors' Health Centre, opened in 1996 to provide geriatric medical and mental-health assessment and consultation for Chinese elders who require culturally responsive care in their own language.

Other important, if smaller-scale, outreach programs grew out of the original Chinese initiative. Mount Sinai medical staff, for example, "adopted" two families of Vietnamese refugees, assuming responsibility for their financial needs, while the hospital became the designated dental centre for these oppressed "boat people" following their arrival in Toronto. As their plight became known, hospital staff also began demonstrating concern for political refugees from the Soviet Union, especially the medical professionals unable to practise in Canada because of poor English skills. Several of these individuals were Russian Jews, who, though highly trained specialists, were limited to doing odd jobs at the hospital. In 1975, Drs. Murray Miskin, Alan Pollard, and Irving Koven established a course, unprecedented in a Canadian hospital, to help foreign physicians prepare for the examinations of the Educational Council for Foreign Medical Graduates (ECFMG). Once the three succeeded in getting funding from the Jewish Immigrant Aid Society and the Department of Manpower, they opened the doors of the program to other doctors, many of them political refugees from Chile. To overcome the refugees' next hurdle of securing internships, the hospital applied to the appropriate bodies for the creation of three additional (non-funded) internships above its annual quota, to be assigned to foreign physicians upon successful completion of the ECFMG examinations.[35]

Research

Ever since the first Atkinson Charitable Foundation grant in 1954 permitted the start of individual research efforts at New Mount Sinai, the board, administration, and medical staff of the hospital had been unwaveringly dedicated to the principle that the highest-quality patient care could only flourish in an environment in which research and education also thrived. In the 1950s, as we have seen, research was very much a part-time activity, conducted in their spare time by physicians with an abiding interest in a particular subject related to their clinical practice. The prestigious Medical Research Council of Canada came into existence only in 1959, and, even at the University of Toronto's Medical Sciences Building, research laboratories were few and the equipment fairly meagre. In truth, in the years following the Banting and Best dis-

Under the direction of obstetrician/gynecologist Dr. Sidney Tobin, a formal research program began. (MSH Image Centre)

covery of insulin and until the mid-1960s, the scale of research at all Toronto hospitals, with the exception of the Hospital for Sick Children, was generally unremarkable.

Nonetheless, New Mount Sinai staff members were very keen to become involved, and, considering that no formal department or exclusive space had been allocated to research, many physicians managed to be productive in individual projects. In 1958, the hospital's research committee designated eight hundred square feet on the top floor as a research department and promoted the training of a full-time researcher. Dr. Jan Blumenstein, a former Mount Sinai intern who went on to acquire a Ph.D., was appointed the first full-time physician-scientist in the department. Blumenstein was a survivor of a Nazi concentration camp, who had been brought to Toronto as a youth by Dr. Charles H. Best, co-discoverer of insulin, and had been nurtured in the scientific community. Blumenstein's own research interests involved white-blood-cell function and leukemia, ever one of the hospital's principal fields of interest. A Research Advisory Committee was set up, representing all medical departments and reporting to a parallel committee of the board, and both bodies, plus a panel of external referees, had to approve any basic or clinical research undertaken at the hospital. When Blumenstein left in 1970, Dr. Sidney Tobin, a New Mount Sinai obstetrician/gynecologist with long-standing research interests,

Dr. Paul Walfish has received inter-national recognition for academic research in endocrinology during thirty-five years at Mount Sinai. (Highlights *magazine*)

assumed leadership of the Research Advisory Committee, a post he held for the next twelve years.

Some active researchers during the final decade in which New Mount Sinai occupied 550 University Avenue included: Dr. Tobin, who studied hydatidiform mole, a malignant tumour that develops from the placenta during pregnancy; surgeon Irving Koven, who contributed a new theory of hemorrhagic shock called interstitial diffusion; gastro-enterologist Victor Feinman, who focused on several areas of liver research; Dr. Roberto Santalo, who became recognized as an international authority on the biochemistry of cell nuclei; rheumatologist Joseph Houpt, who researched biochemical changes in gout; and otolaryngologist Peter Alberti, who studied various aspects of hearing loss in the elderly.[36]

Most prolific of all, however, was Dr. Paul Walfish. Walfish was the first chief resident in Medicine under Dr. Mitchell Kohan when the University of Toronto came into the hospital in 1962. Sponsored there-after as a travelling fellow in endocrinology, he returned from Boston in 1964 to a teaching position at the University of Toronto and one as geo-graphic full-time physician at New Mount Sinai and head of the Division of Endocrinology. Armed with an early Medical Research Council of Canada Fellowship, he promptly outfitted a tiny lab in an unused pantry on the twelfth floor and persuaded the hospital to buy a Nuclear Chicago Photo-Dot Scanner to assess nodules and functions of the thyroid gland and other organs, thereby beginning nuclear medicine at New Mount Sinai.

In conjunction with the imaging, Walfish also began measuring various hormones in the blood, using the emerging new radio immunoassay methods, soon focusing on the problem of congenital hypothyroidism, in which the thyroid gland is inactive from birth. This was the ideal clinical problem to confront, because manifestations of the condition, which causes mental retardation in one out of every 8,000 to 10,000 newborns, were almost impossible to recognize before the age of three to six months, by which time irreparable brain damage had already occurred. Walfish's goal was to develop an appropriate test, using the sensitive assay for thyroid hormone (called T4) discovered by Dr. Jean Dussault at Laval University in 1972, and to institute a screening program to pick up the condition just after birth. Sampling umbilical-cord blood and later a few drops from a heel prick permitted the early diagnosis and treatment that saved thirty to forty infants a year from mental retardation. By 1976, the program was extended throughout Metro Toronto, with the Red Cross picking up all samples and delivering them to Mount Sinai. By 1978, screening became province-wide.

The list of Walfish's other major research contributions, notably those associated with thyroid conditions, is long and impressive. A 1974 collaboration with pathologist Dr. Harry Strawbridge, who had already developed other cytology techniques, produced a method of fine-needle aspiration for assessing thyroid nodules. Cooperation with members of other departments, including ultrasound expert Dr. Murray Miskin, head-and-neck surgeon Dr. Irving Rosen, and, in more recent years, clinical biochemist Dr. Sylvia Asa and head-and-neck oncologist Dr. Jeremy Freeman, has resulted in Mount Sinai's international reputation as a leading centre for the diagnosis and treatment of thyroid cancer. In recognition of his research and medical contributions to thyroidology, Walfish received the City of Toronto's Award of Merit in 1983 and the Order of Canada in 1991.

As the volume of hospital-based research expanded during the early 1970s, the vital issue of funding demanded more urgent attention. Since governments didn't support such research directly, it became increasingly necessary to find alternative sources for raising, maintaining, and disbursing scarce research dollars. Until this time, Mount Sinai had always functioned more or less adequately on the annual research support of long-time loyal sources: its own Auxiliary, the Leukemia Research Fund, a variety of charitable foundations, and the income from endowments. Research expenditures, which had rarely exceeded $73,000 annually when Dr. Sidney Tobin became chairman of the Research Advisory Committee, quickly grew to $250,000 per year as the quality of the work began to attract external grants.[37] Yet by 1975 it was clear that significant changes had to be made if Mount Sinai was to make the research strides it envisioned for the future.

After eighteen months of negotiation between representatives of the University of Toronto, the board, medical staff, and the Research Planning Committee, two conclusions were reached that would have important implications for the future. The Mount Sinai Institute was established as an independent charitable foundation on April 23, 1975, to become the recipient of all monies contributed to the hospital.[38] This tax-driven move would avoid deficit financing, while attracting private endowments, legacies, gifts, and bequests. Furthermore, it was determined in consultation with the Faculty of Medicine that the main thrust of future clinical research funded by the Mount Sinai Institute would be in two major programs, immunology and gerontology.[39] In designing the new hospital, planners allocated 12,000 square feet of space in the basement to support these latest research ventures.

The six new labs quickly filled to capacity as the Research Advisory Committee willingly funded bright young researchers, affording them a start in their respective fields. Two research exchange programs in immunology and oncology were also launched to share knowledge and investigators with other health-science centres, both in Israel and Toronto.[40]

By the end of the decade, however, the board recognized that it was at a crossroads. From being an institution whose research efforts had been virtually ignored, Mount Sinai had evolved to the point where its scientific endeavours were beginning to be taken seriously, at least on the national scene. There was no question that the will to undertake research was firmly ensconced at 600 University Avenue. For the board and the administration, such scientific pursuits clearly represented an unequivocal priority, which explains why, during the period that Sidney Tobin led the Research Advisory Committee, those authorities never once refused funding for a project endorsed by his panel and its independent referees, even when approval meant having to campaign privately for the money.[41] Still, in order to reach the next level, to achieve international stature, the hospital and its board would have to make an overwhelming commitment to build a true research institute, not merely a funding foundation with an extravagant title. In order to accomplish this task, it was first necessary to attract a suitable full-time director of research with illustrious scientific credentials. The next step would be a massive increase in research space, requiring a substantial addition to the building.

Clearly, this was a monumental undertaking. But, as if in homage to the controversial decision unflinchingly made years before by the hospital's convincing pitchman and *éminence grise*, Ben Sadowski, it was barely debated and quickly resolved. If Mount Sinai was going to perpetuate its primary goal of excellence, there was simply no other alternative than to advance full steam ahead.

7

On the World Stage

W hen boyish-looking business mogul Irving Gerstein was appointed chairman of the board in July 1979, he became the third generation of his family to help direct the fortunes of Mount Sinai Hospital. This legacy of loyalty was set in motion by his maternal grandmother, Diana Appleby, who was among the *Ezras Noshem* founders of the Yorkville hospital, and grandfather Frank Gerstein, an early supporter and board member of New Mount Sinai. It continued with the avid participation of Irving's parents, his mother, Dr. Reva Gerstein-Raitblatt, a former president of Mount Sinai's Auxiliary, and father, Bertrand Gerstein, also a past president and chairman of the board. Although only thirty-eight years old when he assumed the board's top job after a two-year stint as treasurer, the younger Gerstein had been actively involved since the end of his student days with the hospital's swift, if bumpy, journey to its present status. In the course of his seven-year term as chairman, he, along with Gerald Turner, would steer Mount Sinai's ascent to an entirely new pinnacle of achievement and recognition.

In the years following the completion of the new hospital, a prime focus of the board that Gerstein now led had been the subject of research, and Mount Sinai's potential for assuming a much broader

Forward-looking chairman of the board Irving Gerstein committed Mount Sinai to building a major research institute. (Mount Sinai Hospital)

scientific role. As we have seen, under the guidance of Dr. Sidney Tobin, activity in basic research had grown substantially, and a rigorous review-and-reporting system had been firmly set in place. Both the hospital board and its administration were understandably proud of these developments. In several important centres around the world, basic biological research was blossoming, and the consequent advances were beginning to have a powerful impact on patient care. To participate in the research wave that would draw the laboratory bench closer to the bedside was a formidable challenge, which had been one of the fundamental dreams of Mount Sinai's founders. Neither the board nor the administration, however, was in pursuit of merely competent research; they aspired to nothing short of excellence, even greatness. Quite logically, therefore, they sought advice from those who had already achieved it.

With the blessing of Duncan Gordon,[1] chairman of the board of the Hospital for Sick Children, Mount Sinai conscripted Drs. Aser Rotstein and Lou Siminovitch as part of a Research Advisory Board. Rotstein was the director of the world-famous Hospital for Sick Children Research Institute. Siminovitch, creator of the Department of Medical Genetics at the University of Toronto, was Sick Kids' geneticist-in-chief and a towering figure in the world scientific community, considered by many to be one of the architects of Canadian medical science. Among vast accomplishments, he had contributed to the Nobel Prize-winning work in molecular genetics of his mentors Jacques Monod and André Lwoff of the Pasteur Institute in Paris and later helped shape the front-ranking Ontario Cancer Institute at Princess Margaret Hospital. Informal and friendly despite his fame, yet known to hold tough, uncompromising standards of science, Siminovitch had had no previous association with Mount Sinai. Nevertheless, he was keenly interested in helping to mount this ambitious research project, and became an enthusiastic participant.

At a particularly key meeting of the advisory board, Siminovitch was evaluating some of the research programs already under way at Mount Sinai, pointing out the current investigators' limited support by the Medical Research Council of Canada, the country's most prestigious granting organization. As Siminovitch tells it, "the penny dropped" when a board member asked, "Are you telling us that this is not first-rate research?"

"That's what I'm telling you," Siminovitch replied.

With barely a pause to digest that painful verdict, Irving Gerstein interjected another question. "What would it take to start a world-class research institute?" Siminovitch made some quick calculations on the back of a napkin.

"Fifty thousand square feet and two million dollars for the first year's overhead." The hasty estimation represented an expenditure of at least $18 to $20 million, but Gerstein and executive director Gerald Turner glanced at each other, then at the napkin, and, without further discussion, made the commitment right there.[2]

"We knew selling the idea of the research institute to the hospital board would be easy," Gerstein now says in defence of the almost absurdly prompt decision. According to the chairman of the board, the concepts of basic research may have been too abstract to grasp readily, but the notion that renowned researchers also attract the best people, who will look after you when you are sick, was something everyone understood, and a conviction that Mount Sinai had explicitly endorsed from the beginning.[3] Clearly, Gerstein did know his constituency, since concrete demonstration of this assumed support was quickly forthcoming.

Dr. Louis Siminovitch is one of only twenty-five Canadian medical scientists to be inducted into the Canadian Medical Hall of Fame. (Randy Bulmer)

Making its largest commitment ever, the hospital Auxiliary, galvanized by president Elaine Culiner, immediately promised to raise $3 million for the project.

An international search for a research institute director of the appropriate calibre ensued, and a well-worn cliché was proved by the two-year quest when the hospital scoured the world before finding their man right across the street – in Dr. Siminovitch himself. It's not that Mount Sinai wouldn't have snapped up the celebrated Dr. Siminovitch on first pass and, in fact, Sidney Liswood, then president of the fund-raising arm of the institute, had informally proposed such an arrangement at the outset.[4] But at the time Siminovitch still had a two-year obligation to the Hospital for Sick Children, at which point he would turn sixty-five, an age when most people plan a leisurely retirement, yield to the next generation, and usually decline such immense responsibilities and workloads. So, when first approached to take on the directorship, Siminovitch demurred.

However, after a serious offer to another potential candidate fell through, Mount Sinai's bid to attract the much-honoured geneticist was revived with a new urgency, and, in 1983, the selection committee officially offered him the post of research director. Siminovitch still recalls with amazement how his agreement to not only head, but conceive and create, the new institute was sealed with nothing more formal than a handshake from Gerald Turner. "From now on," Turner told him, "you're in charge of research. Not a cent of foundation money will be spent without your approval."[5] Siminovitch continued his work at the Hospital for Sick Children until 1985, directing one of the world's first laboratories studying genetic links to cancer, at which time he crossed University Avenue to establish a new professional home at Mount Sinai and build a scientific institution on an international plane.

Given considerable latitude to create the institute as he saw fit, Siminovitch chose to concentrate on five areas, selected because they presented the foremost challenges for understanding the mechanisms of disease. For each of the five divisions, he would recruit a new department head, who would be allotted a given amount of space. In turn, each division head was required to recruit other scientists for that department. No government money would be available for the institute infrastructure. More unusual, however, was the determination by Turner and Siminovitch that the hospital budget would not cover even such basic overhead costs as heat and light. Instead, individual investigators, in addition to attracting their own salary awards and peer-reviewed grants, would be responsible for those expenses. Finally, the most crucial and hitherto revolutionary edict of accountability decreed that none of the researchers was to be granted tenure. Only the productive results of external reviews every three years would ensure their job security and continuing worth to the institute.

Despite these stringent conditions, Siminovitch, with his impeccable credentials and connections, confidently went courting. And like iron filings to a magnet, the best and the brightest basic-science investigators flocked to the new institute and its illustrious director. In their wake, as predicted, came outstanding clinicians, anxious to interact with the researchers. For many of these scientists, the creation of the research institute provided impetus for a reverse brain drain, allowing them to reject offers to go to the United States in favour of coming to Mount Sinai and highlighting Canadians on the frontiers of research.

For the Division of Molecular and Developmental Biology, Siminovitch enticed from the Ontario Cancer Institute Dr. Alan Bernstein, an international authority in cell biology and human genetics.

*Howard Hughes Medical Institute award winners, from left: Drs. Tony Pawson,
Alan Bernstein, Janet Rossant, and Alex Joyner. (MSH Image Centre)*

Bernstein immediately brought on board Dr. Tony Pawson from the
University of British Columbia, an expert in protein biochemistry and
oncogenes, the genes involved in cancer production. From Brock
University, Bernstein attracted Oxford- and Cambridge-trained developmental biologist Dr. Janet Rossant, a two-time winner of the prestigious Steacie Award from the Natural Sciences and Engineering
Research Council of Canada. Dr. Alexandra Joyner, one of Bernstein's
first graduate students, came from the University of California at San
Francisco, where she had just completed a post-doctoral fellowship. An
unprecedented honour was bestowed on this close-knit team of
Bernstein, Pawson, Joyner, and Rossant in June 1991 when the four
received a coveted $1-million grant from the Howard Hughes Medical
Institute in Bethesda, Maryland, for their collaborative work into the
genetic basis of disease.

From Queen's University in Kingston, Ontario, Siminovitch
acquired Dr. Robert Kerbel to lead the Division of Cancer and Cell
Biology. With him came biochemist Dr. Jim Dennis and genetic cell
biologist Dr. Alain Lagarde and, from the Hospital for Sick Children, Dr.
Martin Breitman. The Division of Immunology and Neurobiology

Research institute senior scientist
Dr. Nobumichi Hozumi focuses on the
molecular and genetic mechanisms of
leukemia and bone development.
(MSH Image Centre)

would be led by another Queen's scientist, Dr. John Roder, whose research had led to the development of a human monoclonal antibody. From the Ontario Cancer Institute, Roder brought Dr. Atusuo Ochi and neurobiologist Dr. Nobumichi Hozumi, whose work with Dr. Susumu Tonegawa on how the body makes millions of different kinds of defensive antibodies would soon earn the latter the 1987 Nobel Prize for Medicine. Later, Dr. Steven Gallinger, a Medical Research Council Fellow, joined this group, integrating with the Department of Surgery to pursue tumour immunology.

A fourth division was to be in Epidemiology, the study of the prevalence of disease, an area that Siminovitch deemed essential to the functioning of a hospital where patterns of disease bear such an intrinsic relationship to clinical practice. For that division, Siminovitch selected an individual already at Mount Sinai, Dr. Alexander Logan, a nephrologist and hypertension specialist trained in epidemiology. The last division, Perinatology, had been identified by the National Research Council (NRC) as a high-priority area for research and was a perfect fit for Mount Sinai, which had just been designated a provincial centre for the care of high-risk mothers and newborns. Dr. Charles Bryan of the Hospital for Sick Children, a high-profile perinatologist who had won the NRC's competition for Special Initiatives, came across to head that division. The now-expanded opportunity for research in this area was a factor in attracting perinatal authority Dr. Knox Ritchie, soon to be the new chief of Obstetrics and Gynecology, and later, perinatal researcher Dr. Stephen Lye, who would focus on the genetic causes of premature labour.

A symbolic "groundbreaking" ceremony took place in October 1983 for the new research institute structure, which was actually constructed both atop and adjacent to the hospital on the Murray Street side. Five floors were each extended by nine thousand square feet, adding shelled-in space for future expansion. Two of these floors, the eighth and ninth, were then filled in across both the old and new sections. These floors were designated as The Mount Sinai Research Institute. To minimize interference with hospital functioning, the research centre was constructed from pre-cast, factory-manufactured components, which were hoisted into place by a massive Nadrofsky crane. Construction of additional space in the basement for an animal colony, the perinatology research program, and the respiratory research program proceeded simultaneously.

On July 4, 1985, the day they moved from the Ontario Cancer Institute into their new labs at Mount Sinai, scientists Alan Bernstein and Nobu Hozumi held a race. The winner was required to unpack all his belongings, set up his equipment, and then be the first to conduct a standard experiment of DNA research, a test called a nick translation. The successful completion of this experiment would reveal a good deal about critical details of laboratory conditions, such as the quality of the distilled water. Similarly, it would point out potentially serious problems and shortcomings. Bernstein's lab won the competition, but what he remembers most about the good-natured contest was not its speed, but the fact that the test worked better for both investigators than it ever had before.[6] It would prove to be a good omen. From its first days, the new research institute's star began to rise. One indication: In 1986, the National Cancer Institute of Canada awarded its only two distinguished Terry Fox Program Project Grants to researchers at Mount Sinai.[7]

According to Bernstein, the early successes resulted from a combination of some foresight, a good personality mix, and the never-to-beunderestimated luck of being in the right place at the right time. With the spirit of pioneers embarking on something both new and unique, the young scientists themselves worked collaboratively, exploiting each other in the best sense of the word, and growing individually as a result. In the luck category, it was significant that no one else in Toronto was then doing the kind of leading-edge developmental and molecular science for which these scientists who had been attracted to Mount Sinai were rapidly becoming known. Once the scientific community heard about this concentration of talent, therefore, it began to pay careful attention. For the institute's staff, the evidence of growing recognition was subtle but clear: Whereas those who attended international scientific meetings in the first year or two were automatically assumed to be from New York when they announced their eponymous institutional home as The *Mount Sinai* Research Institute, the response in short order changed to "Which Mount Sinai? New York or Toronto?"[8]

A hallmark of the new institute was its unique relationship with the hospital. Traditionally, institutes for basic science research that are associated with hospitals exist as totally separate entities. At the opposite extreme was the model that existed previously at Mount Sinai, when research was invariably an outgrowth of different clinical departments. Siminovitch's philosophy sought a balance between the two: to steadfastly maintain the pursuit of scientific excellence for its own sake, while still building important ties to the clinical departments. In one sense, the institute's focus on DNA research eased the introduction of Siminovitch's policy, since basic research in that field readily translates into clinical utility. The scrutiny by the institute's Dr. Irene Andrulis of the genetic avenues for determining prognosis following breast-cancer surgery, for example, promised important applications for individualizing treatment options. But the balancing act also required agreement by the clinical chiefs that no new clinicians would be recruited to the hospital who were not also first-rate researchers.

The institute also began to "grow their own" researchers by putting certain clinicians with a research bent into a lab under the guidance of the established scientists for a couple of years, almost as "students." The no-tenure rule was enforced, with the sole ticket to a research appoint-·

ment and lab space being excellence. The determining factor was what the institute's founding director refers to, only half facetiously, as "Siminovitch quality control." Inevitably, there were resignations, several voluntary, others encouraged, as some early housecleaning made way for a new wave. In some instances, maelstroms erupted as indignant physicians made impassioned appeals to the board about high-handed judgements of their research work. But Gerald Turner's handshake with Siminovitch decreed that the outcomes of such petitions were a foregone conclusion. The director had the last word about who and what would be part of research at Mount Sinai.

What the new institute soon attracted in enthusiastic and gifted personnel, however, it lacked in adequate endowment. The first year's budget was $6 million, of which $4.2 million came from external grants. That essential amount was bound to grow quickly.* Obviously, what the institute urgently needed was a major benefactor, and it is fully in the tradition of Mount Sinai that the guardian angel who emerged from the wings had a rich history with the hospital.

Samuel Lunenfeld was one of the founders of New Mount Sinai and a lifelong supporter of medical research. As a twenty-one-year-old accounting graduate, board treasurer Hy Isenbaum had first met Lunenfeld when he was assigned to the business affairs of Ben Sadowski, who quickly familiarized his young accountant with the future plans for the hospital, encouraging him to become involved. As Isenbaum did so, he came into the orbit of Lunenfeld, as well as his daughter and son-in-law, Sybil and Reuben Kunin, but he hadn't seen any of the family in the many years since they had all left Toronto and moved to Geneva, Switzerland.

A governor of the Weizmann Institute of Science in Rehovot, Israel, Isenbaum was strolling across that campus one day in 1985 when he bumped into Reuben Kunin. Asking about Sam, Isenbaum learned that the old man was very ill and near death. The family, Kunin added, wanted to do something to honour and perpetuate their father's name through

---

* In 1996, the annual budget was $20 million.

*Philanthropist Samuel Lunenfeld
was a lifelong supporter of medical
research. (© 1949 Yousuf Karsh)*

the charitable foundation that they had created, so Isenbaum immediately suggested a gift to the new research institute at Mount Sinai.

One stipulation of the Lunenfeld gift was that the name of the institute be changed to the Samuel Lunenfeld Research Institute, a condition that unleashed tremendous consternation among the scientists who had already begun to establish international reputations representing the Mount Sinai Research Institute. The general consensus was that the new name would never catch on, and would be the undoing of the institute, and both Siminovitch and Bernstein recall bitter debates accompanied by much hand-wringing on the subject. In the end, when cooler heads prevailed, neither disaster materialized, and the research institute quickly became known around the world, as it is today, usually abbreviated simply as the Lunenfeld.

High-Risk Perinatology

At the same time that the Lunenfeld was taking shape, the clinical side of Mount Sinai was also on the move. As early as 1976, the consulting firm of Woods Gordon had carried out a study of hospital beds in Metropolitan Toronto. One of the recommendations had been that the Ministry of Health, in cooperation with the University Teaching Hospitals Association (UTHA), develop a high-risk perinatal unit in one of the downtown hospitals. During the next two years, this joint committee refined its needs and called for briefs from five hospitals that had expressed an interest in housing such a unit.[9]

Unlike large American and international cities, Toronto was unusually slow in the development of a high-risk perinatal centre capable of providing specialized care for both mother and baby before and after birth. So entrenched was the worldwide reputation of Toronto's Hospital for Sick Children in outstanding care of newborns with problems that the notion was perpetuated that access to first-rate neonatal care rendered perinatal care unnecessary. In other words, hospitals all over the community could deliver babies who were at risk because of prematurity or other conditions, as long as the newborns were transferred afterwards to Sick Kids. Indeed, with the exception of Dr. Paul Swire, Sick Kids' head of neonatology, who campaigned for a perinatal unit for many years, the children's hospital did nothing to discourage this idea during the 1970s, even as late as 1978 when Women's College Hospital opened the city's first perinatal centre.[10]

Once that pioneering unit got under way in Toronto, however, the wisdom of having specialized care available for both mother and at-risk newborn in a single location became patently obvious to all concerned. Not only did this arrangement permit anticipation and possible prevention of problems before the birth, but it also provided instantaneous care for both mother and baby by a team of highly trained sub-specialists right on site. Even babies who did require transfer for surgical or heart problems could be stabilized first by neonatologists present at the delivery. The issue soon became not *whether* Toronto needed a perinatal centre, but how to service *all* the perinatal problems in a region where sixty thousand births occurred every year, something that the Women's College unit couldn't possibly handle adequately. Naturally, Mount Sinai was anxious to compete for the ministry-approved unit, since its maternity department maintained the busiest practice in the province – at almost five thousand deliveries annually – and was one of only two institutions where birth rates were increasing.[11]

Led by Irving Gerstein, the team of Gerald Turner, Dr. Fred Papsin, chief of Obstetrics and Gynecology, and assistant executive director Ted

Freedman mounted a meticulously researched, painstakingly planned, and aggressively waged campaign for the unit. The Mount Sinai proposal included complete statistical analysis, detailed plans for the renovation of the seventh-floor maternity department, intentions for staff recruitment, and, in order to send a clear signal of the hospital's eagerness, a promise of financial backing. The Ontario Ministry of Health and the UTHA were suitably impressed with all the homework. So was the out-of-province advisory team in perinatal medicine that evaluated all the hospital candidates. In January 1981, the ministry announced that it was awarding the program to Mount Sinai.

Like the titanic leap to build a research institute, winning the high-risk perinatal unit for Mount Sinai represented a turning point for the hospital. Both events catapulted the institution into academic realms that had taken most others far longer to attain. Throughout the competition, it hadn't gone unnoticed by the hospital negotiating team that a regional perinatal centre not only would be a showplace for the country, providing a vital service for women and babies, but almost certainly would inspire a new academic program at the University of Toronto's Faculty of Medicine. This would be a first for Canada. Even in centres where perinatal care already existed, such as Vancouver and Halifax, the universities had not yet played a major role.[12] Moreover, with the research institute also in the works during the same period, and the prospect of funded academic research in perinatology on the horizon, the awarding of the unit promised further scope for academic excellence at Mount Sinai.

In addition to a physical overhaul of the obstetrical floors, construction of the new unit produced major changes in personnel, equipment, and responsibility. Within two years, the south end of the seventh floor had been transformed into a tertiary-care perinatal centre containing thirty neonatal intensive-care isolettes for premature or sick newborns, twenty medium-risk, or Level II, neonatal isolettes, and thirty high-risk pregnancy beds. Floors 7 North and 12 South were also redesigned to house the normal maternity population. By the time all the work was complete, the financial investment that Mount Sinai had astutely pledged as demonstration of its commitment to the project was largely

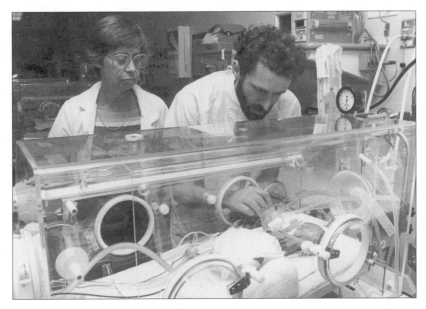

Neonatologists Drs. Heather Bryan and Edmond Kelly attend a tiny Mount Sinai patient. (MSH Image Centre)

recouped when the Variety Club donated $3.4 million to support the new centre.[13]

Dr. Pamela Fitzhardinge from the Hospital for Sick Children became chief of Pediatrics for the new unit in 1982. Formerly a leading light at the Montreal Children's Hospital, she was an internationally known neonatologist. Soon to follow were neonatologists Drs. Heather Bryan, Robert Mirro, and respiratory specialist Dr. Ann Jefferies, all of whom began training a core of nurses in the specialized skills needed for care of premature babies. Ros O'Reilly, who had joined the New Mount Sinai nursery as a staff nurse in 1966, was put in charge of nursing.

Because perinatology was relatively new in Canada, it took longer for the hospital and university search committee to select an obstetrician with the appropriate clinical and scientific qualifications to head that end of the unit. Following an international hunt, Dr. Knox Ritchie, an obstetrical perinatologist associated with the Royal Victoria Hospital and Queen's University in Belfast, Northern Ireland, was invited to consider the post. He was a product of the famous Nuffield Institute in Oxford, England, an international mecca for those interested in fetal physiology.

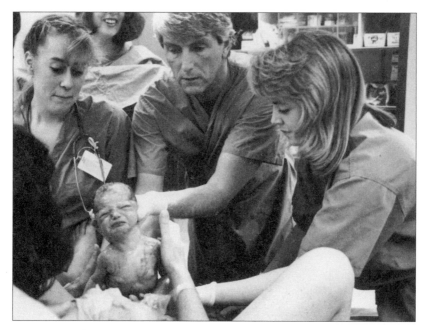

Dr. Knox Ritchie, centre, obstetrician and gynecologist-in-chief, helps usher into the world one of 4,239 babies born annually at Mount Sinai. (Randy Bulmer)

Urged by a colleague to visit Toronto "if only to see how well off you are here," Ritchie crossed the Atlantic with little intention of accepting the offer as chief, but agreeable to advising Mount Sinai on setting up the new unit. To his surprise, what he encountered in Toronto was unlimited potential for perinatology that eclipsed everything he had seen in the United Kingdom. Impressed, too, by a supportive hospital board and a forward-thinking administration whose vision for the future of this area matched his own, Ritchie elected to stay and build new departments at Mount Sinai and the University of Toronto, as well as participate in basic science research at the Lunenfeld. Mount Sinai, he quickly discovered, was already known for its strong, highly motivated team of obstetricians, some of whom – notably Drs. Fred Papsin, Abe Bernstein, Paul Bernstein, and Elliott Lyons – were already active in high-risk pregnancy treatment.[14] According to Ritchie, the entire department required little more than "fine tuning," including the addition of doppler ultrasound capable of measuring blood flow in the umbilical artery, to get it up and running as a centre for first-rate perinatal care.

The team that cared for Mount Sinai's first set of quintuplets, born in June 1989 and delivered by Dr. Paul Bernstein (5th from right). (MSH Image Centre)

That state wasn't long in coming. A high-risk pregnancy clinic that had only one patient booked on opening day in 1985 soon grew to the limits of what the staff could handle. Little more than a year after it was fully established, the Mount Sinai unit was designated by the National Institutes of Health as the only Canadian participant in a major North American study of recently developed ventilating equipment, which was being tested on premature babies.[15] And on October 11, 1988, the unit's team proudly delivered Mount Sinai's first set of quadruplets, followed in June 1989 by the first quintuplets.

Over the next few years, a group of stellar individuals joined the program in obstetrical perinatology and fetal therapy. All were at the top of their field as clinical specialists but, additionally, had acquired extensive and rare academic and research qualifications. On the clinical side, the contributions of Drs. Dan Farine and Robert Morrow and, later, Drs. Greg Ryan and Gareth Seaward quickly placed Mount Sinai in the forefront of the new University of Toronto Division of Maternal Fetal Medicine. In 1988, this group introduced invasive fetal intervention procedures, such as cordocentesis, which permitted sampling of fetal blood in order to monitor and treat rare blood disorders threatening both mother and baby. The number and complexity of these proce-

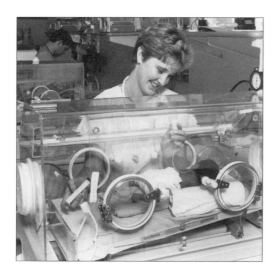

Dr. Jill Boulton, current acting pediatrician-in-chief, visits one of her wee patients in the Neonatal Intensive Care Unit. (Randy Bulmer)

dures have grown to the point where Mount Sinai is the acknowledged centre for the province in fetal intervention programs.[16]

The first recruit to the perinatal research sector was physiologist Dr. Lee Adamson, who became a key figure in the planning of that part of the institute. She was followed by Dr. Stephen Lye, current director of perinatal research and a well-known authority on the microbiology of the uterine muscle and the labour of childbirth. With these additions, according to Dr. Ritchie, who since 1992 has led both the Department of Obstetrics and Gynecology at the University of Toronto and its Division of Perinatology, Mount Sinai moved to an international stage, its fellowship program attracting top students from around the world.

Orthopedic Surgery

Throughout the 1980s, the exploits of Mount Sinai's Orthopedic division continued to make headlines. A not-unexpected side effect of the celebrity was that orthopedic transplant pioneer Dr. Allan Gross began to be assiduously courted by other hospitals. Only once did Gross come close to being lured away, when he received an offer in 1979 to become chief of the new Hospital for Joint Diseases and Orthopedic Institute in New York City, as well as full professor and chairman of the Department of Orthopedic Surgery at the Mount Sinai (New York)

School of Medicine. The complicated decision of whether to abandon the hospital "family" he had joined as an intern in 1962 was clearly evident in a long, angst-filled letter he wrote to Sidney Liswood. Addressed to "Uncle Sid" (the two are not related), Gross's letter extended paeans of gratitude to Mount Sinai for its unqualified support over the years, interspersed with justifications for considering a move to what he referred to as "potentially one of the best jobs in orthopedic surgery in North America."[17] In the end, a combination of family considerations and loyalty to an institution in which he had sunk deep roots, as well as the likelihood of equivalent academic opportunity in Toronto, led him to decline the offer and remain at Mount Sinai. By 1981, Gross was selected to head a combined division of orthopedic surgery with the Toronto General, and, in 1986, he was named professor and chairman of the division at the University of Toronto, a position he would hold for the next ten years.

Early in 1985, Gross led the team that performed knee transplants on a forty-two-year-old Israeli soldier and a twenty-one-year-old Chicago woman, both of whom travelled to Toronto for the pioneering surgery following unsatisfactory local treatment for their serious injuries. International publicity surrounding these successes spawned requests from as far away as Australia for the revolutionary procedure. That summer, a Lansing, Michigan, nurse whose knees were destroyed in a car crash received a new lease on life and made medical history when she became the first recipient of a simultaneous double-knee transplant.

Another landmark operation took place at Mount Sinai in the summer of 1987. A twenty-five-year-old woman from Roanoke, Virginia, whose hip had been broken in a water-skiing accident two years before, received the first fresh-tissue hip transplant performed in Canada. American surgeons had set the hip with pins, but, because of insufficient circulation and the extensive trauma, part of the woman's bone had died and subsequently collapsed, stiffening the joint and leaving her in constant pain. Too young to receive an artificial hip, which had limited durability, she became a candidate for transplanted bone and cartilage from a donor.

Blue Jays Fever

As North American newspapers and scientific journals were kept busy reporting the accomplishments at Mount Sinai, so were the local sports pages. In 1980, the Toronto Blue Jays baseball franchise decided to hire a general practitioner as team doctor in order to provide care for every possible ailment, from sore throats to torn ligaments. The Jays chose Dr. Ron Taylor, a former major-league relief pitcher, whose impressive arm and cool head had assisted the St. Louis Cardinals to clinch the 1964 World Series against the New York Yankees. Five years later he was on the mound again as the New York Mets prevailed in a Series win against the favoured Chicago White Sox. At the age of thirty-five, Taylor, who had already earned a degree in electrical engineering during his years in the minor leagues, hung up his baseball cleats and began medical school at U of T, interning at Mount Sinai in 1979.

The Blue Jays' association with Taylor coincided with Mount Sinai's opening of the S. C. Cooper Sports Medicine Clinic, developed jointly by the departments of Family and Community Medicine, Rehabilitation Medicine, and Orthopedic Surgery. Taylor, with his first-hand experience and keen interest in the subject, was named director. More than just a treatment facility for sports-related injuries, the clinic targeted preven-

Former major league pitcher Dr. Ron Taylor, left, is back in the World Series, this time as the Toronto Blue Jays' team doctor along with Allan Gross. (MSH Image Centre)

tion and education and was geared to every calibre of sports enthusiast, from weekend jock to élite athlete. The well-publicized fact that the clinic's staff of physiotherapists, occupational therapists, family doctors, podiatrist, and consulting orthopedic surgeons provided the same services for the sports-loving public as they did for injured Blue Jays or visiting professional baseball players was enough to get the clinic known in the city.

Along with Taylor, Dr. Allan Gross soon joined the Blue Jays roster as team physician, and, for the next several exciting years when the team reached baseball's loftiest heights as World Series champions, accounts of repairs on assorted Blue Jays' body parts that were overseen by Gross were a regular feature in Toronto newspapers.

National Breast Screening Study

A significant event whose repercussions still reverberate was the decision in January 1980 to make Mount Sinai the first site of the National Breast Screening Study. Led by Dr. Anthony Miller, head of the Epidemiology Unit of the National Cancer Institute of Canada, the five-year study, which involved ninety thousand women between the ages of forty and fifty-nine, was designed to evaluate whether mammography screening would reduce the mortality rate from breast cancer. Although eight other centres across Canada eventually joined the study, Mount

Radiologists Drs. Imre Simor and Roberta Jong became well known for their expertise in interpreting mammograms. (Randy Bulmer)

Sinai was selected to be the first as a result of its strong focus on breast disease. The most advanced dedicated mammography equipment as well as the necessary expertise were already in place at the hospital. Radiologist Dr. Imre Simor, then regarded as the best interpreter of mammograms in the country, was assisted in reading the films by Dr. Roberta Jong, who today heads this division at the University of Toronto. Furthermore, breast clinic director Dr. Alan Bassett was one of only two Canadian surgeons restricting his practice to the breast. (In 1987, Dr. Saul Sidlofsky would take over the sub-specialty of breast surgery upon Bassett's retirement.) Bassett, a staunch proponent of the value of a quality physical examination in breast-cancer detection, was invited to develop the protocol for that component of the study, and it was he who trained the nurse-practitioners who carried out the examinations at the other screening centres across Canada.

Heralded as the definitive appraisal of the value of mammography, the Canadian National Breast Screening Study was intended to clear up troubling questions about radiation levels following an American breast-screening study conducted in New York in the 1960s. Mount Sinai's mammography equipment, it was reported at a hospital press conference announcing the start of the program, produced only one-fortieth the dose of radiation of that New York study and a further 20 per cent less than the standard amount used since 1975.[18] Despite negative publicity about the cancer-causing potential of the mammography screening itself, about 100 women volunteered to participate within the first two weeks, a number that grew to 2,800 by August 1981. Even with the eventual results mired in controversy, Mount Sinai's early involvement in the National Breast Screening Study and the hospital's subsequent increase of patients with breast disease further entrenched its commitment in this area, and stimulated much of the ground-breaking research and expansion of services of more recent years.

Nursing

With the retirement of Marie Sewell Rice as director of Nursing in November 1980, Mount Sinai's Nursing department underwent its most

Vice-president of Nursing Helen Evans abolished the role of nursing supervisor at Mount Sinai. (MSH Image Centre)

dramatic reorganization since the arrival of Ella Mae Howard in 1955. While the latter had been unusually progressive in vigorously promoting continued education for her staff, she was nevertheless very much a champion of the old school of traditional nursing that included a take-your-medicine mode of leadership and an acceptance of rigid hierarchy. As Howard's protégée, Rice followed much the same path, although her personal style provided for increased consensus among staff and a more relaxed attitude toward tradition. The miniskirt uniform, for example, that so scandalized Howard that she banished its wearers from the hospital[19] was far less troublesome to her successor, whose term as director witnessed the gradual introduction of pantsuits, the abandonment of caps, pastel instead of regulation white uniforms, and, finally, street clothes for some nurses and hospital scrubs for others. Male nurses also became an increasingly common sight on the floors.

But it was the arrival of Helen Evans in 1980 to succeed Rice that marked a milestone in nursing practice at Mount Sinai. A graduate of the Toronto General Hospital School of Nursing, with a degree from the University of Western Ontario and an M.Sc.N. from Boston University, Evans was a zealous defender of the changes being advocated for the profession in the latest nursing literature, especially within the organizational structure of hospitals. Her solid academic credentials were complemented by a wealth of practical experience. Previously in charge of the school of nursing at the Hospital for Sick Children as well as that hospital's operating rooms, and later a director of Nursing at North York General Hospital, Evans was known for her intellectual firepower and was becoming a growing force in provincial and national nursing affairs as the president of the Ontario College of Nurses. In the year following her appointment to the top nursing job at Mount Sinai, she was elected president of the Canadian Nurses Association.

Evans's mission was to enhance the professionalism of nursing practice at Mount Sinai. To accomplish this, she resolved to move away from the traditional multiple layers of accountability inherent in the old hierarchical and bureaucratic organizational structure. For the first time ever in an Ontario hospital, evening and weekend supervisors were completely eliminated. This tier of nursing staff had, until now, been unassailable. The fact that so many major hospitals maintained their own nursing schools, which provided the parent institutions with a steady stream of student-staff, rendered such senior supervisors essential. They were needed to watch over the students, make critical decisions for them, and help assess their patients. Such an arrangement, however, had never existed at Mount Sinai. Even after the establishment of the autonomous Nightingale School of Nursing in 1962, the hospital had always relied on fully trained nurses rather than on students to staff its units. Still, by abandoning supervision and rejecting what had been a familiar cornerstone of nursing policy, Evans was introducing a radical measure that was very slow to be adopted by other hospitals.[20]

The essence of her plan was to reassign responsibility and authority closer to the bedside, where the results of decisions would ultimately be felt. Evans felt strongly that the position of supervisor, which she herself had held at one time, was anachronistic, and did not sufficiently recognize the ability of trained nurses to think critically or independently.[21] Furthermore, where trained nurses were employed, supervisors frequently devoted much of their time to non-nursing matters such as admission procedures or pharmacy duties. The fact that the standard had always been thus was simply not enough reason for Evans to perpetuate it. She designated one senior nurse to be on call in the event that a staff person required a resource, but removed all other supervisory positions.

Similar motives gave rise to another important decision to eliminate the central staffing office. Until now, if a unit was short-staffed, this office allocated someone to fill in. Staffing responsibility now reverted to the unit itself, which would henceforth be obliged to assemble its own list of appropriate substitute personnel who were experienced in that unit's specialty areas. The significance of the change was to end the expectation that all nurses were generalists. Recognition of professionalism in nursing practice, according to the iconoclastic Helen Evans, didn't mesh with viewing nurses as identical widgets who could arbitrarily be moved from Labour and Delivery to ICU to Emergency.

Individuals who were previously called head nurses now became nursing unit administrators (NUA). This shift amounted to much more than just a title change. Unlike the starched and uniformed head nurse, whose role had been primarily clinical, the NUA now acquired a managerial function with responsibility for hiring and firing, for budgeting within the unit, and for overall fiscal accountability. Clinical responsibility, meanwhile, was increasingly assumed by the bedside staff nurse. In conjunction with these changes, most NUAs at Mount Sinai readily adopted business attire, although those in surgery were a little more reluctant to abandon their uniforms.[22]

A small number of clinical nurse teachers had been employed by the Nursing department in the late 1970s, but, with the arrival of Helen Evans, these experts assumed a much larger role at Mount Sinai. Before continuing-education and specialization courses became widely available through colleges and universities, clinical teachers with advanced university degrees were brought in to educate and update staff in various technical areas. In addition, a new breed of nurse professional with a patient focus was added to the team. Called clinical nurse specialists, these master's-prepared experts were nurse counterparts to specialist physicians. Consulted for the management of difficult cases, each nurse was an expert in a particular clinical population of patients. Among the first clinical nurse specialists at Mount Sinai were Donna Shields-Poe in maternal-child care, Martha Rogers in medical-surgical services, and Colleen O'Brien in pain management.

As a fresh broom swept through Mount Sinai, the old nursing hierarchy was dismantled and a new corporate-style version took its place. Helen Evans was named Mount Sinai's first vice-president of Nursing, acknowledging her senior administrative role. Each nursing service now maintained its own executive, with the nurse managers or NUAS reporting to a director of that service. Pioneers in this new arrangement were Sharon McKenny (Medicine), Sue Olsen (Obstetrics and Gynecology), Joanne Daniel (Surgery), and Jamie Clark (ICU, Emergency).

Aside from the initial anxiety over change, and some early resistance from physicians who were accustomed to receiving calls from a single supervisor instead of collecting them from individual units, the reorganization and practice changes were both welcomed and applauded. Doctors remarked to Evans that the nurses had "come alive" as the result of her efforts. Encouraged throughout by the robust support of a hospital administration that historically had valued nursing highly, Evans now saw Mount Sinai as fertile ground for attendant advances in scholarship. A unique innovation in 1982 was the addition to Mount Sinai's nursing executive stratum of a director of nursing research. Filling a position that was almost unheard of in Canadian hospitals, Dr. Iola Smith came to Mount Sinai armed with a Ph.D. and an academic background teaching research and statistics at the University of Western Ontario's Faculty of Nursing. Smith's mandate was to ensure that nursing practice at the hospital was based upon a sound scientific foundation, not merely on tradition.[23]

A handful of hospitals in Canada had instituted what Smith calls "studies and projects," whose outcomes would benefit only those few patients actually being studied, but her goal was to foster research that would have a farther-reaching application.[24] In the seven years that she remained at Mount Sinai, the department did begin to attract external funding for research and contribute to the nursing literature. Yet, as midwife to this academic realm, Smith remembers devoting much energy to laying the groundwork for an academic nursing program, educating nurses about its relevance, and cultivating a non-threatening profile that reduced the initial uneasiness with "ivory tower" research.[25] On all counts she succeeded, in the opinion of Kathleen Macmillan, who arrived at Mount Sinai as a clinical teacher in surgery in 1983, and who recalls the excitement of discovering that the principles she had studied at the master's level in the Faculty of Nursing were actually being applied at the bedside, as well as the strong sense, evident at coffee breaks and lunch hours, that the nurses at Mount Sinai felt they were engaged in important work.[26] Long after she retired in 1987, the kudos for Helen Evans, who created the climate for this state of affairs, persist. And as Kathleen Macmillan, who went on to teach at the University of Ottawa and consult to the Ontario Ministry of Health, enjoys pointing out, many of the current nurse leaders across Canada were originally "Helenized" at Mount Sinai.[27]

Appointments

In July 1981, Dr. George Wortzman, a prominent Winnipeg-born neuro-radiologist who had trained at the Montreal Neurological Institute, came across from the Toronto General Hospital, where he had been on

Dr. George Wortzman, left, appointed radiologist-in-chief in 1981, with department colleagues Drs. Marvin Steinhardt, Bernard Shapiro, and Imre Simor. (MSH Image Centre)

staff since 1959, to succeed Dr. Bernard Shapiro as chief of Radiology. From the original three members, the department Wortzman inherited had grown substantially to nine full-time radiologists and five sub-specialists. But as the new chief, Wortzman's first order of business was to plug holes left as a result of the departure of two vital members following an internal departmental dispute.[28] The problem arose over the fact that some of the specialist radiologists maintained outside offices, which were consuming a growing portion of their time. Compounding that issue was the fact that fees collected within these offices were not part of the pool maintained by the whole department. A subsequent firestorm was quelled only when the board passed a by-law forbidding radiologists to carry on outside practices. When the dust settled, Dr. Joel Kirsh was brought in to head Nuclear Medicine (he would later head that division at the University of Toronto), and Dr. Morris Goldfinger took over Ultrasound. With these new additions, the department rapidly expanded to 135,000 examinations per year.[29]

In 1982, the head of Radiology at the University of Toronto, Dr. Edward Lansdown, began exploratory talks with chiefs at the three University Avenue hospitals – Mount Sinai, Toronto General, and Sick Kids – about the possibility of sharing the most advanced scanner available, a Magnetic Resonance Imager, in which magnetic fields rather than X-rays generate images.[30] By this time, payments from the Ministry of Health for capital expenditures had reduced to all but a trickle, and the overwhelming cost of the new machine ($2-million capital cost plus about $600,000 to install the machine's nine-ton magnet) demanded a united effort. Mount Sinai offered to house the unit, since its reinforced basement site would have reduced much of the installation expense for the massive machine, but the General balked at the idea.[31] The discussion then continued for several more years. Eventually, the Tri-Hospital Magnetic Resonance Centre opened at the Toronto General Hospital in February 1987 – after a site was specially prepared in the Mulock–Larkin Wing at University Avenue and College Street.[32] Another noteworthy addition to the Department of Nuclear Medicine occurred in 1985, when Mount Sinai became the first Canadian hospital to install a Dual Photon

Absorptiometer to measure bone mass and thereby screen for the serious condition of osteoporosis.[33]

Upon reaching the age of sixty-five in 1982, Dr. Nathan Levinne stepped down after twenty-one years as family practitioner-in-chief and an association with Mount Sinai that went back to Yorkville Avenue. Appointed to replace him as chief was Dr. Yves Talbot, who came to Toronto from the Kellogg Centre for Advanced Studies in Primary Care at McGill University. With a distinguished background in many areas of family medicine, ranging from pediatrics to palliative care, Talbot helped develop several progressive programs, including *Vive la Différence*, an unusual course for University of Toronto medical students that was designed to expose them to different lifestyles and to challenge their assumptions about life. Future doctors taking the course spent time with prison inmates, severely physically or mentally disabled people, elderly individuals confined to nursing homes, and gay couples, all in order to sensitize them to the real world of primary-care medicine.

Talbot's passion for teaching underscored his development of the hospital's Family Medicine program as an academic discipline. Bringing more geographic full-time family doctors on staff, he was able

Thanks to the efforts of Drs. Warren Rubenstein, left, and Yves Talbot, Mount Sinai became a North American leader in developing Family Medicine as an academic discipline. (MSH Image Centre)

*Thoracic surgeon Dr. Robert Ginsberg
was appointed surgeon-in-chief
in 1983. (MSH Image Centre)*

to introduce advanced techniques in medical education for residents in family medicine as well as for teachers of the specialty. Along with Dr. Warren Rubenstein, who directed Mount Sinai's newly formalized residency program, and Dr. David White, Talbot also took a leading role in revising the curriculum for the training of family doctors, especially emphasizing obstetrics in an effort to reduce the alarming drop-out trend among family doctors from this increasingly high-tech field. Furthermore, it was Talbot's philosophy that guided the direction of the Emergency department as a vital part of Family Medicine, rather than as a separate department unto itself. Today, Mount Sinai's Emergency department, directed by Drs. Eric Letovsky and Howard Ovens, is the home of the highly regarded Family Medicine/Emergency Medicine residency program.

Some shuffling within the Department of Surgery commenced in 1982, when Dr. Robert Stone, head of General Surgery for six years, succeeded Dr. Allan Gross as surgeon-in-chief after the latter became head of the Mount Sinai/Toronto General Combined Orthopedic Service. A year later, when Stone left to assume the position of chief of Surgery at the Toronto Western Hospital, thoracic surgeon Dr. Robert J. Ginsberg was appointed surgeon-in-chief at Mount Sinai. Former head of Thoracic Oncology at the Toronto General Hospital, Ginsberg was recruited following a two-year successful effort to secure the

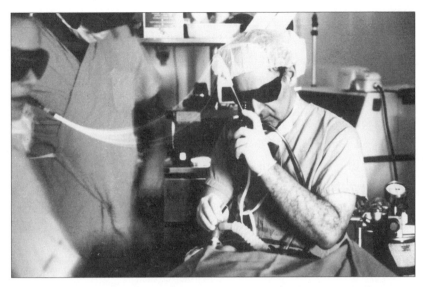

Dr. Melvyn Goldberg was part of the team that performed Toronto's first heart-lung transplant. (Randy Bulmer)

University of Toronto's second Thoracic Surgery Unit for Mount Sinai. The twenty-five-bed combined medical-and-surgical pulmonary service, including a four-bed step-down unit, opened on 14 North on January 1, 1984.

Because of the expertise of both Ginsberg and Mount Sinai thoracic surgeon Dr. Melvyn Goldberg in lung cancer, the Thoracic Unit became part of the Toronto Lung Cancer Study Group, thereby drawing over $400,000 in annual funding from the U.S. National Institutes of Health for the inclusion of Mount Sinai patients in clinical trials. Within six months, the unit was bustling with activity, having established the first bronchoscopic laser centre in Ontario, delivered two postgraduate courses for both thoracic surgical nurses and practising thoracic surgeons from all over North America and Europe, and introduced multidisciplinary services and palliative-care support for the management of the unit's patients. Ginsberg and Goldberg were also part of the Toronto General/Mount Sinai team involved with Toronto's first heart-lung transplant on June 25, 1984.

During Ginsberg's tenure as surgeon-in-chief, Mount Sinai developed the most comprehensive laser-surgery program in Toronto, providing hospital patients with hitherto-unavailable treatment options in virtually every surgical specialty. Ophthalmology and Otolaryngology had been the first departments to introduce lasers into the operating rooms as early as 1974, where they were used for retina and glaucoma problems and for delicate vocal-cord surgery.[34] But by 1988, lasers offered a bright ray of hope for many more patients, when the hospital purchased Canada's only laser lithotripsy unit, designed to pulverize painful urinary stones in a program directed by urologist Dr. Kostantinos Psihramis. And when Mount Sinai's thoracic-surgery group included an argon tunable dye laser as part of a revolutionary photo-dynamic therapy treatment of airway and lung tumours, it was one of only two centres in the country to do so.[35] Lasers, moreover, were used increasingly by Mount Sinai's gynecologists to remove various lesions in the reproductive tract.

Dentistry

Dentistry has the distinction of being both the oldest and the youngest department at Mount Sinai. It was the oldest because, even before the birth of the small hospital on Yorkville Avenue, a collective of volunteer Jewish dentists had provided organized dental services for indigent refugees in a clinic located at Sheuer House, a Jewish community centre at the corner of Baldwin and Beverley streets. Once the clinic moved to Yorkville Mount Sinai, dentists played a prominent role at the hospital, especially in its first decade, due to a prevailing and widely held theory within the dental profession that infections of the teeth and gums were the underlying cause in many problems of general health. In the early 1930s, a respected American expert, Dr. Rosenow from the Mayo Clinic, had drawn a capacity crowd of the Toronto Academy of Dentistry to Eaton auditorium on College Street for a lecture to demonstrate the validity of this theory, known as "focal infection," or "elective localiza-tion." If you had "rheumatism," for example, as joint diseases were then commonly known, treatment almost invariably included extraction of all your teeth. Dentists were consequently called in as consultants for many hospitalized patients, and thousands of teeth were needlessly

Dr. Charles Oliveri-Munroe became the first non-volunteer dentist-in-chief at Mount Sinai in 1973. (Highlights *magazine*)

sacrificed in attempts to cure an assortment of diseases. Given their importance to the medical staff of the Yorkville hospital, therefore, the Jewish dentists were able to enlist the support of Dr. Wallace Seccombe, dean of the University of Toronto's Faculty of Dentistry, in their petition to secure a seat on Mount Sinai's Medical Advisory Council. Dr. Harry Landsberg was their first representative.[36]

With such primitive beginnings, it is interesting to note that Dentistry also qualifies as the youngest department at Mount Sinai, because it was the last to affiliate with U of T in 1973 under its first non-volunteer full-time chief, Dr. Charles Oliveri-Munroe.

Negotiating the transition from the purely voluntary treatment that evolved over the years from wholesale extraction of teeth and care of needy emergency patients, to a structured program of teaching, research, and a much-altered service function was not without problems, many of which centred on a woeful lack of space. But at the time of Munroe's arrival, the electric mood throughout the hospital, which had been generated by rapid growth and increasing public and academic recognition, was equally prevalent in the Department of Dentistry, and the new chief eagerly set about recruiting his own high-calibre staff. Cross-appointed from the University of Toronto was Dr. Norman Levine, then head of Pediatric Dentistry at the Faculty of Dentistry. He invited Mount Sinai to begin a program for mentally and physically challenged adults, many of

Neurologist Dr. Allan Gordon, left, and current dentist-in-chief Dr. David Mock collaborate frequently to diagnose and treat cranio-facial pain. (Henry Feather)

whom had complex medical problems or required general anesthesia for dental treatment. Aside from services at Sick Kids and the Hugh MacMillan Centre, both of which treated children exclusively, no such service existed in the province. With such an obvious need, the program instantly blossomed into the first academic one in the department. Taken over in 1982 by Dr. Michael Sigal, current chief of Pediatric Dentistry at the university, today it provides treatment for patients from around the country and training for undergraduate and postgraduate residents in a variety of dental sub-specialties.

A second program was unofficially launched in 1976 through the regular collaboration between oral pathologist Dr. David Mock, neurologist Dr. Allan Gordon, otolaryngologist Dr. Robin Blair, and psychologist Kenneth Doody. The group began meeting to discuss patients whose pain in any location above the shoulders was either difficult to manage or to diagnose. Formalized in 1980 as the Cranio-Facial Pain Unit under co-directors Drs. Mock and Gordon, Mount Sinai's current chief of Dentistry[*] and head of the division of Neurology, respectively, the unit today includes representation from Anesthesia, Psychiatry, and Rehabilitation Medicine. Treating more than two thousand patients annually, this unique multidisciplinary program is closely linked with the Faculty of Dentistry's Basic Science Pain Unit, a world leader in the field.

---

[*] Dr. Mock succeeded Dr. Charles Oliveri-Munroe as chief of Dentistry in 1991.

As additional expertise was attracted to the growing department, new strengths developed. Oral and maxillofacial surgery flourished because of director Dr. Gerald Baker's proficiency in tempomandibular joint procedures and innovative implants for cancer patients and accident victims whose jaws had been resected. Orthodontics, first introduced in New Mount Sinai's Dentistry department in the 1950s by volunteers Drs. Murray Simon and Bert Levin as an inexpensive clinic for low-income patients, continued to thrive under Dr. Earl Haltrecht. And research, notably periodontist Dr. Howard Tenenbaum's bone-physiology studies, one of which will be part of a forthcoming space-shuttle mission, has brought Mount Sinai's Dentistry department renown in basic science that belies its small size.

Microbiology and the Norwalk Virus

After the 1977 departure from the Department of Pathology of microbiologist Dr. John A. Smith, who coordinated the first formal infection-control-and-surveillance program at Mount Sinai, this division of the hospital laboratories remained in flux for several years, straining under the weight of inadequate leadership and friction among the remaining technologists. A solitary infection-control nurse, Carol Goldman, had struggled since 1978 to maintain the monitoring of infection rates along with the myriad other tasks associated with preserving the standards of practice for infection prevention, but she had little staff support. In 1984, a search committee began looking for a new chief. One member was Dr. Hillar Vellend, head of the bi-hospital (Mount Sinai–Toronto General) Division of Infectious Diseases and today Mount Sinai's director of graduate education in Medicine and head of the Division of Internal Medicine. Vellend had encountered Dr. Donald Low, a Winnipeg internal-medicine and infectious-disease specialist, when the latter was training in microbiology in Toronto and recommended that he be recruited to revitalize the labour-intensive domain of microbiology.

The importance of the discipline of microbiology, whose critical mandate is to protect patients from the hospital environment, was just

*Guarding against dangerous anti-
biotic-resistant bacteria has become a
growing responsibility for Dr. Donald
Low. (MSH Image Centre)*

beginning to be explored at this juncture. Epidemiology, the study of
the prevalence of disease, was still widely regarded as a quality-assurance issue. To Low, however, it was a fundamental component of
microbiology, possessing clear relevance to both the investigation and
prevention of infection within hospitals. That point had been reiter-
ated in the summer of 1985 just before Low left St. Boniface Hospital
in Winnipeg for Mount Sinai, when a major outbreak of entero-virus
in the neonatal unit there killed two babies and triggered meningitis
and encephalitis in several others. The only infectious-disease specialist not away on holidays, Low was required to manage both the crisis
and the subsequent investigation, for which he enlisted the help of the
Centers for Disease Control in Atlanta, Georgia. On his arrival in
Toronto, having weathered that storm, Low insisted that Microbiology be separated from Pathology and made a distinct department
with a direct line to the administration. He also reasoned – wrongly as
it turned out – that he would not likely face another such dire emergency any time soon.[37]

On November 14, 1985, just four months after his arrival at Mount
Sinai, Low was informed by infection-control nurse Carol Goldman
that "something weird was going on in the Emergency department."
Several nurses and house staff had suddenly fallen ill with severe gastro-
intestinal symptoms of nausea, vomiting, and diarrhea, coupled with

debilitating fatigue. A preliminary investigation, consisting of a questionnaire for all ER staff followed up with telephone interviews, disclosed even more cases, including patients who had passed through the ER. At first, food poisoning was suspected, and the Toronto Department of Public Health was brought in to assist in examining the kitchens. Meanwhile, specimens from the afflicted people were dispatched for examination by electron-microscopy, and emergency meetings were convened with senior medical staff and the Medical Advisory Council.

By five o'clock on the following day, the magnitude of the problem was far more evident. For one thing, the results of a questionnaire to every employee at the hospital now revealed that the outbreak was not limited to the ER, but was present in every single department, mostly among staff, but among patients as well. Second, food from the kitchens was ruled out as the source of the problem. Tests identified the disease as a Norwalk-like virus, a finding that was completely unexpected. Although nursing homes with concentrations of the sick elderly had experienced such outbreaks before, no general hospital had ever reported a widespread Norwalk virus. With staff seriously depleted through illness, and the cause of the outbreak still a mystery, CEO Gerald Turner, Low, and the administrative staff made an unprecedented decision. In order to contain the damage and extinguish the virus as expeditiously as possible, Mount Sinai Hospital would close its doors until further notice, permitting neither staff nor patients to move between hospitals until seventy-two hours after resolution of their last symptoms.

As the crisis began to unfold over the next several days, there was a frenzy of activity: twice daily meetings of the investigative committee, daily press conferences overseen by vice-president Murray MacKenzie, appeals to the Federal Laboratories in Ottawa and Atlanta for a medical SWAT team of field epidemiologists to assist with surveillance, collection of data, and identification of the source of the virus. Especially worrisome was the fact that all previous outbreaks of Norwalk virus recorded in the medical literature had been associated with one identifiable source, such as contaminated water or food. Since meticulous detective work in the lab had exonerated both, it was postulated that this might be the first such outbreak with an airborne spread. Notices were placed in

Toronto newspapers, imploring everyone who had visited the hospital after November 8 who suffered bouts of diarrhea or vomiting to telephone a special hotline. Curiously, among the many callers were those who had had no physical contact with either patients or staff, such as people delivering flowers or camera persons from media crews. Each, however, had walked through the Emergency department.[38]

By the time the pernicious pathogen was finally on the run and the hospital fully reopened on November 25, mountains of data had been assembled and countless hours spent analysing results and testing theories. In the end, the epicentre of the mysterious Norwalk virus was determined to be the Emergency department, with all evidence pointing to airborne transmission. But the real lesson of the Norwalk virus (known in hospital lore as the "No Work Virus," because more than nine hundred health-care workers and a hundred patients were stricken) was that early and aggressive action in such emergencies limits spread of disease before it acquires a firm foothold. As a footnote to the Norwalk virus story, ever since its participation in the crisis, the Centers for Disease Control in Atlanta has used the Mount Sinai episode as a model in their epidemiology training courses.[39]

At the same time that Microbiology was declared independent from Pathology with the arrival of Dr. Donald Low, Biochemistry also split off to become a separate department under Dr. Alan Pollard. An additional transition in Pathology occurred with the retirement of Dr. Harry Strawbridge in the spring of 1986, and the subsequent appointment of Dr. Kenneth Pritzker as pathologist-in-chief. Although the announcement in the Auxiliary publication, *Highlights*, made no mention of it, the selection of Pritzker for the top job in Pathology held special significance for the hospital.[40] Across a span of seven decades, strong family ties to Mount Sinai have been a recurrent and familiar theme. In many instances, such ties have been figurative ones, in the sense of faithful and continuing bonds of community loyalty. But the connection of the Pritzker name to the hospital, and especially to Pathology, is surely one of the most notable of the literal family ties. A staff pathologist at Mount Sinai since 1972 and head of the Connective Tissue Research Group,

Pathologist-in-chief Dr. Kenneth Pritzker heads a Pacific Bridge project studying the impact of environment, viruses, and genes on cancers affecting Chinese populations. (Randy Bulmer)

Kenneth Pritzker was the son of Harold Pritzker, pathologist-in-chief at both Yorkville Mount Sinai and New Mount Sinai hospitals.

Psychiatry

The comprehensive psychotherapy-based program in Psychiatry that began to flourish once the new hospital opened in 1974 was a world apart from the earlier one. Dr. Daniel Silver joined the department in that year to oversee the long-awaited in-patient unit, which soon attracted international attention for its management of borderline disorders, a catch-all phrase describing a category of such difficult behaviours as acting out, sexual impropriety, suicide attempts, and others. A consultation-liaison service also got under way to provide a link with medical and surgical departments, but cooperation from these quarters was slow to develop. Senior staff under Dr. Stanley Greben during this decade included Drs. David Berger, Ray Freebury, Jack Brandes, and Graeme Taylor. Staff psychiatrists Joel Sadavoy and Howard Book each led a team within the in-patient unit. Sadavoy, who had taken some of his training at Mount Sinai and had expertise in geriatrics, then left in 1980 to become head of Psychiatry at Baycrest.

In 1985, Greben stepped down and Dr. Mary Seeman, an international authority on schizophrenia, was appointed psychiatrist-in-chief.

Psychiatrist-in-chief Dr. Mary Seeman was Mount Sinai's first female chief of service. (Henry Feather)

Under Seeman's aegis, several significant developments took place. The department added a Clinic for HIV-Related Concerns run by Dr. Steven Woo, a staff psychiatrist and passionate proponent of services for AIDS patients and their families, partners, and friends. Incorporating Mount Sinai's long-standing psychotherapy approach as well as community outreach, the only clinic of its kind in Canada soon began to garner awards from the American Psychiatric Association for its excellence.

A second addition was the psychiatric Day Hospital, which patients attended each day for a specified period, returning to their homes at night. With more treatment now available on an out-patient basis, the in-patient unit then contracted down to fifteen beds, its current size.

Consultation-liaison with medical and surgical departments hadn't been meeting with much success until Dr. Peter Brown began devoting his attention to the service in 1988.[41] His eventual collaboration with oncologist Dr. Pamela Goodwin launched the hospital's important work in the psycho-social impact of living with breast cancer. The immediate success of this cooperative link provided a much-needed boost to expand interdepartment association, and the consultation-liaison soon expanded to include the gastro-intestinal program and other medical and surgical units.

A highly skilled scientist, possessed of compassionate, humanistic values, Seeman was so warmly regarded at Mount Sinai that, when she

Caring for the emotional ills of the AIDS community became a principal concern of psychiatrist Dr. Steven Woo. (MSH Image Centre)

eventually left in 1993, her department created an award in her name to be given to the resident or junior staff psychiatrist best exemplifying her exceptional combination of qualities. Seeman's successor, Dr. Joel Sadavoy, had returned from Baycrest in 1991 to implement a geriatric program at Mount Sinai. Building on his predecessor's goal of augmenting the academic thrust of the department, Sadavoy has forged closer ties with the research institute, especially in the area of psychosomatic medicine (a link between psychiatry and organic medicine) and, with a rapidly aging population, the increasingly important sphere of geriatric psychiatry.

Palliative Care

A letter landed on the desk of executive director Gerald Turner early in 1977, sent by a woman who had recently nursed a close relative through a terminal illness.[42] The writer, moved by a television documentary about the ground-breaking work in palliative care at the Royal Victoria Hospital in Montreal, wanted to know if Toronto's Mount Sinai offered anything similar. The receipt of this query followed closely upon a new program at the hospital, the establishment of an Ad Hoc Committee for the Total Care of the Terminally Ill, a consultation team of physician, nurse, psychiatrist, social worker, rehabilitation therapist, nutritionist, and clergy that had been convened to advise *staff* on caring for the terminally ill. At that time, however, no program existed to specifically support *patients* and their families. It wasn't until nine years later that the situation changed.

In October 1986, a second Palliative Care Consultation Team was mobilized to work directly with patients and families as well as with their primary-care physicians. Team members included part-time medical consultant Dr. Trudy Chernin, psychologist Kenneth Doody, and clinical nurse specialist Colleen O'Brien. O'Brien, a former head nurse in Montreal's Royal Victoria Palliative Care Service, had come to Mount Sinai to work in oncology, where she advised in the area of pain management. This group was supplemented by chaplains Rabbi Sheldon Steinberg and Betty Calvin and social worker Michelle Chaban. The first year in which the service operated, it attracted only twenty-six consultations from medical and nursing staff scattered throughout the hospital.

The fact that palliative support for patients and families at Mount Sinai got off to such a slow start was not in the least unusual, and indeed was part of a worldwide phenomenon of active resistance to such care. Long after the general acknowledgement that obstetrical practices required an overhaul so that families could experience a "good birth," the equivalent possibility of a "good death" continued to meet with stubborn opposition. This reaction was no mere denial of death on the part of physicians trained to preserve life – mostly oncologists dealing with terminal cancer. Rather, it reflected the belief by medical staff that providing adequate pain management *was* palliative care.[43] This traditional barrier had stood in the way of earlier acceptance of a comprehensive program, but, with the enthusiastic encouragement of assistant executive director Ted Freedman, Mount Sinai began building an impressive new service. In 1988, family physician-in-chief Dr. Yves Talbot recruited Dr. Lawrence Librach from the Toronto Western Hospital, where the latter had founded a palliative-care team. Librach, a family doctor whose interest in the emerging field began early in his medical career, was a disciple of Dr. Balfour Mount, the prophet of palliative care in Canada and founder of the fabled unit at the Royal Victoria Hospital in Montreal.

Dr. Lawrence Librach heads Toronto's
foremost palliative-care program.
(MSH Image Centre)

The highly specialized skills that Librach brought to Mount Sinai encompassed far more than the latest and most effective techniques for pain management, although the manual he would soon compile on that subject quickly became among the best-selling medical texts in the country.[44] The broad reach of his expertise embraced a philosophy of care that addressed not just the physical needs of the dying patient, but also the emotional, social, and spiritual ones. Issues such as family dynamics, handling children, nutrition and skin care, cultural and religious concerns surrounding death, questions about the dying process, and numerous other emotionally charged problems all figured into every patient's care plan. Dispensing support, offering counselling, and linking patients and families with the proper services at the proper time were critical elements of the multifaceted treatment.

Librach began with an education program for all medical personnel and a strong public-relations effort to spread the message of palliative care. Within the first year after his arrival at Mount Sinai, referrals from medical and nursing staff increased from 26 to 129. By the following year, the number rose to 200. For a brief period, there were five in-patient palliative-care beds on 17 South, but, when cutbacks eliminated these, efforts were concentrated on a strong home palliative-care program. Dr. Frank Ferris joined Librach in 1991 to share operation of this service.

Over the years, the program has expanded to include the equivalent of four and a half full-time physicians treating an average of 170 patients a year, with home consultations and continuing care twenty-four hours a day, seven days a week. Some 80 per cent of terminally ill patients are now able to remain comfortably in their homes until the end. The Mount Sinai service also facilitates, where necessary, patients' entry into palliative-care units in other hospitals and supervises up to five hundred home-care cases per year, many referred from Princess Margaret Hospital and Sunnybrook Regional Cancer Centre. In addition, Dr. Librach is a founder and Mount Sinai a partner in the Jewish Hospice Program,[*] launched in 1990, whose purpose is to attend to some very specific issues of delivering palliative care in a Jewish manner, observing, among other things, appropriate Orthodox religious rites as well as the unique sensitivities of Holocaust survivors.

As a recognized leader in the field of palliative care, Dr. Librach, who heads that division at the University of Toronto, along with the rest of the Mount Sinai team, has been actively involved in the growing academic and research side of palliative medicine. The department, moreover, founded the Metropolitan Toronto Palliative Care Council and was instrumental in creating the Canadian Palliative Care Association, which determines and publishes national standards for palliative care. Additionally, cooperative links with the Department of Psychiatry have generated bereavement and family-therapy programs by Drs. Ed Pakes and Jonathan Hunter. The division's most recent initiative is the opening in 1996 of the Rabbi Sheldon Steinberg Library, providing the community with literature on all aspects of palliative care.

Otolaryngology

For decades, the major medical preoccupations of Mount Sinai's pioneers in otolaryngology had been tonsillitis and mastoid disease, the common, often life-threatening, scourges that provided the bread and

---

[*] The other participants are Baycrest Centre, Jewish Family and Child Service, and Senior Care.

butter for such early ear-nose-and-throat specialists as Dr. I. R. Smith, one of the three original specialists at Yorkville Mount Sinai, followed later by Drs. Ivan Vaile, Joseph Gollom, Louis Kane, Bill Goodman, and David Green. Once antibiotics all but vanquished these conditions, the specialty began to grow in stature, notably during the years coinciding with the term of New Mount Sinai Hospital, until it soon encompassed surgery for, and diagnosis of, a whole variety of hearing and nasal disorders as well as management of cancer. It was during this period of rapid development that Dr. Gollom, the hospital's chief of department, had dedicated himself to acquiring a fellowship in his specialty at the age of fifty.

After the appointment of Peter Alberti as chief and the subsequent move to 600 University, the department had expanded rapidly with the addition of sub-specialty expertise. Dr. Arnold Noyek, a former Mount Sinai intern and award-winning research fellow in bone-scanning, focused on radiology techniques in support of otolaryngology. He joined with Dr. Jerry Chapnick, and the two began to share much of the head-and-neck surgery associated with thyroid and parotid gland problems that to date had been handled exclusively by head-and-neck surgeon Dr. Irving Rosen. Other cooperative relationships with the departments of Dentistry and Neurology were cemented by Dr. Robin Blair in order to manage, among other conditions, the treatment of oral lesions. Under the leadership of Dr. Jack Friedberg, laser surgery soon allowed far more accuracy and delicacy, with considerably less bleeding or scarring than was previously possible in procedures involving the vocal cords.[45]

Another prime thrust of the department was the expansion of the sophisticated hearing-test facility called the Otologic Function Unit, launched by Dr. Alberti and directed by audiologist Krista Riko, which became a major referral centre for noise-induced hearing loss for the Workers' Compensation Board. The establishment in 1979 of the Saul A. Silverman Hearing Research Laboratory allowed Drs. Sharon Abel, Martyn Hyde, and Hans Kunov, three Ph.D. researchers, to begin trailblazing studies and clinical research associated with hearing loss, especially early detection of impairment in infants. When it became a shared

Dr. Jeremy Freeman, co-director of head-and-neck oncology at Mount Sinai, North America's largest treatment centre for thyroid and para-thyroid oncology. (Henry Feather)

service with the Toronto General in 1983, adding the Western Division in 1990,[*] Mount Sinai's Otologic Function Unit became the largest of its kind in Canada.

A unique resource for the adult hearing impaired was first established in 1984 in the hospital's apartment residence at 222 Elm Street. Revolutionary at the time was the Gerstein Aural Rehabilitation Centre's provision of the latest information about electronic devices for those with hearing impairment. Patients attended workshops to both sample and learn how to use a whole range of equipment, including room amplification systems common in theatres and religious institutions, closed-caption television, and telephone amplifiers. Another sophisticated service of the centre was computerized assistance in the selection of hearing aids.

In 1980, the addition of Dr. Jeremy Freeman, a specialist in the field of head-and-neck oncology, bolstered the capacity for complicated cancer surgery begun by Dr. Irving Rosen. Later, Dr. Ian Witterick joined that team. Facial plastic and cosmetic surgery became formalized under the direction of Drs. Jerry Chapnick and Kris Conrad. In 1988, a bright new Ambulatory Care Centre opened, dedicated to difficult diagnoses and

---

[*] The Toronto General and Toronto Western merged in 1986 to become the Toronto Hospital.

treatment in several areas: general otolaryngology, complicated airway problems, head-and-neck surgery, and communication disorders. Shortly after the appointment of Dr. Noyek as chief in 1989, the division launched the ambitious Canadian International Scientific Exchange Program (CISEPO) to foster interactive associations in research, education, and clinical programs with leading medical schools in the Middle East and, in doing so, to promote peace in this troubled region.

Ophthalmology

Like so many Mount Sinai leaders of his generation who had graduated with as much distinction from the School of Hard Knocks as from advanced specialty training, Dr. Bernard Teichman determined when he had become the new chief of Ophthalmology in 1966 that Mount Sinai's division would become recognized for its excellence. One of the first requirements for fulfilling that goal was to redesign the physical layout for the new hospital. The comprehensive department Teichman outlined, embracing state-of-the-art visual-fields equipment and ceiling-mounted microscopes in the operating room, quickly became a model for other hospitals in Toronto that were revamping or adding to their own departments.

The slate of part-time ophthalmologists already at Mount Sinai when Teichman arrived, including Drs. Harold Sniderman, Louis Kazdan, Morris Shusterman, Harold Stein, Louis Myers, Sigmund Vaile, Martin Kazdan, and Louis Kagan, was soon supplemented by two sub-specialists who would guide the future direction of the division, Dr. Fred Feldman, an expert in glaucoma, and Dr. Mark Mandelcorn, a specialist in diseases of the retina. The Toronto General was originally the main base of Drs. Martin Kazdan and Sigmund Vaile, who ran the only ophthalmologic ultrasound unit in the city. But when both decided to move across the street in 1968, join the teaching program, and become full time at Mount Sinai, U of T division chief Dr. Clement McCullough (with whom Bernard Teichman had resumed good relations) permitted the two to bring the unique apparatus that was vital for diagnosing orbital tumours or detached retinas along with them.[46]

The most recent focus of the Division of Ophthalmology has been in ocular plastics, a sub-specialty of corrective and reconstructive surgery for the treatment of a variety of diseases affecting areas immediately surrounding the eye, including eyelids, tear ducts, and sockets. Mount Sinai is now the oculoplastic centre for the University of Toronto. Spearheaded by Dr. Jeffrey Hurwitz, who followed Teichman as chief in 1986, this area has spawned considerable academic research, which is currently being carried out by Drs. Raymond Stein, a third-generation ophthalmologist at Mount Sinai,[*] James Oestreicher, Robert Pashby, and Martin Kazdan.

Governance

In September 1986, Hy Isenbaum assumed the chairmanship of the board of directors. A chartered accountant by profession, Isenbaum and his partner, Max Soberman, had been the hospital's auditors since the 1950s, and the new leader had as unclouded a view of the financial picture as anyone. In the course of his long involvement, Isenbaum had witnessed the complete transformation of Mount Sinai from a small community institution to a citadel of pride, buttressed by the three vital pillars of a first-class hospital: patient care, teaching, and research. With the dependable dedication of two, and in some instances three, generations of supporters, the seemingly impossible goal of his predecessor and mentor Ben Sadowski had been fully accomplished.

Yet now that the dream was a reality, it had to be nourished, and a clear-eyed Isenbaum announced at the beginning of his term that his mission would be to raise enough capital funds to keep Mount Sinai fiscally sound.[47] This task, Isenbaum warned *Highlights* in a declaration of manifold understatement, "wouldn't be easy." The annual endowment that was required for the research institute alone was $3.5 million, an amount that was surely destined to grow. Then there were rapidly rising costs of capital equipment necessary for Mount Sinai to keep

---

[*] Dr. R. Stein is the son of Dr. Harold Stein and the grandson of Dr. Maxwell Bochner.

Board chairman Hy Isenbaum strived to enhance the financial stability of Mount Sinai for generations to come. (Randy Bulmer)

pace in high-tech diagnosis and treatment, as well as clinical and teaching programs hungry for constant development.

Of course, asking the public for money was familiar territory for Mount Sinai. Since the noble initiatives of the *Ezras Noshem* volunteers, the hospital's board and its powerful Auxiliary had raised funds repeatedly and in a creative variety of ways to support hospital projects and supplement gradually dwindling government aid. Donors, moreover, had been remarkably steadfast and magnanimous over the years. Not untypical was the sentiment expressed in a 1978 letter to Sidney Liswood from a patient of Dr. Barnet Berris who, in gratitude for his restored health, had donated generously to a particular area of research at Mount Sinai. Liswood had responded to the contributor, offering to install a plaque in the building in recognition. "There are only two who should be aware of our investment," the donor wrote back to Liswood in gentle rebuke. "I am confident that word has already reached the good Lord above us, and Ottawa will be advised at the end of the year."[48]

The capital campaign envisioned by Isenbaum, however, would be unique in several respects. For one thing, the goal of $75 million was a completely unprecedented amount. To put this huge undertaking into perspective, it must be understood that no institution of Mount Sinai's size (527 beds) had ever launched such an ambitious project before. In all their years, neither of the neighbouring hospital behemoths, the Toronto General or the Hospital for Sick Children, had ever attempted to raise so vast an amount of money at one time. Nor, with the exception of U of T, McGill, and UBC, had any Canadian university mounted a campaign of such magnitude.[49] And although there was certainly initial scepticism at the board when Isenbaum announced his intended goal,[50] it was soon overcome when Mount Sinai Auxiliary president Tobie Bekhor threw down the gauntlet with a $5-million pledge from that formidable organization.

Another defining characteristic of the campaign would be to heavily cultivate the national corporate sector, while continuing to protect and enlarge the hardy perennial border of community support. In all instances, the "take the money and run" ethic common to all large hospital campaigns, including Mount Sinai's previous once-a-decade campaigns for buildings or equipment, would no longer suffice. Instead, the message to corporate and private donors alike could have been applied to the board, medical staff, core supporters, and patient population ever since the hospital's inception: They would become Mount Sinai's "Friends for Life." Finally, everything about this campaign would be highly sophisticated, from the professional fund-raising talents of Jon Dellandrea, former vice-president of development for the University of Waterloo, who was brought in to head the foundation, to the integration into the campaign of the hospital's public-relations director, Jodi Macpherson, and her department, all newly installed in the executive wing.

Led by chairman Albert Reichmann, the campaign cabinet of Jon Dellandrea, Kenneth Rotenberg, Gerald Shear, Norman Hollend, Lloyd Fogler, Ephraim Diamond, Garth Drabinsky, Douglas Bassett, Bernard Ghert, Hy Isenbaum, and Gerald Turner demonstrated extraordinary commitment and leadership as well as irrepressible optimism on a level

The Mount Sinai "Friends for Life" campaign cabinet. Standing, left to right: Jon Dellandrea, Kenneth Rotenberg, Gerald Shear, Norman Hollend, Lloyd Fogler, A. Ephraim Diamond, Garth Drabinsky, Douglas Bassett, Gerald Turner. Sitting: Bernard Ghert, Albert Reichmann, Hy Isenbaum. (Communique Public Relations)

that professional fund-raiser Dellandrea had never before witnessed. And, despite a voluntary halt to the campaign shortly after it began, due to the five-month emergency of Operation Exodus[*] in late 1990, that passion was amply rewarded. At its zenith during one forty-two-week period, the Friends for Life campaign was bringing in an average of $1 million a week.[51] Furthermore, within three years after the enthusiastic fund-raisers hit the track running, the $75 million had been fully pledged. Even if Mount Sinai's aspirations were huge, it certainly appeared – at least initially – that there was an endless capacity to sustain them.

---

[*] Operation Exodus was a worldwide effort begun in April 1990 to airlift Jews from the Soviet Union to Israel after Soviet authorities suddenly opened the doors for them to emigrate.

8

Rainbows and Storm Clouds

The wrenching changes that hospitals now face in the late 1990s did not come about suddenly or without warning. For almost two decades, a succession of reports from task forces and commissions had repeatedly recommended more efficient ways to manage the province's bloated health-care budget, and, although few measures had been implemented, Mount Sinai, like its sister institutions across Ontario, was fully resigned by the late 1980s to relinquishing its once-cherished entitlements to government funding for every worthy program. Until this time, except for a brief downturn in the Canadian economy in 1981, a stretch of sustained growth often characterized by excess and conspicuous consumption and financed at high interest rates had permeated all sectors of society, including health care. But, with the particularly punishing effects of a worldwide recession in 1990–91, there was now little doubt that this pattern would soon become a thing of the past.

In Toronto, the term "downsizing" entered the lexicon, as unemployment topped 10 per cent, and for the first time city food banks found themselves overwhelmed. The province's first NDP government, elected in 1990, reiterating its predecessor's goal to shift the focus and much of the funding of health care away from institutions into the community and direct more attention to prevention and health maintenance,

Lloyd Fogler, board chairman
1991–97, concentrated on the new
realities of hospital restructuring.
(MSH Image Centre)

promptly closed almost 20 per cent of Metro Toronto's acute-care hospital beds.[1] Still, the costs of health care continued to escalate, thanks to a proliferation of expensive technology and a rapidly aging population.

Diminished expectations aside, however, few would have predicted the sweeping nature of the transformation ahead: painful winnowing of budgets, institutional realignments, system-wide redesigns, revised funding formulae, as well as new academic requirements, all of which would converge during the next decade to yield not only a daunting challenge in the short term, but a permanent alteration to the face of hospitals and the manner in which they delivered care. Taking the helm in September 1991 at Mount Sinai to confront these seismic changes was a new chairman of the board, lawyer Lloyd Fogler. A fourteen-year member of the board's executive committee, Fogler would ride the wave of enforced medical-service rationalization, providing tough, savvy, and vigilant leadership during one of the most difficult decades in Mount Sinai's history.

With the new economic climate well entrenched, it came as no surprise when foundation president Jon Dellandrea, writing in the hospital's 1990–91 annual report, revealed that the goal of the Friends for Life campaign was too low. "Already we are looking at the need to raise at least another $50 million . . . if we are to maintain our present patient care, teaching and research commitments into the 21st century," he

The Marvelle Koffler Breast Centre: compassion, privacy, and luxurious comfort plus a total range of ambulatory services associated with the diagnosis and treatment of breast disease. (MSH Image Centre)

observed.[2] Making new and retaining old Friends for Life would henceforth play a pivotal role in Mount Sinai's existence. Over the next several years, many programs would be refined and reorganized, but none would be achieved without deeply committed donor support.

One such project expanded the Emergency department, which had been struggling with the burden of bed closures, creating a need for an Emergency Admissions Unit for seriously ill patients awaiting an available bed.[*] An upgraded endoscopy suite with the most advanced equipment available was another generous consequence of patient gratitude and support. And it was the Koffler family's lifelong involvement with Mount Sinai, coupled with the donor's personal encounter with breast cancer, that culminated in the hospital's extraordinary Marvelle Koffler Breast Centre, a peerless facility that brought together expertise from eight separate departments, combining it with leading-edge research in one elegant and tranquil twelfth-floor location.

---

[*] The Ray D. Wolfe Emergency Admission Unit closed in November 1996 as part of a realignment that moved the unit's eleven beds to Level 17 (Medicine/Geriatric).

Quite apart from the acceptance of this increasing reliance on corporate support and private philanthropy to improve and expand patient services was the need to recognize that the hospital's future was largely dependent on maintaining indefinitely the remorseless intensity and momentum of the campaign. Furthermore, responding to these pressures would now inform every decision and undertaking in Mount Sinai's operation, from redeveloping and enhancing ambulatory services, to focusing on priority programs of excellence, to initiating and strengthening collaborations with other institutions.

New Neighbours

An opportunity for a significant collaboration had first come to Gerald Turner's attention some months after a June 1985 consultant's report warned that the province's flagship cancer-treatment centre, Princess Margaret Hospital, built in 1958 to accommodate four thousand patients a year, faced a critical need for additional space and would require a new home. A relocation committee, headed by Dr. Burnett Thall, was preparing to present a resolution to Health Minister Murray Elston, recommending that the new Princess Margaret Hospital and Ontario Cancer Institute be erected adjacent to the Sunnybrook Health Science Centre on Bayview Avenue. Another committee member, Dr. Martin Barkin, then president of Sunnybrook, endorsed the north-Toronto site. Mount Sinai's Turner wasn't included in the deliberations, but requested that Thall postpone a final recommendation pending Turner's submission of an alternative proposal for a downtown location on the University Avenue property owned by Ontario Hydro, immediately north of Mount Sinai Hospital.

Turner wasn't alone in his uneasiness with regard to the possibility of Princess Margaret and the Ontario Cancer Institute moving so far away from the University of Toronto complex of teaching hospitals. As an institution that concentrated heavily on medical and surgical oncology, Mount Sinai relied on the radiation and oncology services of Princess Margaret for its patients. What's more, much of the focus of the Samuel Lunenfeld Research Institute was cancer-related. Turner feared that accessibility for both quality patient care and research activities might be compromised if the cancer hospital was removed from the downtown core. He mobilized supporters at the Toronto General and the Hospital for Sick Children who agreed with this assessment.[3] Together with Mount Sinai and Women's College, these four teaching hospitals referred fully one-fifth of Princess Margaret's cancer patients.[4]

Health Minister Elston then appointed a commission, headed by fact-finder and former deputy health minister Alan Backley, to evaluate the merits of three possible downtown locations. These included the Toronto General's last bit of unused space facing Elizabeth Street, some vacant land next to the Wellesley Hospital at Princess Margaret's current Sherbourne Street location, as well as the now-favoured Hydro property. Mount Sinai's detailed proposal made the case that the University Avenue land next door would allow the PMH to exist as an autonomous institution, while encouraging beneficial collaborations, and, more important, would grant it ready access to the emergency- and critical-care it sorely needed nearby. Optimal coordination of cancer care within a group of academically oriented centres would also be supported by a University Avenue address. Research institute director Lou Siminovitch underscored the importance and benefits of close association between his facility and the Ontario Cancer Institute. And finally, to relieve pressures caused by the desperate shortage of radiation treatment facilities while the construction was under way, Mount Sinai agreed to install a satellite radiotherapy unit housing four machines in its Level-2 basement.

The decision-making process dragged on until the summer of 1987, and Health Minister Elston blamed the delay on such complicating issues as the fate of the Wellesley Hospital, which had a close relationship with the cancer institution next door, the cost of buying, then renovating, the historic Hydro properties, which required architectural preservation, and the pressure from city bureaucrats in North York, Peel, and York region, who continued to urge provincial health officials to select the Bayview site in accordance with the shift of the population to the suburban north.[5] Meanwhile, Gerald Turner, now the newly elected chairman of the Ontario Hospital Association, lobbied tirelessly for the University Avenue choice.

In August, the verdict was delivered. The $177.5-million Princess Margaret Hospital and Ontario Cancer Institute would relocate next door to Mount Sinai Hospital in the heritage Hydro Electric Power Commission and Ontario Hydro Commission buildings, which had been constructed in 1915 and 1935 respectively. "The site was chosen because of the unique grouping of hospitals in the area," said Murray Elston at a press conference announcing the decision. "A large number of Princess Margaret's patients are initially diagnosed and undergo treatment at these hospitals. . . . This site will also allow the most efficient use of University of Toronto resources and will strengthen a research and academic oncology centre of worldwide stature."[6]

In succeeding in his bid to secure the Princess Margaret Hospital and Ontario Cancer Institute next door, Gerald Turner preserved cancer treatment and research close to the university and its core hospitals. In doing so, he also accomplished what was arguably the most significant coup of all for Mount Sinai. The public hue and cry over the lengthening queue for radiotherapy services would end with the immediate renovation of the second level of Mount Sinai Hospital, a space directly contiguous with the new facilities to be built on the Hydro site. But the designated area of 17,500 square feet for the satellite radiotherapy unit was the site of Mount Sinai's busy Ambulatory Department of

New next-door neighbours Princess Margaret Hospital and the Ontario Cancer Institute begin construction. (MSH Image Centre)

Rehabilitation Medicine, which would now have to be relocated. Any such move, moreover, would have to accommodate the depth of the department's therapeutic swimming and exercise pool.

The configuration of Mount Sinai hospital is such that only vertical expansion is possible above the Murray Street tower. Therefore, in order for the Rehabilitation department and its pool to be situated on an upper level, it was necessary to construct *two* new floors. When negotiations were complete, Mount Sinai gained a totally new, state-of-the-art Ambulatory Rehabilitation department on Level 11, plus an extra unfinished floor on Level 10, shelled in for future research laboratories. Total space amounted to 50,600 square feet, all built at no cost to the hospital as part of the Princess Margaret project.[7]

The proposed realignment of services with Princess Margaret Hospital was less successful, despite months of joint meetings and negotiations. Critical Care was assumed by Mount Sinai, and Microbiology and Virology did combine in a newly enlarged department under the direction of Dr. Donald Low, as did several non-clinical programs such as Purchasing and Occupational Health and Safety. A joint program in Psychiatry had a brief existence until the end of 1996, when Princess Margaret downgraded its department to a program of Psycho-oncology within its Department of Medicine. Another proposed collaboration in radiology was not supported by the Princess Margaret medical staff, who feared a loss of institutional identity resulting from such a move.

Research

During the construction of the PMH/OCI next door to Mount Sinai, Dr. Alan Bernstein succeeded Dr. Lou Siminovitch as director of the Samuel Lunenfeld Research Institute, and, in 1994, the original five-division structure of the institute was reorganized. The old division of Molecular and Developmental Biology dissolved in favour of a new program in Molecular Biology and Cancer, headed by Dr. Tony Pawson, a senior scientist who had been showered with international acclaim throughout the institute's first decade for his widely heralded breakthrough into the mechanism of cell signalling, or how cells "com-

Long-time philanthropist Anne Tanenbaum, seen here with Dr. Alan Bernstein, funded five research chairs in molecular medicine and neuroscience at Toronto institutions. (Randy Bulmer)

The award-winning research of senior scientist Tony Pawson may be useful in designing drugs to block the growth of tumour cells. (Randy Bulmer)

municate" with both normal and malignant cells. Under the umbrella of Pawson's division, and with the expectation of broadening its scientific expertise, a new laboratory of surgical oncology was established within the institute to permit young cancer surgeons to conduct clinical research.

The same potential synergy was the motive for enlarging the Lunenfeld's original division of Perinatology into a blended program of Developmental and Fetal Health under the co-leadership of Dr. Stephen Lye, who focused on the physiology of embryonic development, and Dr. Janet Rossant, an authority on fetal genetics. The intention was to draw together two areas that, in traditional research circles, spoke different scientific languages. The former division of Clinical Epidemiology also expanded with the addition of further research into breast cancer, diabetes, and biostatistics.

To further propel the Lunenfeld into its second decade, Bernstein planned a fourth division in Molecular Medicine and Genome Research aimed at deciphering the complex human genetic blueprint, studying inherited predisposition to certain diseases and ultimately investigating new gene-based therapies. The additional ten labs and one hundred scientists would represent yet another opportunity to forge strong links with Mount Sinai's clinical departments. But this division, earmarked for the adroitly acquired tenth-floor shelled-in space, would have to await the availability of a major financial infusion.

Since 1990, when, quite by chance, Dr. Rossant noticed a research-grant application from Bristol-Myers Squibb on a bulletin board where she was delivering a lecture, members of the Lunenfeld had become increasingly sophisticated and accomplished in winning major industry support for their research. Indeed, with 20 per cent of its support from industry and with two spin-off companies generating milestone payments to fuel further research, the institute had reached the point where it was fast becoming a role model for other institutions.[8] But the corollary of growing success in research is that it continually yields higher and higher costs. And, as Dr. Bernstein discovered, finding funds for the new tenth-floor labs and Centre for Molecular Medicine and Human

Genome Research, a prospective $10-million expansion, required some special skills not generally honed inside the laboratory.

Bernstein, nevertheless, learned quickly. Invited by a provincial civil servant to speak at a government function on the subject of "Why Ontario Is a Good Place to Do Research in Biotechnology," the genial scientist accepted, noting in passing that, assuming the truth of the proposition, the province should expect to contribute to the cost of such research. A cash-strapped Ministry of Health would be unable to assist, noted the civil servant, but perhaps the federal Ministry of Trade's infrastructure program could be persuaded to contribute, even though that program had never before supported biotechnology. The exchange launched Bernstein's long, sometimes Byzantine, involvement with four levels of government. Coached in the fine art of lobbying by steel magnate Lawrence Tanenbaum, the research institute board chairman, and a staunch research supporter, and by allies made along the way, Bernstein and the Samuel Lunenfeld Research Institute eventually emerged with $5 million for the Centre for Molecular Medicine and Human Genome Research. That grant, together with $10.3 million over five years, the largest industry funding agreement in Canadian history, won competitively from Squibb, and a generous private donation, allowed the centre to open in 1997.[*] With a $10-million gift, cited by University of Toronto president Robert Pritchard as "one of the most important in the history of Canadian philanthropy," Anne Tanenbaum (mother of Lawrence Tanenbaum), whose large family had been closely associated with the hospital for decades, established a Joint Chair in Biomedical Research at Mount Sinai, whose occupant was to head the new centre.[†]

---

[*] At that time, the centre was renamed The Joseph and Wolf Lebovic Centre for Molecular Medicine and Human Genome Research.

[†] In October 1995, the $10-million Anne and Max Tanenbaum Joint Chair in Biomedical Research created five research chairs in molecular medicine and neuroscience at the U of T Faculty of Medicine, Mount Sinai Hospital, Baycrest Centre for Geriatric Care, the Hospital for Sick Children, and the Toronto Hospital.

*Expansion of research in all medical
divisions was the goal of Dr. Eliot
Phillipson, chief of Medicine 1987–97.
(Randy Bulmer)*

Despite the expansion of Mount Sinai's "crown jewel," the research
institute nevertheless continues to be a source of financial stress for the
hospital and its board. When the wing was built between 1983 and 1986,
construction cost $28 million, out of which fund-raising pledges payable
over a number of years tallied approximately $24 million. But the hospi-
tal quickly sagged under the accumulated weight of high interest rates,
and soon found itself owing the full amount. Furthermore, while the
institute's operational budget derived largely from peer grants, Mount
Sinai assumed an annual obligation for infrastructure that rapidly
doubled from $3 million the first year to its current $6 million. One of
Lloyd Fogler's first decisions upon becoming chairman in 1991 was to
bring down the worrisome bank loan. But by that time, budgets were so
tight that, even with continual fund-raising, the debt was reduced only
marginally each year. By 1996, it became necessary to sell the hospital's
non-core assets, the apartment buildings and a parking garage, in order
to further knock down the debt. Yet, in order to eliminate it completely
and properly endow the institute for the future, Mount Sinai would have
to continue to struggle on a relentless fund-raising treadmill.

Medicine and Surgery

Mount Sinai's traditionally robust leadership in the Department of

Dr. Bernard Zinman heads leading-edge research into diabetes at U of T. (MSH Image Centre)

Medicine was destined to continue with the appointment in 1987 of Eliot Phillipson as physician-in-chief. A gold medallist from the University of Alberta's Faculty of Medicine, Phillipson had spent sixteen years as a clinician scientist associated with the Toronto General Hospital, his research in respirology focusing on the brain's regulation of breathing. With the Department of Medicine securely anchored on foundations laid by Dr. Barnet Berris, who first developed its academic stature, and Dr. Arnold Aberman, who created the financial resources to sustain research, Phillipson now undertook to identify crucial areas in which to build significant research, as well as to superintend the complete revision of the graduate and undergraduate teaching programs. Like his predecessor, Phillipson would be named the Sir John and Lady Eaton Professor and Chairman of the Department of Medicine at the University of Toronto in 1993.

Although Mount Sinai had always maintained an active Division of Endocrinology within the Department of Medicine, there had been minimal activity in diabetes research. Aside from being extremely common, particularly in the Jewish and Chinese communities served by Mount Sinai, the disease had become a focus of the hospital's growing Perinatology program. Since pregnant diabetic women, as well as women who developed gestational diabetes, received treatment in the high-risk obstetrical unit, there was ample opportunity for research in the area. To that end, Phillipson recruited Dr. Bernard Zinman to lead the Division of Endocrinology and Metabolism. Today the director of the University of Toronto's Banting and Best Diabetes Centre, Zinman was named head of Mount Sinai's new ambulatory Diabetes Clinical Research Unit, built on the seventh floor in 1990.

The unit acquired an instant high profile when it became one of twenty-nine North American centres participating in a massive ten-year National Institutes of Health–sponsored study, the Diabetes Control and Complications Trial, for which Zinman was U of T's principal investigator. When the study ended a year early in 1993, because the startling results were so conclusive, it revealed that using a more intensive therapy than conventionally recommended to treat Type I diabetes dramatically reduced the devastating complications of the disease, an outcome hailed in the press as "the most important advance since insulin." The unit also assumed a unique project in the northern community of Sandy Lake, Ontario, whose goal was to examine the high incidence of Type II diabetes among native populations and find culturally appropriate ways to control or prevent it.

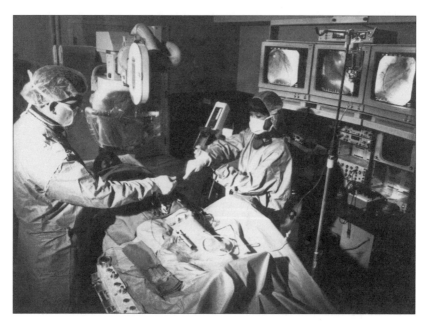

Performing a cardiac catheterization at the Miles Mount Sinai Cardiovascular Clinical Research Laboratory. (MSH Image Centre)

A second medical division that Phillipson knew gained considerable coin if alloyed with research was Cardiology, a vital clinical service then run by Dr. Brian Gilbert. What was lacking in the Toronto arsenal was a high-tech cardiac laboratory, equipped with specialized X-ray, ultrasound, and catheterization monitoring systems and dedicated exclusively to research, whose findings could possibly have a major impact on the treatment of cardiovascular diseases. The Cardiac Catheterization Laboratory established on the sixteenth floor in May 1992 became the first of its kind in North America. Directed by cardiologist Dr. Allan Adelman, it was built entirely through donations to the foundation and Friends for Life campaign, although a $5-million grant from Miles Canada Inc. the following year ensured continuing operating expenses.

Dr. John Parker, a Harvard-trained cardiologist specializing in congestive heart failure, joined the Cardiac Catheterization Laboratory in 1992 to lead the exploration of left-ventricular function and the effect of different drugs on failing heart muscle. Clinical scientists Dr. John Floras and Dr. Gary Newton followed in 1995 and 1996 respectively, to further staff this critical component of the University of Toronto's Centre for Cardiovascular Research. The cardiac clinical service was also reinforced during these years with the addition of cardiologists Drs. Jewel Gold, Zion Sasson, and Robert Wald.

Under Dr. Phillipson's direction, Rheumatology and Respirology, always strong clinical presences at Mount Sinai, also acquired impressive research components, the result of Dr. Katherine Siminovitch's investigation into the molecular genetics of rheumatic and auto-immune diseases and Drs. Arthur Slutsky's and Noe Zamel's hot pursuit of the gene responsible for asthma. Following Siminovitch's discovery of a genetic marker for a fatal condition called Wiskott-Aldrich syndrome in 1994, genetic counsellors from across North America began contacting Mount Sinai for help in prenatal diagnosis of the disorder.[9]

Another pivotal opportunity for extensive research evolved from the appointment in 1990 of Dr. Zane Cohen to succeed Dr. Robert Ginsberg as surgeon-in-chief. Cohen and his colleague Dr. Robin McLeod, who

Chief of Surgery Dr. Zane Cohen
coordinated a multi-disciplinary
approach to gastro-intestinal diseases
at Mount Sinai. (MSH Image Centre)

came to Mount Sinai with him, had achieved international reputations in the area of colo-rectal surgery at the Toronto Hospital, General Division (the Toronto General Hospital merged with the Toronto Western Hospital in 1986 to become the Toronto Hospital Corporation). Cohen's own research concerned intestinal transplantation, while McLeod focused on multiple clinical trials. Cohen's willingness to transport this expertise across the street depended on Mount Sinai's agreement to build a vastly expanded multidisciplinary program in gastro-intestinal diseases, involving medicine, surgery, and research.

A mountainous obstacle threatening the pair's move was Mount Sinai's lack of resources and beds necessary to fulfil these ambitions. The impasse presented far-reaching implications for the hospital's future direction, and consequently remains a memorable episode. Asked to describe the "culture" of Mount Sinai, many of the medical staff from a variety of departments offer up the events surrounding this expensive recruitment as examples of the institution's remarkable absence of swashbuckling egos, and its collegial sense of working for the greater good of the whole, which has always been a principal value of those associated with the hospital. In this instance, it was only because other departments sacrificed some of their own beds, operating time, and funding that this important program was able to be accommodated.

The special skill of Dr. Demetrius Litwin, minimal-access surgery through a laparoscope, has dramatically reduced recovery time and hospital stay for many patients. (MSH Image Centre)

Cohen's installation as chief created an interesting statistic that clearly illustrated Mount Sinai's continuing upward trajectory and prefigured the hospital's growing research ambitions. No other hospital in Canada could claim that within its major departments, Medicine (Eliot Phillipson), Pathology (Kenneth Pritzker), Obstetrics and Gynecology (Knox Ritchie), and Surgery (Zane Cohen), were four chiefs who simultaneously held grants as principal investigators from the country's most respected granting agency, the Medical Research Council of Canada.[10]

To accommodate Cohen's team, several changes occurred within the hospital. In-patient and ambulatory facilities of the Division of Gastro-enterology merged to form combined units, with a thirty-bed medical-surgical unit on 11 North and ambulatory on 4 North close to the surgical offices. To head the medical Division of Gastro-enterology, Phillipson added Dr. Gordon Greenberg in 1991 and Drs. Hillary Steinhart and David Baron shortly thereafter. In surgery, Cohen brought on gastro-intestinal surgeons Drs. Jean Couture and Carol Swallow, as well as Dr. Demetrius Litwin to develop an innovative program of laparoscopic minimal-access surgery (using sophisticated video and endoscopic instruments inserted through tiny holes in the body). Aggressive recruitment in other surgical sub-specialty areas began to change the face of the department, notably with the addition

Surgeon-scientist Dr. Steven Gallinger explores the occurrence and frequency of genes associated with hereditary gastro-intestinal diseases. (Randy Bulmer)

of Dr. Keith Jarvi's unique expertise in male-factor infertility and other aspects of andrology. The high-profile orthopedic and sarcoma programs expanded with the arrival of Drs. Jay Wunder, Carol Hutchison, and Erin Boynton, while Dr. Robert Bell, director of the sarcoma program, was selected to head surgical oncology for an integrated department with the Toronto Hospital, which was located at Mount Sinai. Thoracic surgery, which turned over completely following Dr. Ginsberg's departure, added Drs. Gail Darling, Michael Johnson, and Alan Casson.

An explosion of academic productivity within the Department of Surgery ensued, as all of these new recruits joined the Lunenfeld to conduct basic research, much of it in the realm of molecular genetics. One of the most significant projects, the Familial Adenomatous Polyposis (FAP) Registry, originally directed by colo-rectal surgeon Dr. Hartley Stern, had been the only undertaking of its kind in Canada to track and study patients and their families with pre-cancerous polyps of the large intestine.[11] Now enlarged and renamed under clinician-scientist Dr. Steven Gallinger to include a registry for other varieties of hereditary colon cancer, the Familial Gastro-Intestinal Cancer Registry has contributed to Mount Sinai's reputation as a world leader in the study and treatment of cancer and inflammatory bowel disease.[12]

Dr. Barry Smith was pediatrician-in-chief from 1989 until 1996.
(Randy Bulmer)

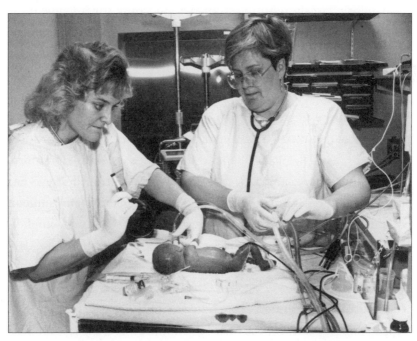

Clinical nurse specialist Jackie Livingston, left, and nurse Janet Narcisco attend
a tiny preemie in Mount Sinai's Neonatal Intensive Care Unit. (Randy Bulmer)

Dramatic maternal-fetal interventions led by program director Dr. Dan Farine have produced miracle babies at Mount Sinai. (MSH Image Centre)

Other Appointments

The 1989 appointment of clinician-scientist Dr. Barry Smith as pediatrician-in-chief coincided with a period of sustained growth in the field of neonatology, largely resulting from the kind of cutting-edge clinical research that Smith and colleagues at the Hospital for Sick Children had been involved with for many years. A product of Queen's University in Kingston, Smith had previously directed neonatology at Harvard Medical School before returning to Sick Kids, where he investigated treatments for respiratory distress syndrome (RDS), a potentially lethal problem that threatened many premature babies. In 1991, he introduced to Mount Sinai's Neonatal Intensive Care Unit the use of laboratory-produced surfactant as a new treatment for RDS. Controlled studies had shown that treating immature lungs with this complex mixture of lipids and proteins substantially reduced mortality rates and other complications associated with mechanical ventilation, the previous standard therapy for RDS.[13]

During the combined watch of Drs. Smith and Knox Ritchie, Mount Sinai's focus on fetal intervention also expanded considerably. (Smith stepped down as chief in 1996 to become the dean of Queen's University Medical School.) Perinatologist Dr. Robert Morrow performed Ontario's first intravascular-intrauterine (into the umbilical cord) blood

Physiatrist-in-chief Dr. Rajka Soric leads Rehabilitation Medicine, a major department for many years at Mount Sinai, now reduced to an ambulatory program due to restructuring and budget constraints. (MSH Image Centre)

transfusion in 1992 to save an unborn child from severe anemia or death caused by Rh incompatibility.[14] A great leap forward in ultrasound technology, permitting detail that could now signal such problems as fluid build-up in fetal lungs, led to the dramatic therapy of inserting tiny chest shunts in affected fetuses to drain dangerous fluid into the amniotic sac. Ever since this procedure was first carried out on a twenty-two-week-old fetus in 1992, Mount Sinai's fetal intervention team, which is now led by Dr. Dan Farine with Drs. Greg Ryan and Gareth Seaward, has acquired more experience in it than any other hospital in Canada.[15]

A maternal-fetal clinic for high-risk pregnancies also became the only one of its kind in which a variety of sub-specialists – such as rheumatologist Dr. Carl Laskin, who treats recurrent miscarriage and auto-immune disorders, internist Dr. Laura McGee, an expert in the medical disorders of pregnancy, and cardiologist Dr. Jack Colman, an authority on heart complications – converged in one location, not merely for the convenience of patients, but to facilitate collaboration and communication between several team members who would potentially be involved with the patient's care.

Four other departments came under new leadership early in the new decade. Dr. Joseph Fisher succeeded Dr. Gerald Edelist as anesthetist-in-chief in 1990, and Dr. Rajka Soric, a member of the Department of

Neuroradiologist Dr. Edward Kassel
became chief of Diagnostic Imaging
in 1992. (MSH Image Centre)

Rehabilitation Medicine since 1982 and coordinator of its undergraduate and postgraduate training, became physiatrist-in-chief early in 1992. When Dr. George Wortzman stepped down as chief of Radiology in 1989, the hospital cast a wide net in search of a chief of Diagnostic Imaging Services for the proposed shared imaging department to be developed with the Princess Margaret Hospital/Ontario Cancer Institute. With $5 million promised to upgrade equipment and expand facilities following the hospital Auxiliary's most ambitious pledge in its history, Mount Sinai's department was poised to become one of the leading North American centres in imaging technology. In the summer of 1992, neuro-radiologist Dr. Edward E. Kassel became the new chief as the expansion got under way. Nevertheless, the joint service with the cancer hospital failed to materialize at this juncture.

The Department of Family Medicine, whose reputation for innovative, unorthodox approaches to education, as well as superb family-doctor-led obstetrics, became well established under the stewardship of Dr. Yves Talbot. It continued in those directions and also moved into leading-edge research with the appointment in 1993 of Dr. Warren Rubenstein as family-physician-in-chief. Rubenstein, a one-time Mount Sinai resident, directed the hospital's thirty-bed Family Practice Unit, an unprecedented concept in which patients' own family doctors rather than specialists delivered primary care. Not only did the unit maintain

Vice-president of Nursing Judith Shamian directs a department with a strong academic focus. (Randy Bulmer)

continuity of care for patients, but, for teaching purposes, it provided an acute-care environment under the supervision of the family doctor – an atmosphere far more reflective of the reality of community hospitals, where students would likely transport their skills.[16]

Nursing

Following the retirement of Helen Evans in 1987 and the one-year tenure of Susan Smith in the department, Dr. Judith Shamian became Mount Sinai's vice-president of Nursing in August of 1989. Originally trained in Israel, with a doctorate from Frances Payne Bolton School of Nursing in Cleveland, Ohio, Shamian had most recently directed Nursing Research at Toronto's Sunnybrook Hospital. As a special adviser to the World Health Organization, she also acted as consultant for the development of nursing in Eastern Bloc countries.

Her arrival at Mount Sinai coincided with a period of great challenge for nursing departments nationwide. A troubling shortage of nurses, which had escalated since 1985, had reached crisis proportions. Since this shortage came at the same time as the acquisition of several new clinical services, notably an expanded Intensive Care Unit, the need to strengthen the department was clearly an urgent priority. Shamian set about not only to recruit nurses, but to complete the transition initiated by Helen Evans to a fully professional department reflecting excellent patient care combined with first-class academic standards.

The review of nursing at Mount Sinai resulted in a provocative move: the creation of an all-registered nursing staff. At the same time that other institutions, compelled by cost-cutting imperatives, were reducing their numbers of expensive RNs and hiring unlicensed individuals to fill some of their non-nursing functions, Mount Sinai determined to achieve the same cost-per-case ratio with better care by maintaining the highest possible qualifications. Intensive training for a new classification of team member, the service assistant, whose job would now consolidate several non-professional functions, from porter to nutrition aid, permitted the hospital to preserve its dwindling resources at the bedside where they were most needed.[17] Despite initial scepticism about the move, both within the hospital and without, Mount Sinai by 1993 was the only hospital in Canada whose nurses were all RNs.

Revamping the structure of the department by appointing four master's-prepared program directors with strong clinical backgrounds while eliminating separate divisions of education and research would also ensure that henceforth all research and educational endeavours would be driven exclusively by care for the patient instead of existing as sidelines. Until this time, the use of computers within the hospital had been largely confined to management and financial systems. Yet the most progressive academic thinking included nursing informatics, the application of technological data to clinical care. Information that might include the quantity of gauze pads used post-operatively or the number of nurse-hours associated with a particular condition, could now be reflected in such vital clinical decisions as treatments, use of supplies, nursing-care requirements, and outcomes. The many changes were new, far-reaching, and, in the case of the implementation of nursing informatics by Dr. Lynn Nagle, somewhat intimidating, but they placed Mount Sinai at the forefront of a revolution in nursing practice.

In 1992, the newly named Gerald P. Turner Department of Nursing was selected as a World Health Organization Collaborating Centre for

Nursing, the only hospital department in the world to earn this distinction, and a resounding international acknowledgement of the department's outstanding accomplishments and leadership. Headed by Dr. Shamian with the assistance of Dr. Irmajean Bajnok, one of the program directors of nursing at Mount Sinai, and, later, David Zakus, whose Ph.D. in health administration focused on international health, the centre has carried Mount Sinai's name and expertise in areas of leadership, administration, and clinical practice to parts of Africa, Eastern Europe, China, South America, the Caribbean, and elsewhere around the world.

With its intense academic focus and strong ties to the Faculty of Nursing at the University of Toronto, Mount Sinai's Nursing department seemed the most likely home for the country's first endowed chair for nursing research. Established in October 1996 in partnership with the university, the Heather M. Reisman Chair in Perinatal Nursing Research was presented to Dr. Ellen Hodnett, director of Mount Sinai's Perinatal Nursing Research Unit. But the highest tribute to Judith Shamian's Nursing department came with the imprimatur of peers upon it. When the Registered Nursing Association of Ontario created a new award for Employer of the Year in 1997, a year marked by upheaval and discontent within the nursing profession, the first recipient was Mount Sinai Hospital.

High Honours

On the last day of 1991, board chairman Lloyd Fogler received a letter from Dr. John Dirks, outgoing dean of the Faculty of Medicine, expressing gratitude for the working relationship the dean had enjoyed with both Fogler and his predecessor, Hy Isenbaum, during his term at the University of Toronto. Referring to "your marvellous institution," Dirks wrote, "The progress that has been made at Mount Sinai during the last five years has been truly extraordinary. It is now an academic institution that has the widest possible recognition.... You provide exemplary clinical care at the highest levels of academic development."[18]

If Mount Sinai's rapid rise to the front ranks of Canadian hospitals was now being exuberantly touted in the corridors of power, it would soon receive much more public acclaim. In October 1992, following a rigorous peer review, Mount Sinai became the first hospital in Canadian history to be granted a four-year accreditation award with distinction.[*] Unlike any other evaluation, this broad assessment, conducted by the Canadian Council on Health Facilities Accreditation, which measures a hospital's performance against national standards, has always been singled out as the one most indicative of an institution's degree of public accountability. In announcing its decision, the council summarized, "The Mount Sinai Hospital is truly an outstanding health-care facility. The Board of Trustees and the staff of the hospital deserve to be proud of this facility and its reputation. The community is fortunate in having such a valuable resource as the Mount Sinai Hospital."[19]

More honours would soon follow. An updated edition of the much-scrutinized survey, *The Best Hospitals in America*, concluded that Mount Sinai was "probably the best all-around hospital in the country."[20] A handbook for job hunters listed the hospital as one of Canada's best employers for women, noting that 70 per cent of upper-level managers were female.[21] Even the popular survey of more than 300,000 readers of the local tabloid, *NOW*, repeatedly concluded that Mount Sinai was "Toronto's Best Hospital."

Changing Times

With the first four-year accreditation, the crowning achievement of thirty-eight years of dedicated service to Mount Sinai, Gerald Turner stepped down as president and CEO on March 31, 1993. Since the hospital had first opened on University Avenue, there had been only two professional administrators, Turner and his predecessor, Sidney Liswood, both of whom, with single-minded intensity, had devoted their entire careers to building Mount Sinai Hospital. The immeasurable value of this

---

[*] A year later, Mount Sinai's close associate institution, the Baycrest Centre for Geriatric Care, became the second health-care facility to receive this honour.

Mount Sinai president and CEO
*Theodore Freedman leads Mount
Sinai through tough times.*
(MSH *Image Centre*)

abiding loyalty was not lost on the board of directors, whose membership now included sons and daughters as well as grandchildren of some
of the hospital's founders. In selecting a successor, their committee
named Theodore J. Freedman, Turner's executive vice-president and
chief operating officer. With twenty-four years' experience in the administrative wing at Mount Sinai, Freedman was already a *bona fide* member
of the hospital's "family," having played an integral part in its development. Like Liswood and Turner, he possessed a strong personal as well as
professional investment in Mount Sinai's future welfare. In the same tradition, Joseph Mapa, who had also begun his career as an administrative
resident back in 1977, moved into Freedman's former position. Along
with three corporate vice-presidents, Janine Girard-Pearlman, Georgia
Gerring, and Martin Stein, this leadership team prepared to weather the
most dramatic winds of change to hit health care yet.

The first strong gust arrived late in 1993, when the Metropolitan Toronto
District Health Council (MTDHC) finally set in motion an essential
metamorphosis of the city's forty-four hospitals. The whole concept of
hospitals required fundamental change, from individual piles of bricks
and mortar each in business for itself to an interconnected network of
people: a variety of health-care professionals prepared to deliver care in a
cooperative array of institutional and community settings. In response

to radical changes in medical technology (such as minimal-access surgery), resulting in shorter hospital stays, plus a dramatic increase in procedures that could be performed on an out-patient basis, the need for expensive in-patient beds was in rapid decline. Most hospitals had already closed beds to reflect these dynamic shifts. But other factors, including the elimination of duplication of services, had to figure into an improved, more-integrated health-care system.

When the MTDHC's first blue-ribbon Hospital Restructuring Committee was convened in the fall of that year, Mount Sinai stood ready to demonstrate its indispensability within the broader hospital community, the University of Toronto, and the University Avenue complex of hospitals. Enumerating its unique strengths for the committee, Mount Sinai's submission explained how the hospital had been assured repeatedly by peer reviewers that its Samuel Lunenfeld Research Institute was one of the finest of its kind in the world. Particularly significant was the fact that bench-to-bedside interaction between clinicians and researchers enabled the institute to be an intrinsic part of the hospital and not a separate facility. Clinical care at Mount Sinai was also widely regarded as superior, which was largely the result of the hospital's ability to assemble a roster of top talent to populate the stellar research institute. Moreover, from a standing start in the early 1960s, Mount Sinai had risen to become a major teaching centre at the University of Toronto's Faculty of Medicine. Finally, it was essential for Mount Sinai to identify for the benefit of the committee its special relationship with the Jewish community, and its need to preserve that relationship through independent governance. Well known by the Canadian public for an exceptional quality of caring and an ethic of humanity unparalleled in most clinical environments, Mount Sinai was solidly grounded in the Jewish values of its founders and the historical injunction to always maintain them.

Along with this account of principles, Mount Sinai demonstrated a clear commitment to fulfilling the necessary practical goals of the committee. A veteran and enthusiastic seeker of collaborative clinical opportunities and rationalized services with its neighbouring institutions and U of T partners, the hospital now spearheaded additional innovative ones, including a series of commercial links with its Department of Laboratories, a pilot telecommunications computer system called HealthLink in conjunction with six other hospitals, a "preferred provider" partnership agreement that would make Doctors' Hospital an ambulatory centre for Mount Sinai, and a number of joint activities with organizations in the Asian community. Still other ventures undertaken at this time included an undergraduate teaching academy shared with Women's College Hospital and a Tri-Hospital Orthopedic Program, directed by Dr. Allan Gross, involving Mount Sinai, Women's College, and the Toronto Hospital, which instigated a more-seamless provision of orthopedic patient care, education, and research.[22]

In the spring of 1995, while the exhaustive two-year study by the MTDHC Restructuring Committee was under way, a Conservative government was elected in Ontario. Fiercely committed to deficit reduction and massive reform of health care, education, and social programs, it announced cuts of 18 per cent over three years to hospital funding. Shortly thereafter, at the end of September 1995, the committee released its final report. It recommended that the number of Toronto's acute general teaching hospitals was to be reduced from six and consolidated at three sites: St. Michael's (with programs transferred from the Wellesley Hospital), Sunnybrook (with merger and relocation of the Women's College Hospital), and the University Avenue Hospitals (composed of Mount Sinai, the Toronto Hospital, and Princess Margaret). Establishment of new ambulatory-care centres (the Doctors' Hospital would be folded into the Toronto Hospital, Western Division, *not* Mount Sinai), closure or consolidation of eleven acute-care hospitals, and reorganization of chronic-care facilities were among the sweeping recommendations. Mount Sinai was specifically affected by two of them: a proposal to amalgamate University Avenue Emergency departments at a yet-to-be-determined location and a plan to dramatically alter the rehabilitation medicine network in the city, transferring its academic centre to Queen Elizabeth Hospital.

Nevertheless, without the authority to implement any of these recommendations, the MTDHC saw few of them adopted, although budget constraints caused Mount Sinai to close the in-patient rehabilitation unit it had pioneered in 1977, retaining ambulatory service only. Not surprisingly, a serious obstacle to further rationalization of programs was the issue of adequate funding. While it was easy enough for hospitals to agree among themselves that one would be responsible for brain surgery and another for delivering babies, things became sticky when it came to handing over the resource allocation that went along with the program. In the end, Mount Sinai deemed the success of its submission to the restructuring committee to have been only marginally successful.[23] A gnawing worry was the description of the University Avenue hospitals. Said board chairman Lloyd Fogler, "We anticipated that it wouldn't be long before someone suggested taking the 's' off hospitals."[24]

That fear seemed to materialize when the Toronto Hospital began urging the MTDHC, which was charged with ratifying the restructuring committee's report, to consider one "superboard" for the three neighbouring institutions. Once more, Mount Sinai waged its battle for independent governance with the MTDHC, taking the tough position that its separate identity could never be on the table. Volunteer organizations at Mount Sinai, of which the board was a vital segment, have, from the hospital's founding, played a huge role, accounting in no small measure for its success. Much of the drive for that volunteerism, which annually raises millions of dollars, donates 100,000 hours of dedicated support within hospital departments, and safeguards Mount Sinai's high standards of patient care, is denominationally motivated. There was legitimate concern that the traditionally close-knit volunteer network would be substantially reduced and perhaps lost if the hospital's identity disappeared or was submerged in another institution. In the long run, concluded Mount Sinai's executive committee and administration, it was entirely in the public interest to preserve the extraordinary enthusiasm of volunteers at all levels (including the board) in order to preserve quality of care, teaching, and research.

On November 30, 1995, the MTDHC finalized its report. With reference to the University Avenue Hospitals, it declared, "An acceptable governance mechanism must be developed to facilitate decision-making related to the consolidation, distribution and ongoing management of programs and services among the three hospitals. It is expected that each hospital will continue to have its own governing board."[25]

Following the MTDHC's decision to reject an overarching board, there was a brief period of calm on the subject. But by midwinter things began to heat up, as the Toronto Hospital sought to merge with Princess Margaret Hospital. At the eleventh hour, that deal was quashed by the PMH, but the Toronto Hospital did assume executive control over the cancer hospital. On paper, the two institutions remained separate, but otherwise, they were, *de facto*, one. Yet again, alarm bells began to sound in Mount Sinai's executive corridor, as the question arose of how this development would affect the discussions among the University Avenue hospitals, carried on over two to three years, to create an "articulated cancer-care program" for Toronto as part of the necessary restructuring. Thus far, the hospital expected to play a major role in comprehensive cancer care, notably in its areas of acknowledged expertise: breast, sarcoma, head and neck, and gastro-intestinal oncology and surgery. But now that Mount Sinai was in bed with an elephant, there was a very good chance that the beast might choose to roll over.

In April 1996, unwilling to endure further foot-dragging by some hospitals on the restructuring issues and frustrated by critics determined to resist change, the new Conservative provincial government, as part of its highly controversial Omnibus Bill 26, created its own Health Services Restructuring Commission, with a four-year mandate to review *all* provincial health services – including hospitals, but also encompassing community care, home care, long-term care, and the provision of nursing and physician services. Intending to move as expeditiously as possible through the province, focusing first on hospitals, the commission, chaired by Dr. Duncan Sinclair and Chief Executive Officer Mark Rochon, was legislated to assess the previous MTDHC Report, contribute its own evaluation, and then *enforce* decisions applying to hospitals. Thereafter, it would make recommendations to the Health Ministry on the reconfiguration of the other elements of health services in Ontario.

After only two months, the commission rendered its first verdict, ordering the closing of three of the five hospitals in Thunder Bay, Ontario, leaving one for acute care and one for chronic care in the city of 110,000.[26] More unpalatable medicine was dispensed in Sudbury, when, in the face of the ministry's earlier assurance that denominational hospitals would be untouched, the commission boldly ordered the merger of the city's Catholic and general hospitals. (The Catholic Hospital Association immediately launched a legal action to set aside the order requiring closure.) Next, the commission's "travelling executioners," as they were dubbed by the press, moved on to Toronto.

In the midst of this sabre-rattling, Mount Sinai continued to take an aggressive role both to ensure mutually respected rules of engagement in matters relating to consolidation on University Avenue and to produce the adjustments and balances needed for a wholly integrated system of hospital care. Both goals, Mount Sinai believed confidently, were fully compatible with its threshold issue, a determination to remain independently governed. New alliances included a joint Department of Anesthesia with the Toronto Hospital, with Dr. Alan Sandler at the helm, a joint Department of Obstetrics and Gynecology under Dr. Knox Ritchie, a University of Toronto Joint Centre for Bioethics, led by Dr. Peter Singer, and preparations for a Tri-Hospital Department of Medical Imaging in partnership with the Toronto Hospital and Princess Margaret.

Although disappointed by the commission's choice to ignore the denominational background of the Sudbury Catholic hospital that was ordered closed in the summer of 1996, Mount Sinai hadn't entirely pinned its own restructuring expectations on its status as a Jewish hospital. Unlike the provincial chain of mostly church-owned Catholic hospitals, which display religious symbols in every patient room, Mount Sinai is a single institution unaffiliated with any governing religious body, providing a level of Jewish services and comfort only to those who ask for them. Its steadfast position, which enjoyed strong support both at the university and within the Health Ministry, was that the hospital's excellence and its quality of care, teaching, and research entitled it to remain independent.[27] Indeed, the common weal would be better served if it did, added the chairman of the board with a sense of moral authority that could only flow from heading "perhaps the best all-around hospital in the country," "if only as a denominator to keep everybody else honest and set a standard."[28]

That's when the elephant stirred.

While preparing its own submission to the restructuring commission in September 1996, Mount Sinai determined to examine the submissions of its neighbours. Believing that an understanding had been reached on the matter, during unfailingly cordial negotiations, hospital officials were startled to discover that the Toronto Hospital/Princess Margaret colossus continued to attack the independent governance of Mount Sinai as a barrier to the efficiency of rationalization.[29] Once again, for what it hoped would be the last time, the hospital firmly and forcefully made its case, gaining in the process, according to Fogler, grudging respect, a willingness to live with Mount Sinai's insistence on separate governance, and finally the initial resource-transfer agreements so critical to health-services reform.

Relentlessly, as the restructuring kettle continued to boil, the provincial government whittled away transfer payments to hospitals. Since 1991, Mount Sinai had been forced to reduce its staff, programs, and beds by $38 million, although, until the end of 1996, every effort had been made to concentrate on budget reductions related to non-clinical departments as a bulwark against modifying patient care. However, with funding for 1997–98 pared a further $13 million, it could no longer avoid applying cost-cutting measures to actual patient-care programs. For the first time, three planning councils were created in the areas of Medical/Community, Perinatology, and Surgery, each co-chaired by the corresponding chief of department and a corporate vice-president. In keeping with the participatory philosophy of the administration, the councils were empowered to make clinically related reductions on their own turf and to meet specific targets of approximately $3 million each.

Still, the challenge of funding cuts went far beyond finding suitable places to slash costs. It involved stepping up vigilance at all staff, executive, and board levels to make sure that Mount Sinai not be starved of the justifiable sustenance needed to maintain a superior clinical, teaching, and research institution. Having witnessed other hospitals incrementally squeezed to the point where they had toppled, Mount Sinai was absolutely determined never to be among them.[30] Accordingly, in 1997 it turned to its foundation, now headed by chairman Bernard Ghert and president Nicholas Offord, which began to gear up for another massive fund-raising campaign.

Biological Threats

Although facing the glint of the cost-cutting knife and weathering the painful realities of restructuring while trying to maintain the highest possible standards of care were the crises accompanied by the most *Sturm und Drang*, they represented only part of the threat to Canadian hospitals in the middle years of a very turbulent decade in health care. Another menacing peril was the appearance of so-called "super-bugs," the multi-drug-resistant infectious diseases that were a consequence of the promiscuous prescription of antibiotics mingled with the notoriously mercurial nature of microbes. Although by no means immune to the deadly problem, Mount Sinai was at least better equipped than most hospitals to deal with it.

Two bacteria were of particular concern. Methicillin-resistant *Staphylococcus aureus* (MRSA), which had been raging through American hospitals since the early 1980s, was harmless to healthy people, but in immune-compromised patients potentially caused many life-threatening infections, including toxic-shock syndrome, bloodstream infections, or pneumonia. MRSA was resistant to all antibiotics except one, vancomycin, an expensive and not-always-effective drug, chillingly labelled "the antibiotic of last resort." The second bacterium was worse. Much more easily spread through airborne transmission than MRSA, vancomycin-resistant enterococci, or VRE, succumbed to no known chemical weapon at all.

Dr. Donald Low, now Mount Sinai and Princess Margaret's joint chief of Microbiology, had been part of the team that successfully fought Canada's first major outbreak of MRSA at the Toronto General Hospital in 1981. In the aftermath of that frightening episode, Low began

From left, Drs. Allison McGeer and Donald Low and infection-control nurse Karen Green confer while battling a case of VRE. (MSH *Image Centre*)

investigating the spread of MRSA with a former colleague, molecular biologist Dr. Barry Kreiswirth, then in New York City researching public-health problems. All hospitals in that American city's five boroughs sent specimens of the bacteria to Kreiswirth, who in turn shipped them to Low for further study. Among the specimens that Low received in 1987 was one never before encountered in the United States, a bacterium completely resistant to the antibiotic of last resort. The deadly organism was VRE. Within two and a half years of its discovery in a single New York hospital, it had surfaced in 50 per cent of that city's hospitals; within five years, it had spread worldwide.[31]

In 1990, Low recruited Dr. Allison McGeer, an international authority on VRE, to head infection control at Mount Sinai and Princess Margaret. The two, along with infectious-disease specialist Dr. Tony Mazzulli and infection-control nurses Carol Goldman, Karen Green, and Darlene Cann, developed strict and aggressive protocols for identifying and containing outbreaks of MRSA and VRE. As well, in collaboration with infection-control technologist Barbara Willey, Low devised the first laboratory test, now used internationally, to identify VRE. Mount Sinai subsequently became the coordinating centre for a nationwide study designed to assist other health-care providers in identifying the signs of antibiotic resistance, while the peripatetic team of Drs. Low and McGeer assumed the role of expert advisers to other hospitals, nursing homes, and health-care institutions across North America.[32]

Despite greatly heightened vigilance since the study began in 1993, the reality is that the appearance of these insidious bacteria in Canadian hospitals continues unabated, in great measure because of international travel. While there have been some frantic efforts to develop new antibiotics, the ominous implication is that even-more-virulent strains may be on the horizon, as nature cleverly adapts to whatever curve ball medicine attempts to throw. And for that reason, there was relief but no joy at Mount Sinai in February 1996 when the hospital's first outbreak of VRE was quickly contained.

There is little doubt that by any standard, the pressures of the 1990s have been daunting. Although the March 6, 1997, report of the Health Services Restructuring Commission ultimately did confirm Mount Sinai's independent governance, it also directed the hospital to participate in a task force to make rapid and binding decisions of further realignment of services and programs among the University Avenue complex of hospitals. More change, more streamlining, more upheaval would surely follow.

That said, today's environment at Mount Sinai Hospital is not one of doom and gloom. This is an institution that knows a thing or two about stumbling over obstacles and getting back up, that takes enormous pride in its many accomplishments, earned in such a remarkably short time, and that plans confidently to build on its strengths for the future, knowing full well that excellence will always be in high demand. When the dust settles early in the new millennium, after the restructuring commission has completed the remainder of its work, Mount Sinai expects to remain a leader in the front ranks of Canadian health care, medical education, and research, committed to the needs of the community it has served for three-quarters of a century.

Anyone in pursuit of a symbol for Mount Sinai Hospital's evolutionary leap during the past seventy-five years would find it outside the sixth-floor office suite of pathologist-in-chief Dr. Kenneth Pritzker. Splendid glass doors, featuring the workmanship of glass artist Ron So, contain graceful arcs of lead and shimmering jewel-coloured shapes that resemble a futuristic mobile suspended in a transparent expanse. Just beyond this sophisticated entranceway is a tiny reception area, furnished with two mismatched oak chairs and a wrought-iron table whose wooden top appears to have once supported a sewing machine. The antique grouping looks slightly out of place in the sleek corridor, and a visitor, despite the surrounding hum of the latest technology, can't help but feel the sensibility of another era.

It comes as no surprise that the humble furniture in the midst of this contemporary setting originally graced the Yorkville Avenue workplace of Mount Sinai's first pathologist-in-chief, Dr. Harold Pritzker. Not only have these remnants of that epoch endured through many years and several relocations, but they are still valued as treasured reminders of the past, and have been placed as sentinels to the vastly different business of the present day.

So, too, does a muscular heart of dedication and compassion continue to beat during a time of tough talk and tumultuous stock-taking. Although there are no soothing bromides for deep budget cuts or the upheaval of drastic change, it is certain that the long tradition of optimism and determination that once drove the rugged individualists who began Mount Sinai Hospital will not soon be dispatched to the dust bin of history. Both within the hospital and outside in the Canadian community it serves, the irrepressible will for Mount Sinai to prosper and flourish, grounded in a single core value of uncompromising excellence, remains as substantial and durable as those sturdy Yorkville table and chairs.

Appendix One

The Early Members of Ezras Noshem

Appendix Two

Mount Sinai's Charter, 1923

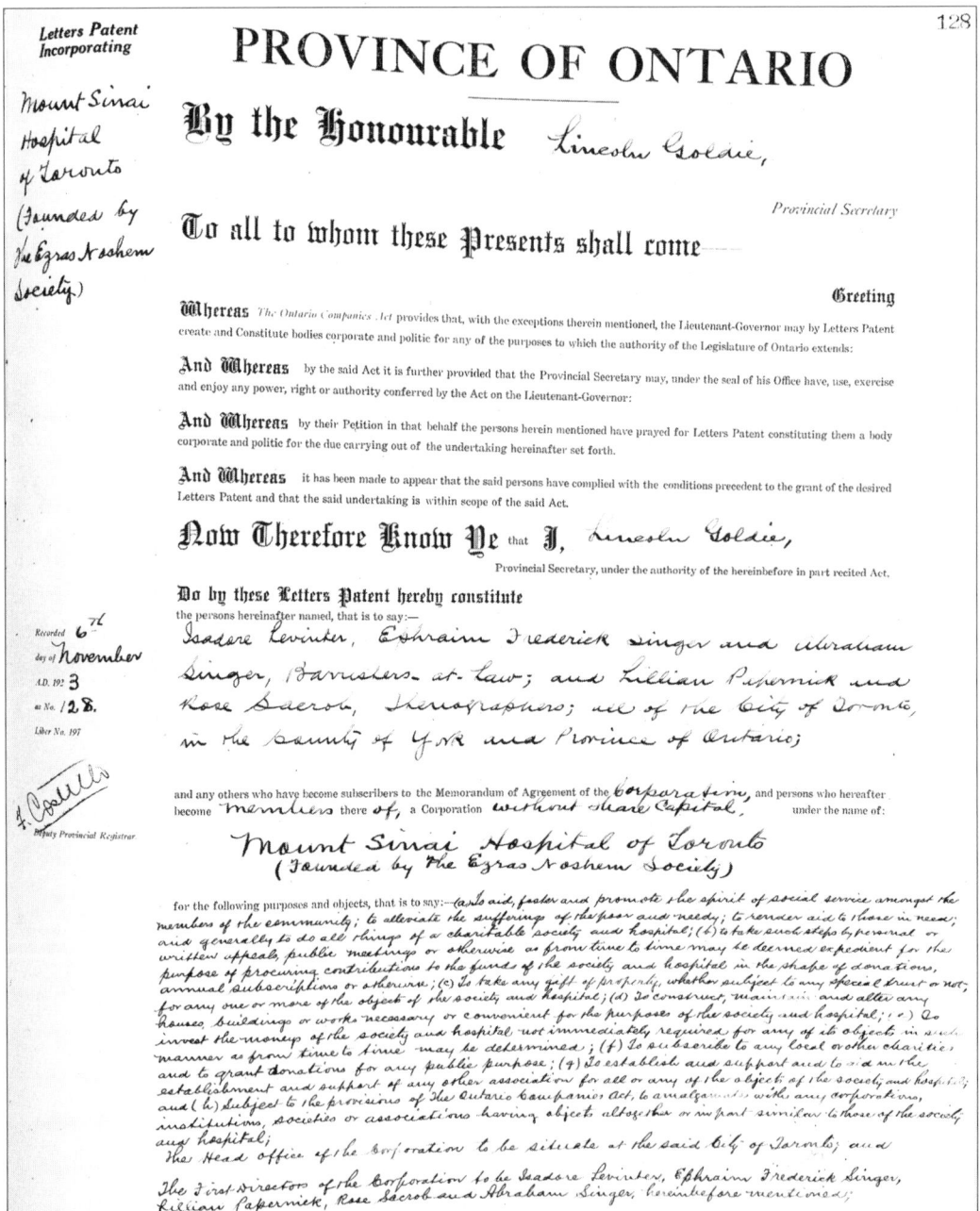

Letters Patent Incorporating

Mount Sinai Hospital of Toronto (Founded by the Ezras Noshem Society)

128

PROVINCE OF ONTARIO

By the Honourable Lincoln Goldie,

Provincial Secretary

To all to whom these Presents shall come

Greeting

Whereas *The Ontario Companies Act* provides that, with the exceptions therein mentioned, the Lieutenant-Governor may by Letters Patent create and Constitute bodies corporate and politic for any of the purposes to which the authority of the Legislature of Ontario extends:

And Whereas by the said Act it is further provided that the Provincial Secretary may, under the seal of his Office have, use, exercise and enjoy any power, right or authority conferred by the Act on the Lieutenant-Governor:

And Whereas by their Petition in that behalf the persons herein mentioned have prayed for Letters Patent constituting them a body corporate and politic for the due carrying out of the undertaking hereinafter set forth.

And Whereas it has been made to appear that the said persons have complied with the conditions precedent to the grant of the desired Letters Patent and that the said undertaking is within scope of the said Act.

Now Therefore Know Ye that I, Lincoln Goldie,

Provincial Secretary, under the authority of the hereinbefore in part recited Act,

Do by these Letters Patent hereby constitute

the persons hereinafter named, that is to say:—

Isadore Levinter, Ephraim Frederick Singer and Abraham Singer, Barristers-at-Law; and Lillian Papernick and Rose Sacrob, Stenographers; all of the City of Toronto, in the County of York and Province of Ontario;

Recorded 6th day of November A.D. 1923 as No. 128. Liber No. 197

H. Carlisle
Deputy Provincial Registrar

and any others who have become subscribers to the Memorandum of Agreement of the Corporation, and persons who hereafter become Members thereof, a Corporation without share Capital, under the name of:

Mount Sinai Hospital of Toronto
(Founded by the Ezras Noshem Society)

for the following purposes and objects, that is to say:—(a) to aid, foster and promote the spirit of social service amongst the members of the community; to alleviate the sufferings of the poor and needy; to render aid to those in need; and generally to do all things of a charitable society and hospital; (b) to take such steps by personal or written appeals, public meetings or otherwise as from time to time may be deemed expedient for the purpose of procuring contributions to the funds of the society and hospital in the shape of donations, annual subscriptions or otherwise; (c) To take any gift of property, whether subject to any special trust or not, for any one or more of the objects of the society and hospital; (d) To construct, maintain and alter any houses, buildings or works necessary or convenient for the purposes of the society and hospital; (e) To invest the moneys of the society and hospital not immediately required for any of its objects in such manner as from time to time may be determined; (f) To subscribe to any local or other charities and to grant donations for any public purpose; (g) To establish and support and to aid in the establishment and support of any other association for all or any of the objects of the society and hospital; and (h) Subject to the provisions of The Ontario Companies Act, to amalgamate with any corporations, institutions, societies or associations having objects altogether or in part similar to those of the society and hospital;

The Head office of the Corporation to be situate at the said City of Toronto; and

The First directors of the Corporation to be Isadore Levinter, Ephraim Frederick Singer, Lillian Paperniek, Rose Sacrob and Abraham Singer, hereinbefore mentioned;

And It Is Hereby Ordained And Declared That (1) The subscribers shall be the first members and it shall rest with the directors to determine the terms and conditions on which subsequent members shall from time to time be admitted; (2) The first directors shall hold office until the first general meeting; (3) The first general meeting shall be held at such time, not being more than two months after incorporation, and at such place as the directors may determine; (4) Subsequent general meetings shall be held at such time and place as may be prescribed by the corporation in general meeting; and, if no other time or place is prescribed, a general meeting shall be held on the fourth Wednesday in January in every year at such place as may be determined by the directors; (5) The directors may, whenever they think fit, and they shall, upon a requisition made in writing by any five or more members, convene a general meeting; (6) The requisition shall express the object of the meeting proposed to be called and shall be left at the office of the korporation; (7) Upon the receipt of such requisition the directors shall forthwith convene a general meeting, and if they do not convene the same within seven days of the receipt of the requisition, the requisitionists or any other five members may themselves convene a meeting; (8) At least seven days' notice of any general meeting, specifying the place, the day and the hour of meeting, and in case of special business the general nature of such business, shall be given to the members in the manner hereinafter mentioned, or in such other manner, if any, as may be prescribed by the corporation in general meeting, but the non-receipt of such notice by any member shall not invalidate the proceedings at any general meeting; (9) If within one hour from the time appointed for the meeting a quorum of members is not present, the meeting, if convened upon the requisition of the members shall be dissolved; in any other case it shall stand adjourned to the same day in the following week at the same hour and place, and if at such adjourned meeting a quorum of members is not present, it shall be adjourned sine die; (10) The president (if any) of the directors shall preside as chairman at every general meeting of the corporation; (2) If there is no such chairman, or if at any meeting he is not present, the members present shall choose one of their number to be chairman of the meeting; (11) The chairman may, with the consent of the meeting, adjourn it from time to time and from place to place, but no business shall be transacted at any adjourned meeting other than the business left unfinished at the meeting from which the adjournment took place; (12) At any general meeting, unless a poll is demanded, a declaration by the chairman that a resolution has been carried, and an entry to that effect in the minutes of proceedings of the corporation shall be sufficient evidence of that fact without proof of the number or proportion of the votes recorded in favour of or against such resolution; (13) If the poll is demanded, the same shall be taken in such manner as the chairman directs, and the result shall be deemed to be the resolution of the corporation in general meeting; (14) With the consent in writing of all the members a general meeting may be convened on shorter notice than seven days and in any manner which such members think fit; (15) The presence in person of at least one-third of the members shall be necessary to constitute a quorum at general meetings; (16) Until otherwise determined by special resolution, every member shall have one vote; (17) A resolution signed by all the directors shall be as valid and effectual as if it had been passed at a general meeting of the directors duly called and constituted; (18) The future remuneration of the directors and their remuneration for services performed previously to the first general meeting shall be determined by the corporation in general meeting; (19) The affairs of the corporation shall be managed by the directors, who may pay all expenses of the incorporation and may exercise all such powers of the corporation as are not by The Ontario Companies Act or by this memorandum required to be exercised by the corporation in general meeting, subject, nevertheless, to any regulations of this memorandum, to the provisions of that Act and to such regulations or provisions as may be prescribed by the corporation in general meeting, but no regulation made by the corporation in general meeting shall invalidate any prior act of the directors which would have been valid if such regulation had not been made; the continuing directors may act notwithstanding any vacancy in their body; (20) No director shall vacate his office by reason of his being a shareholder or member of any corporation which has entered into any contract with or done any work for the corporation of which he is a director, but he shall not vote in respect of such contract or work, and if he votes, his vote shall not be counted; (21) A retiring director shall be eligible for re-election; (22) If at any meeting at which any election of directors ought to take place the places of the vacating directors are not filled, the meeting shall stand adjourned till the same day in the next week at the same hour and place, and if at such adjourned meeting the places of the vacating directors are not filled, the vacating directors, or such of them as have not had their places filled, shall continue in office until the ordinary meeting in the next year, and so on from time to time until their places are filled; (23) (a) The board of directors shall consist of nineteen members, four of whom shall be ladies elected by the Ezras Noshem Society of Toronto, a Company incorporated under The Ontario Companies Act by charter dated the seventh day of July, A.D. 1922, one of whom shall be the president of the said society ex officio; the remaining members of the board shall be elected at the first general meeting of the corporation from the male members of same; the female members of the board shall be elected annually from the members of the Ezras Noshem Society and shall hold office on the board from and after the regular annual meeting of the board; (b) the male members of the board of directors shall be elected in three groups of five each for the period of two, four and six years respectively; (c) At the following elections held for two years the members elected shall hold office for a period of six years; (24) The Corporation may, from time to time, in general meeting increase the number of directors, and may also determine in what rotation any such increased or reduced number is to go out of office (25) Any casual vacancy occuring in, the board of directors may be filled by the directors, but any person so chosen shall retain his office so long only as the vacating director would have retained same if no vacancy had occured; (26) the Corporation in general meeting, by a resolution of three-quarters of the directors of the corporation, may remove any director before the expiration of his period of office, and may, by resolution, appoint another person in his stead; the person so appointed shall hold office during such time as the director in whose place he was appointed would have held the same if he had not been removed; nothing herein however, shall have the effect of decreasing the number of female members under this provision; the Ezras Noshem Society shall immediately elect a substitute; (27)(a) the directors may meet for the dispatch of business, adjourn and otherwise regulate their meetings as they think fit, and determine the quorum necessary for the transaction of business; (b) Questions arising at any meeting shall be decided by a majority of votes; in case of an equality of votes the chairman shall have a second or casting vote; (c) A director may at any time summon a meeting of the directors; (28) the directors may elect a chairman of their meetings and determine the period for which he is to hold office, but if no such chairman is elected, or if at any meeting the chairman is not present, the directors present shall choose one of their number to be chairman of the meeting; (29) The directors, by resolution entered upon the minutes, may delegate any of their powers to committees consisting of such member or members of their body as they think fit and a committee so formed shall, in the exercise of its powers so delegated, conform to any regulations that may be imposed on them by the directors; (30) A committee may elect a chairman; and if no such chairman is elected or if he is not present, the members present shall choose one of their number to be chairman of the meeting. (31) the board of directors shall form the following committees from their membership; (1) executive to consist of the president and six members of the board of directors; the duties of the executive committee shall be the immediate care and management of the hospital; (2) Finance Committee to consist of the vice president and three members of the board of directors, one of whom must be a lady; their duties shall be the supervision of the finances of the Corporation; (3) House Committee to consist of President, vice-president and three elected members of the board of directors, representatives of the Ezras Noshem Society; their duties shall be the immediate supervision of the management of the hospital; (4) Ladies Auxiliary Committee to consist of twenty four members of the Ezras Noshem Society elected annually by that body; their duties shall be to supervise the general welfare of the patients and to recommend to the board of directors improvements and expenditures; (32) There shall be a medical Advisory Committee, appointed by the board of directors consisting of five members of the medical staff of the hospital appointed annually by the directors; their duties shall be to advise the board of directors upon the medical policy of the hospital; (33) A committee may meet and adjourn as it thinks proper; question arising at any meeting shall be determined by a majority of votes of the members present, and in case of an equality of votes the chairman shall have a second or casting vote; (34) All acts done by any meeting of the directors or of a committee of directors, or by any person acting as a director, notwithstanding that it is afterwards discovered that there was some defect in the appointment of any such director or person so acting, or that they, or any one of them, were disqualified, shall be as valid as if every such person had been duly appointed and was qualified to be a director, but it shall not be necessary to give notice of a meeting of the directors to a director who is not in Ontario; (35) In case it is considered desirable to sell or otherwise dispose of the hospital building in the said City of Toronto conveyed to the corporation by the Ezras Noshem Society of Toronto, except by way of Mortgage, it shall be requisite that the approval of the Ezras Noshem Society of Toronto shall be obtained by a majority vote at a special meeting of that Society called for the purpose of considering such sale; (36) The picture, and the stone with names of those who took an active part in the organization and acquiring the property of the Hospital shall remain in the vestibule of the Hospital as long as the Hospital exists; (37) the beds and rooms purchased for the Ezras Noshem Society by various members and their Societies shall remain in the name of the persons and societies of those who purchased them; and (38) the officers of the corporation shall be the president, vice-president, treasurer and secretary to be elected annually by the board of directors at the annual general meeting;

And It Is hereby further Ordained and declared that the said Corporation shall be carried on without the purpose of gain for its members, and that any profits or other accretions to the Corporation shall be used in promoting its objects

Given under my Hand and Seal of Office at the City of Toronto in the said Province of Ontario this Seventeenth

day of October in the year of Our Lord one thousand nine hundred and twenty - three

L.S.

L. Goldie

Provincial Secretary.

Appendix Three

Chairmen of the Board

Ephraim Frederick Singer	1923–1953
Ben Sadowski	1943–1966
Bertrand Gerstein	1966–1971
Monty Simmonds	1971–1974
Alvin Rosenberg	1974–1979
Irving Gerstein	1979–1986
Hy Isenbaum	1986–1991
Lloyd Fogler	1991–1997

Appendix Four

Medical Advisory Council Chairmen

Dr. Maxwell K. Bochner	1928–1966
Dr. Louis J. Harris	1966–1970
Dr. David Bohnen	1970–1974
Dr. Barnet Berris	1974–1977
Dr. Bernard J. Shapiro	1977–1979
Dr. Nathan N. Levinne	1979–1981
Dr. Bernard Teichman	1981–1983
Dr. Stanley Greben	1983–1985
Dr. Peter W. M. Alberti	1985–1987
Dr. George Wortzman	1987–1989
Dr. Kenneth P. Pritzker	1989–1991
Dr. Eliot Phillipson	1991–1993
Dr. Knox Ritchie	1993–1995
Dr. Zane Cohen	1995–1997

Appendix Five

Mount Sinai Hospital Auxiliary

Honorary Officers

Founder President/Life Director: Rose Torno
Honorary Secretary: Ruth Brown

Past Presidents

Rose Torno	Nov. 1953 to May 1958
Ruth Brown	May 1958 to May 1961
Tannis Silverstein	May 1961 to May 1962
Dr. Reva Gerstein, C.M.	May 1962 to May 1964
Ethyle Levine	May 1964 to May 1966
Selma Eisen	May 1966 to May 1969
Judy Sussman	May 1969 to May 1971
Rae Bookman	May 1971 to May 1973
Libby Hoffman	May 1973 to May 1975
Valerie Fine	May 1975 to May 1977
Harriett Bomza	May 1977 to May 1979
Elaine Culiner	May 1979 to May 1981
Penny Offman	May 1981 to May 1983
Rosalind Witkin	May 1983 to May 1985
Carole Herman Zucker	May 1985 to May 1987
Tobie Bekhor	May 1987 to May 1989
Queenie Nayman	May 1989 to May 1991
Fran Binder	May 1991 to May 1993
Sandra Hausman	May 1993 to May 1995

Officers 1995–1997

Immediate Past President:	Sandra Hausman
President:	Julia Paisley
President-Elect:	Barbara Kerbel
Vice-President:	Joyce Chapnick
Vice-President:	Clara Cooper
Vice-President:	Gail Gerstein
Vice-President:	Renee Gozlan
Treasurer:	Henrietta Chesnie
Recording Secretary:	Bonnie Gottlieb
Corresponding Secretary:	Ruth Paisley

Notes

Chapter One

1. J. M. S. Careless, *Toronto to 1918: An Illustrated History* (Toronto: James Lorimer & Co. and National Museums of Canada, 1984), p. 145.

2. Louis Rosenberg, *Canada's Jews: A Social and Economic Study of Jews in Canada in the 1930s* (Montreal: Bureau of Social and Economic Research, Canadian Jewish Congress, 1939), p. 71.

3. Stephen A. Speisman, *The Jews of Toronto: A History to 1937* (Toronto: McClelland & Stewart, 1979), p. 22. Originally strictly Orthodox, Holy Blossom later became the stronghold of Reform Judaism in Canada.

4. James Lemon, *Toronto Since 1918: An Illustrated History* (Toronto: James Lorimer & Co., 1985), p. 13.

5. Ibid., p. 13.

6. Ibid., p. 13.

7. Michael R. Marrus, *The Unwanted: European Refugees in the Twentieth Century* (New York: Oxford University Press, 1985), p. 27.

8. Ibid., p. 33.

9. Speisman, *The Jews of Toronto*, pp. 71, 76; Rosenberg, *Canada's Jews*, p. 33.

10. Careless, *Toronto to 1918*, p. 100.

11. Speisman, *The Jews of Toronto*, p. 83.

12. Lemon, *Toronto Since 1918*, p. 51.

13. Ibid., p. 23.

14. Speisman, *The Jews of Toronto*, p. 90.

15. Coleman Solursh, autobiographical audiotape, January 3, 1985, Ontario Jewish Archives, Toronto.

16. Cyrile I. Gryfe, "Ethnicity and Doctoring in Toronto: A Historical

Perspective from the Jewish Experience" (unpublished paper presented to the Toronto History of Medicine Club, January 25, 1991), p. 8.

17. Speisman, *The Jews of Toronto*, p. 151.

18. Dorothy Dworkin, personal memoir, 1953, Mount Sinai Hospital Archives, Toronto, p. 3.

19. Aaron G. Volpé, "The Healers of Toronto's Past," *The Jewish Standard* (August 15–September 1, 1960): p. 18.

20. Speisman, *The Jews of Toronto*, p. 162.

21. A. I. Willinsky, *A Doctor's Memoirs* (Toronto: Macmillan of Canada, 1960), p. 47.

22. Ibid., p. 24.

23. Speisman, *The Jews of Toronto*, p. 120.

24. David Eisen, *Diary of a Medical Student* (Toronto: Canadian Jewish Congress, 1974), p. 4. Other types of Jewish professionals, while still discriminated against, could still function as private practitioners within their own community.

25. Rosenberg, *Canada's Jews*, p. 304.

26. Speisman, *The Jews of Toronto*, p. 132.

27. Rosenberg, p. 256. In 1921, 94.2 per cent of Canadian Jews over the age of ten listed Yiddish as their first language.

28. Michiel Horn, "Keeping Canada Canadian: Anti-Communism and Canadianism in Toronto, 1928–29," *Canada* 3:1 (September 1975): p. 44.

29. Lita-Rose Betcherman, *The Little Band* (Ottawa: Deneau, 1982), p. 10.

30. Editorial: "German Anti-Semitism," *Globe*, November 8, 1923; Horn, "Keeping Canada Canadian," p. 47.

31. Lemon, *Toronto Since 1918*, p. 53.

32. Ibid., p. 53.

33. Ibid., p. 56.

34. R. D. Gidney and W. P. J. Millar, "Medical Students at the University of Toronto, 1910–1940: A Profile" (unpublished, Toronto, 1995), p. 19.

35. Ibid., p. 4.

36. Ibid., p. 18.

37. David Eisen, *Toronto's Jewish Doctors* (Toronto: Maimonides

Medical Society of Ontario and the Toronto Centennial Committee of the Canadian Jewish Congress and the United Jewish Welfare Fund, 1960), p. 15.

38. Ibid., p. 15.

39. Etta Taube Sherman, personal interview, September 30, 1996.

40. Irene McDonald, C.S.J., *For the Least of My Brethren: A Centenary History of St. Michael's Hospital* (Toronto and Oxford: Dundurn Press, 1992), p. 122.

41. Eisen, *Toronto's Jewish Doctors*, p. 15. Dr. David Bohnen was the first Jewish doctor awarded the prestigious Gallie postgraduate course in surgery in 1943.

42. Willinsky, *A Doctor's Memoirs*, p. 83.

43. Dr. Louis Cole, personal interview, December 11, 1996.

44. Speisman, *The Jews of Toronto*, p. 121 n. 11. They were Drs. A. I. Willinsky and L. J. Solway.

45. "A Jewish Hospital for Toronto," *Canadian Jewish Times*, August 7, 1922, p. 27.

Chapter Two

1. A. D. Hart, ed., *The Jew in Canada* (Toronto and Montreal: Jewish Publications Ltd., 1926), p. 261.

2. Ibid., p. 261.

3. Cyrile I. Gryfe, "Ethnicity and Doctoring in Toronto: A Historical Perspective from the Jewish Experience" (unpublished paper presented to the Toronto History of Medicine Club, January 25, 1991), p. 11.

4. Ibid., p. 11.

5. "Jewish People of Toronto to Have Their Own Hospital," Toronto *Telegram*, February 11, 1922.

6. Aaron G. Volpé, "The Healers of Toronto's Past," *The Jewish Standard* (August 15–September 1, 1960): p. 18.

7. Toronto Historical Board, *Heritage Property Report re: 100 Yorkville Avenue*, June 22, 1992.

8. *Der Yiddisher Zhurnal*, July 20, 1922, Ontario Jewish Archives. Translated by Rabbi Bernard Schulman.

9. Dorothy Dworkin, personal memoir, 1953, Mount Sinai Hospital Archives, Toronto, p. 5.

10. Ibid., p. 6.

11. Ibid., p. 6.

12. Letter from Edmund Scheuer to Maxwell Bochner, date unknown, Mount Sinai Hospital Archives.

13. Gryfe, "Ethnicity and Doctoring in Toronto," p. 25.

14. Joseph Lazarus, "Political Watershed," *The Jewish Standard* (originally published 1930, reprinted July 15, 1992): p. 6.

15. Hart, *The Jew in Canada*, p. 223.

16. Dworkin memoir, p. 6.

17. Ibid., p. 7.

18. David Eisen, *Diary of a Medical Student* (Toronto: Canadian Jewish Congress, 1974), p. 100.

19. Hart, *The Jew in Canada*, p. 223.

20. David Eisen, *Toronto's Jewish Doctors* (Toronto: Maimonides Medical Society of Ontario and the Toronto Centennial Committee of the Canadian Jewish Congress and the United Jewish Welfare Fund, 1960), p. 5. Hart, *The Jew in Canada*, p. 415.

21. Eisen, *Toronto's Jewish Doctors*, p. 6.

22. Hart, *The Jew in Canada*, p. 419.

23. Dr. Irving Koven, personal interview, January 24, 1996.

24. Dworkin memoir, p. 13.

25. Report reprinted in *Canadian Jewish Review*, April 10, 1925.

26. Dworkin memoir, p. 8.

27. James Clark Fifield, *American and Canadian Hospitals* (Minneapolis: Midwest Publishers, 1933), p. 1,449.

28. Dworkin memoir, p. 8.

29. Rubye Orlinsky Halpern, personal interview, December 1995.

30. G. Harvey Agnew, *Canadian Hospitals, 1920–1970: A Dramatic Half-Century* (Toronto: University of Toronto Press, 1974), p. 126.

31. Eisen, *Toronto's Jewish Doctors*, p. 10.

32. Halpern interview.

33. Richard Sutherland, "Days of Shame," *Medical Post*, October 16, 1990, p. 11.

34. Ibid., p. 12.
35. Dr. Fred Langer, personal interview, July 18, 1996.
36. Aaron G. Volpé, "The Healers of Toronto's Past," *The Jewish Standard* (August 15–September 1, 1960): p. 19.
37. Ibid., p. 19.
38. Dworkin memoir, p. 11.
39. Personal papers of Edward Richmond. Toronto Historical Board, *Heritage Property Report re: 100 Yorkville Avenue*, June 22, 1992.

Chapter Three

1. Dorothy Dworkin, personal memoir, 1953, Mount Sinai Hospital Archives, Toronto, p. 16.
2. Sybil Lunenfeld Kunin, Reuben Kunin, personal interview, April 30, 1996.
3. Hy Isenbaum, personal interview, January 12, 1996. Yvonne Sadowski Davies, personal interview, January 30, 1996. Noah Torno, personal interview, February 7, 1996. Kunin interview.
4. Isenbaum interview. Davies interview. Torno interview.
5. Minutes of the New Mount Sinai Hospital Board, October 26, 1944.
6. "Did You Know?" *Highlights*, vol. 13, no. 1, p. 11.
7. Dworkin memoir, p. 18.
8. David Eisen, *Toronto's Jewish Doctors* (Toronto: Maimonides Medical Society of Ontario and the Toronto Centennial Committee of the Canadian Jewish Congress and the United Jewish Welfare Fund, 1960), p. 11.
9. Minutes of the Medical Advisory Council (MAC), July 9, 1934, April 27, 1939, May 14, 1942.
10. Eisen, *Toronto's Jewish Doctors*, p. 13.
11. MAC minutes, June 10, 1941.
12. Dr. Joan Levy Gladstone, personal interview, January 19, 1996.
13. Coleman Solursh, autobiographical audiotape, January 3, 1985, Ontario Jewish Archives, Toronto.
14. Report of the Hospital Practice Committee, 1941.
15. Dworkin memoir, p. 16.

16. Dr. Earl Myers, personal interview, January 25, 1996.

17. Fanny Ziskin Avrin, personal interview, September 20, 1996.

18. Ruth Mather, "Doctor's Office" (unpublished manuscript, 1993), p. 6.

19. Dr. Louis Cole, personal interview, December 11, 1996.

20. Minutes of the New Mount Sinai Board, April 16, 1947.

21. Editorial: "Mt. Sinai Appeal Is to All Citizens," Toronto *Telegram*, January 7, 1949.

22. Editorial: "Two Hundred and Fifty New Beds," *Globe and Mail*, November 24, 1948.

23. Minutes of the New Mount Sinai Board, August 1, 1951.

24. Etta Taube Sherman, personal interview, September 30, 1996.

25. Rose Torno, personal interview, January 11, 1996.

26. Editorial: "Our Newest Hospital," *Globe and Mail*, August 19, 1953.

27. "$7,300,000 Mt. Sinai Called Last Word in Modern Hospital," Toronto *Telegram*, August 13, 1953.

Chapter Four

1. Dr. Isaac Shleser, personal interview, March 6, 1996.

2. Ruth Mather, "Doctor's Office" (unpublished manuscript, 1993), p. 25.

3. Ibid., p. 26.

4. Dr. Charles Tator, personal interview, October 31, 1996.

5. Minutes of the Medical Advisory Committee (MAC), April 7, 1954.

6. MAC minutes, May 2, 1956.

7. Dr. Alan Bassett, "The Tumor Service," *Highlights*, vol. 7, no. 1 (October 1959): p. 3.

8. MAC minutes, October 13, 1954.

9. Letter from S. G. Fines to B. Sadowski, November 30, 1953. Minutes of the Joint Conference Committee, December 3, 1953.

10. Sidney Liswood, personal interview, January 12, 1996.

11. Ella Mae Howard, personal interview, February 1, 1996.

12. Aina Zulis, personal interview, March 26, 1996.

13. Dr. Nathan Levinne, personal interview, February 9, 1996.

14. Howard interview.

15. Minutes of the Joint Meeting Chartered Officers of Baycrest Hospital and Executive Committee, Jewish Home for the Aged, June 17, 1954.
16. Report of the Administrator, 1955, p. 1.
17. *Journal of the Canadian Medical Association*, July 2, 1960, as quoted in "Diabetic Patients Return To School," *Highlights*, vol. 8, no. 3 (April 1961): p. 7.
18. Report of the Administrator, 1959, p. 5.
19. Liswood interview.
20. Minutes of the New Mount Sinai Board, December 10, 1954.
21. Minutes of the New Mount Sinai Board, January 28, 1955.
22. Gerald Turner, personal interview, February 22, 1996.
23. Report of the Administrator, 1955, p. 3.
24. Ibid., p. 6.
25. Dr. Coleman Solursh, autobiographical audiotape, January 3, 1985, Ontario Jewish Archives, Toronto.
26. Turner interview.
27. Dr. Irving Rother, personal interview, March 18, 1996.
28. "Health Education Lectures Conclude Successful Season," *Highlights*, vol. 4, no. 4 (May 1957): p. 7.
29. Minutes of the New Mount Sinai Board, May 13, 1955.
30. Report of the Administrator, 1955. Minutes of the New Mount Sinai Board, September 30, 1955.
31. Dr. Bernard Laski, personal interview, February 27, 1996. "Five-Cent Treatment Almost Wipes Out Thrush, Baby Disease," *Toronto Daily Star*, November 29, 1958.
32. Report of the Administrator, 1959, p. 3.
33. *Sixty Years of Service: A History of the Ontario Hospital Association, 1924–1984* (Toronto: OHA Communications Services, 1984), p. 24.
34. Ibid., p. 25.
35. Annual Financial Report, September 1959.
36. Interim Report of the Department of Radiology, September 30, 1955.
37. Minutes of the New Mount Sinai Board, May 29, 1959.
38. Joseph Gollom, "Mount Sinai Hospital" (unpublished paper, 1974), p. 6.

39. Report from the Nightingale School of Nursing, Archives of Ontario, RG10, reel 166, 1959–1962.

40. Ella Mae Howard, personal interview, January 31, 1996.

41. University of Toronto Archives, A76-0044/022/06.

42. Minutes of the New Mount Sinai Executive, June 19, 1959.

43. Liswood interview.

Chapter Five

1. Minutes of the New Mount Sinai Board, April 6, 1962.

2. Memorandum re: Meeting, May 1, 1962, by Sidney Liswood, Sidney Liswood Papers, MG31 J29, vol. 2, National Archives of Canada (NAC).

3. University of Toronto Archives, A76-0044/037/08.

4. Liswood, Memorandum re: Meeting, May 1, 1962, Sidney Liswood Papers, MG31 J29, vol. 2, NAC.

5. University of Toronto Archives, A76-0044/037/08.

6. Minutes of the Medical Advisory Board, Toronto General Hospital, June 20, 1963.

7. Dr. Michael Sole, personal interview, October 28, 1996.

8. Ibid.

9. Minutes of the New Mount Sinai Board, June 15, 1961.

10. Residence Management Committee Report, September 28, 1962.

11. Dr. Stanley Greben, personal interview, April 2, 1996.

12. S. Greben, "Background History of the Department," 1977, Sidney Liswood Papers, MG31 J29, vol. 5, NAC.

13. Ibid.

14. Dr. Irving Koven, personal interview, January 17, 1996.

15. Dr. Imre Simor, personal interview, March 18, 1996.

16. Ibid.

17. Joseph Gollom, "Mount Sinai Hospital" (unpublished paper, 1974), p. 8.

18. Minutes of the New Mount Sinai Executive Committee, November 8, 1963.

19. Dr. Harry Strawbridge, personal interview, May 31, 1996.

20. Dr. Alan Pollard, personal interview, July 9, 1996.

21. Dr. Barnet Berris, personal interview, June 3, 1996.

22. Minutes of the Medical Advisory Council (MAC), April 13, 1966.

23. Dr. Bernard Teichman, personal interview, November 8, 1996.

24. Ibid.

25. "Recent Senior Medical Appointments," *Highlights*, vol. 16, no. 1 (October 1969): p. 3.

26. Dr. Diana Schatz, personal interview, April 23, 1996.

27. Ibid.

28. Dr. Harry Strawbridge, personal interview, March 27, 1996.

29. Dr. Alan Pollard, personal interview, February 29, 1996.

30. Ibid.

31. Minutes of the New Mount Sinai Executive Committee, Report of Gerald P. Turner, June 21, 1968.

32. "Dear Doctor," May 7, 1970, Sidney Liswood Papers, MG31 J29, vol. 5, NAC.

33. "New Mount Sinai Must Expand," *Highlights*, vol. 13, no. 3 (September 1966): p. 20.

34. Gerald Turner, personal interview, March 4, 1996.

35. Monty Simmonds, personal interview, March 29, 1996. Letter from Agnew Peckham and Associates to Sidney Liswood, August 8, 1967, Sidney Liswood Papers, MG31 J29, vol. 4, NAC.

36. Minutes of the New Mount Sinai Executive Committee, August 10, 1967.

37. Simmonds interview.

38. Peckham to Liswood, August 8, 1967, Sidney Liswood Papers, MG31 J29, vol. 4, NAC.

39. "Construction Begins With Ceremony," *Highlights*, vol. 15, no. 1 (November 1968): p. 6.

40. "Building Campaign in Final Phase," *Highlights*, vol. 17, no. 1 (October 1970): p. 12.

41. Minutes of the New Mount Sinai Executive Committee, October 23, 1967.

42. "Mount Sinai Announces new $30 Million Hospital Project," Toronto *Telegram*, October 25, 1967.

43. "Mount Sinai May Build New Hospital on University," *Globe and Mail*, September 8, 1967.

44. "Ontario Orders 10 Hospitals to Delay Expansion," *Toronto Star*, January 14, 1969.

45. MAC minutes, Accreditation Report of Dr. W. I. Taylor, April 21–22, 1969.

46. Liswood to Dymond, February 26, 1969, Sidney Liswood Papers, MG31 J29, vol. 4, NAC.

47. C. MacNaughton to E. Goodman, March 5, 1969, Sidney Liswood Papers, MG31 J29, vol. 4, NAC.

48. Noah Torno, personal interview, May 1, 1996.

49. S. Martin to B. Gerstein, April 29, 1969, Sidney Liswood Papers, MG31 J29, vol. 4, NAC.

50. Simmonds interview.

51. Ibid.

Chapter Six

1. "Special Ceremony Marks Occasion," *Highlights*, vol. 19, no. 1 (April 1972): p. 6.

2. Ibid., p. 5.

3. Monty Simmonds, personal interview, March 29, 1996.

4. "Gerstein Address," June 26, 1974, Sidney Liswood Papers, MG31 J29, vol. 4, NAC.

5. Simmonds interview.

6. Minutes of the Medical Advisory Council (MAC), November 4, 1970.

7. Annual Report of the Executive Director, June 27, 1974.

8. "Dedication of the Hospital Synagogue," *Highlights* (April 1976): p. 7.

9. "Is Mount Sinai the Last of the Lavish Hospitals?" *Globe and Mail*, March 24, 1979.

10. Dr. George Wortzman, personal interview, September 17, 1996.

11. Minutes of the Mount Sinai Executive Committee, April 14, 1972.

12. Joseph Gollom, "Mount Sinai Hospital" (unpublished paper, 1974), p. 12.

13. Department of Medicine, Reproductive Biology Unit, October 1972, Sidney Liswood Papers, MG31 J29, vol 5, NAC.

14. Dr. Fred Papsin, personal interview, May 13, 1996.

15. K. L. Valtchev and F. R. Papsin, "A New Intrauterine Mobilizer for Laparoscopy: Its Uses in 518 Patients," *American Journal of Obstetrics and Gynecology* (April 1, 1977): p. 738.

16. Minutes of the Mount Sinai Hospital Executive, July 22, 1971.

17. Minutes of the Mount Sinai Hospital Executive, May 12, 1972.

18. Dr. Allan Gross, personal interview, May 14, 1996.

19. Dr. Fred Langer, personal interview, July 18, 1996.

20. "One-of-a-Kind Sarcoma Unit Opens," *Highlights* (Spring 1989): p. 2.

21. Minutes of the Mount Sinai Hospital Executive, June 9, 1977. Dr. Alan Bassett, personal interview, June 25, 1995.

22. Dr. Martin Blackstein, personal interview, June 14, 1996.

23. Minutes of the Mount Sinai Hospital Executive, June 9, 1977.

24. Eleanor Wasserman, personal interview, June 11, 1996.

25. Ibid.

26. Dr. Arnold Aberman, personal interview, May 23, 1996.

27. Betty Calvin, personal interview, July 12, 1996.

28. Renee Fleishman, personal interview, July 21, 1996.

29. Calvin interview.

30. Maria Lee, personal interview, June 24, 1996.

31. Ibid.

32. "Eye Screening Program for the Chinese Community," *Highlights* (April 1976): p. 9. "Chinese Community Health Screening" (February 1977): p. 6. "Chinese Community Outreach Program" (February 1978): p. 5.

33. "Chinese Community Outreach Program," *Highlights* (February 1978): p. 5.

34. "Chinese Community Health Centre Opening Day April 2, 1978," *Highlights* (June 1978): p. 7.

35. Assistance for Foreign Physicians, 1975, Sidney Liswood Papers, MG31 J29, vol. 3, NAC.

36. New Mount Sinai Research Programs, Sidney Liswood Papers, MG31 J29, vol. 6, NAC.

37. Dr. Sidney Tobin, personal interview, July 18, 1996.
38. "Mt. Sinai Institute," *Highlights* (September 1976): p. 6.
39. Mount Sinai Hospital Report to the Community, 1975, p. 8.
40. The Michael Sela Exchange Program in Immunology and the Joseph J. Schiffer Program in Oncology. Research Comes of Age at Mount Sinai, Sidney Liswood Papers, MG31 J29, vol. 6, NAC.
41. Tobin interview.

Chapter Seven

1. Irving Gerstein, personal interview, August 27, 1996.
2. Dr. Lou Siminovitch, personal interview, August 21, 1996.
3. Gerstein interview.
4. Siminovitch interview.
5. Ibid.
6. Dr. Alan Bernstein, personal interview, September 4, 1996.
7. Mount Sinai Hospital Report to the Community, March 31, 1987.
8. Ibid.
9. Department of Obstetrics and Gynecology, 1977–1979, Sidney Liswood Papers, MG31 J29, vol. 4, NAC.
10. Dr. Knox Ritchie, personal interview, September 4, 1996. Dr. Heather Bryan, personal interview, September 24, 1996.
11. Minutes of the Mount Sinai Hospital Executive, January 11, 1979.
12. Ritchie interview.
13. "Official Opening of the Regional Perinatal Centre," *Highlights* (Winter 1986): p. 4.
14. Dr. Pamela Fitzhardinge, personal interview, September 12, 1996.
15. Ibid.
16. Dr. Dan Farine, personal interview, January 15, 1997.
17. Letter from Dr. Allan Gross to Sidney Liswood, Sidney Liswood Papers, MG31 J29, vol. 5, NAC.
18. "Breast Screening Program," *Highlights* (April 1980): p. 2.
19. Ella Mae Howard, personal interview, January 30, 1996.
20. Helen Evans, personal interview, March 27, 1996.
21. Ibid.

22. Kathleen Macmillan, personal interview, September 25, 1996.

23. Evans interview.

24. Dr. Iola Smith, personal interview, October 1, 1996.

25. Ibid.

26. Macmillan interview.

27. Ibid.

28. Dr. George Wortzman, personal interview, September 17, 1996.

29. Ibid.

30. Edward Shorter, *A Century of Radiology in Toronto* (Toronto: Wall and Emerson, 1995), p. 161.

31. Wortzman interview.

32. "Super Magnet Looks Through Body to Find Disease," *Toronto Star*, February 11, 1987.

33. "Osteoporosis – or, is there a fracture in Your Future?" *Highlights* (Summer 1985): p. 6.

34. Dr. Arnold Noyek, personal interview, September 24, 1996.

35. "Lasers – The Ray of Hope," *Highlights* (Fall 1988): p. 3.

36. Dr. Harry Jolley, personal interview, January 26, 1996.

37. Dr. Donald Low, personal interview, September 24, 1996.

38. Carol Goldman, personal interview, October 3, 1996.

39. Low interview.

40. "Staff Appointments," *Highlights* (Winter 1987): p. 4.

41. Dr. Joel Sadavoy, personal interview, October 17, 1996.

42. "Letters to the Editor," *Highlights* (February 1977): p. 2.

43. Dr. Lawrence Librach, personal interview, September 26, 1996.

44. S. L. Librach, *The Pain Manual: Principles and Issues in Cancer Pain Management* (Toronto: Pegasus Healthcare, 1991).

45. "Focus on the Department of Otolaryngology," *Highlights* (October 1980): p. 3.

46. Dr. Bernard Teichman, personal interview, November 8, 1996.

47. "Hy Isenbaum – New Chairman," *Highlights* (Winter 1987): p. 1.

48. Letter to S. Liswood, Sidney Liswood Papers, MG31 J29, vol. 4, NAC.

49. Dr. Jon Dellandrea, personal interview, November 12, 1996.

50. Hy Isenbaum, personal interview, September 3, 1996.

51. Dellandrea interview.

Chapter Eight

1. Irene McDonald, C.S.J., *For the Least of My Brethren: A Centenary History of St. Michael's Hospital* (Toronto and Oxford: Dundurn Press, 1992), p. 293.
2. Mount Sinai Annual Report to the Community, 1990–91, p. 5.
3. Gerald Turner, personal interview, November 27, 1996.
4. Editorial: "Hospital-in-Waiting," *Globe and Mail*, June 22, 1987.
5. "North York Guts Allies in Cancer Hospital Bid," *Toronto Star*, May 28, 1987.
6. "Major Plans for Princess Margaret Hospital," *Medical Post*, August 18, 1987.
7. Mendelow Ghatalia Architects, *Renovation Proposal, Radiotherapy and Rehabilitation*, February 11, 1987.
8. Dr. Alan Bernstein, personal interview, September 4, 1996. SLRI Community Report 1995/96.
9. Report of the President to the Board of Directors, February 1, 1994.
10. Dr. Eliot Phillipson, personal interview, November 12, 1996.
11. Annual Report, 1991–1992.
12. Dr. Zane Cohen, personal interview, November 13, 1996.
13. Annual Report, 1991–1992.
14. "New Lifesaving In-Utero Transfusions for Babies," *Highlights* (Spring/Summer 1992): p. 2.
15. Dr. Jill Boulton, personal interview, December 12, 1996. Samuel Lunenfeld Research Institute Annual Report, 1991–1992.
16. "Family Practice Inpatient Unit Opens," *Highlights* (Spring/ Summer 1992):p.2.
17. Theodore Freedman, personal interview, January 7, 1997.
18. Letter from J. Dirks to L. Fogler, December 30, 1991. Report of the President to the Board of Directors, January 30, 1992.
19. Accreditation Survey Report, Mount Sinai Hospital, April 13–15, 1992.
20. John W. Wright and Linda Sunshine, *The Best Hospitals in America: The Top Rated Medical Facilities in the U.S. and Canada* (New York: Gale Research Inc., 1995), p. 496.

21. Tema Frank, *Canada's Best Employers for Women* (Toronto: Frank Communications, 1994), p. 148.

22. Mount Sinai Community Report, 1993/1994. A Year in Review (1994–95).

23. Lloyd Fogler, personal interview, February 10, 1997.

24. Ibid.

25. As quoted in Report of the President to the Executive Committee, December 12, 1995.

26. "Travelling Executioners to Seal Fate of Ontario Hospitals," *Globe and Mail*, July 15, 1996.

27. Fogler interview.

28. Ibid.

29. Ibid.

30. Ibid.

31. Dr. Donald Low, personal interview, September 24, 1996.

32. "Mt. Sinai Doctors Study Multidrug Resistance," *Highlights* (Winter 1994): p. 5.

Index

Page numbers in *italics* indicate photographs.

Selznick, Dr. Maurice W., 56, 152n

Sewell, Marie. *See* Rice, Marie Sewell

Shack, Dr. L., 93–94

Shamian, Dr. Judith, 251, *251*, 253

Shapiro, Dr. Bernard, 83, *83*, 85, *113*, *205*, 206; as chief of Radiology, 112, 113–14; on Radiology department layout, 96; teaching, 90

Shapiro, Dr. Israel, 42, 45, *46*, 155

Shapiro, Rubin, 30

Sharp, Dr. Allan, 70

Sharp, Dr. Sidney, 70

Sharpe, Gladys, 76, 98

Shaul, Dr. David, 70, 152n, 154

Shaul, Dr. Nathan, 30, *30*, 48

Shaul, Dr. S., 48

Shear, Gerald, 228, *229*

Sherman, Dr. John, 85

Sheuer House, 210

Shields-Poe, Donna, 203

Shleser, Dr. Isaac, 70

Shuber, Dr. Jack, 152n, 154

Shusterman, Dr. Morris, 225

Sidlofsky, Dr. Saul, 111–12, 200

Siegel, Ida, 10, 24, 29

Sigal, Dr. Michael, 212

Silver, Dr. Daniel, 217

Silverstein, Dr. Ezra, 156

Silverstein, Dr. Harry, 69, 84, *85*, 118

Silverstein, Tannis, 107, 273

Siminovitch, Dr. Katherine, 243

Siminovitch, Dr. Lou, 181–82, *183*, 183–86, 234, 236

Simmonds, Monty, *132*, 134, 135, 137–39, *138*, 141; and New Mount

Sinai, 146; and 1967 expansion, 128, 129

Simon, Dr. Murray, 213

Simon, Dr. Saul, 48

Simor, Dr. Imre, 112, 113, *199*, 200, *205*

Sinclair, Dr. Duncan, 259

Sinclair, Dr. J. C., 149

Singer, Ephraim Frederick, *29*, 29–30, 47, 48, 68

Singer, Mrs. E. F., *38*

Singer, L. M., 10n

Singer, Dr. Peter, 260

Singer, Dr. Solomon, 10

Slavens, Dr. Jack, 84

Slutsky, Dr. Arthur, 166, 243

Smith, Dr. Barry, *247*, 248

Smith, Dr. I. R., *30*, 32, 223

Smith, Dr. Iola, 204–5

Smith, Dr. John Angus, 116, 213

Smith, Sidney, 100

Sniderman, Dr. Harold, 225

So, Ron, 265

Soberman, Max, 226

Soboloff, Dr. John, 56–57

Social Services department, 71

Social Work department, 150; and Chinese outreach, 170, 171

Sole, Dr. Michael, 106

Solursh, Dr. Coleman, 69, 84, *85*, 114, *114*; and Family Practice Unit, 89–90; and lodge doctors, 56–57

Solway, Dr. Leon Judah, 30, 33, 35–36, *36*, 68; and free Jewish dispensary, 10

Soric, Dr. Rajka, 249, *249*

Spiegel, Mrs., 21